1993

Narrated Films

Narrated Films

Storytelling Situations in Cinema History

Avrom Fleishman

The Johns Hopkins University Press

Baltimore and London

The Johns Hopkins University Press
701 West 40th Street
Baltimore, Maryland 21211-2190
The Johns Hopkins Press Ltd., London

The paper used in this book meets the minimum
requirements of American National Standard for
Information Sciences—Permanence of Paper
for Printed Library Materials,
ANSI Z39.48-1984.

Library of Congress
Cataloging-in-Publication Data

Fleishman, Avrom.
Narrated films : storytelling situations
in cinema history / by Avrom Fleishman.
p.   cm.
Includes bibliographical references and index.
ISBN 0-8018-4222-0 (alk. paper)
1. Motion pictures. 2. Narration (Rhetoric).
3. Motion pictures and literature. I. Title.
PN1995.F55   1992   791.43′015—dc20
91-12350

To the
memory of
David and
Johanna
Abraham
—they
survived,
they
abide

Maybe we are, in fact, the witnesses—or the artisans
—of a certain death, that of the art of narrating, from which
proceeds the death of storytelling in all its forms. . . . Maybe it
is necessary, *in spite of everything*, . . . to continue to believe
that new forms of narrative, which we are not yet in a
position to identify, are already in the process of
being born. . . . For we have no idea of what
a culture could be in which one no longer
knew what it meant to *narrate*.

—Paul Ricoeur

□

Contents

Contents

Illustrations

Preface

Some of those who turn the following pages will be sur-
prised, perhaps distressed, not so much by what they find
there as by what they do not. "Film narration" has come to
mean, among those who speak and write of cinema, a wide
variety of things having to do with the way a story is communicated. Like every piece of language, the term is the product
of a social practice, and any argument about its proper meaning
may seem like a struggle to control verbal behavior. Although
I shall offer some reasons for using "film narration" in a literal
rather than a metaphoric way, about a distinct range of films
rather than about cinema at large, I am proposing not a linguistic
reform but a shift of attention—to what I take to be somewhat
neglected but especially valuable elements of cinematic practice.

A number of readers, if they stay the course, may register
impatience with a proceeding that seems to offer few contemporary relevancies. There is, to be sure, little about the unconscious or politics, and nothing about sexual politics, in what
follows, but I do not thereby surrender the claim that formal
and narratological analysis can have social implications. By con-
centrating less on cinema's multiple codes of communicating
than on the communicative acts that characters and narrators
engage in, I take as my subject an eminently social process—
the apparently universal collective activity of storytelling. While
I have drawn heavily on the terms and methods of a type of
narratology without markedly sociological orientation, I should
disclose that the underlying "ideology" of what follows has been
shaped by the views of art and life as communal discourse in
the thought of Mikhail Bakhtin and Paul Ricoeur.

Some readers may detect occasional evolutionary overtones in my survey of narration in the course of cinema's history, and sense value judgments in the accounts of its workings in specific films. My evaluative statements will, insofar as I am able to govern them, be directed toward estimating the difference narration has made in larger processes, whether in the course of historical developments or in the making of unique art works (for such I conceive many films to be). These normative judgments will be based less on broad propositions about what films or their narration should be than on pragmatic weighings of how particular techniques work in given situations. There is no implication that narration per se makes a film the better for it, or better than other films that lack it. Nor should my selection of narrated films to illustrate varied storytelling situations be taken as thereby upholding their singular worth, though several are among the most highly regarded and discussed of all time. There is no denying, however, my tacit assumption that narration adds an important element to the array of formal ordering, complex characterization, and narrative significance that makes for high cinematic achievement.

As a series of dramatic or commentative events taking place within films, narration is conveyed by visual and sonic techniques that exist in a dimension and have esthetic effects beyond the storytelling function. My project entails discerning and calling attention to sounds and images as they relate to narration and, secondarily, to the story; it cannot pay due respect to their stylistic beauty or touch on all the cinematic qualities that make films what they are. In apology, I can plead only the necessary limitations of any specialized inquiry, with the potential compensations of focusing on a single but important contributory force in cinematic art. I might add that abstaining from comment on the wider range of expressive techniques has demanded self-restraint and selectivity; I would have liked more of the qualitative texture to enter my analysis—just as I would have welcomed more stills illustrating storytelling scenes, had I been able to obtain them.

My interest in cinema history and certain strains within it began during casual visits to the Cinémathèque Française, but later became serious business at the two dozen movie houses in Paris showing repertory films. Much of the reading was done while I enjoyed the hospitality of a visiting professorship at the University of Hawaii; I cannot pretend that in such surroundings it was done entirely indoors. Most of my knowledge of American films was gained on horizontal viewing tables at the Library of Congress; to its technical assistants, my gratitude. A number of the illustrations are from photos supplied by the Museum of Modern Art's Film Stills Archive. An early manifesto of the views developed here was presented to Seymour Chatman's NEH seminar at Berkeley; my thanks for the hearing and for subsequent comments. Three colleagues, Jerome C. Christensen, Richard A. Macksey, and George M. Wilson, offered useful suggestions and general encouragement, for which I am equally grateful.

Films are designated here by their U.S. release title; where none is available the original title is given, with my translation in parentheses. Release dates are cited from standard directories, but as these are sometimes at variance the dates must be taken as approximations.

Narrated Films

Introduction:
What Is Film Narration, after All?

. . . a movable army of metaphors,
metonymies and anthropomorphisms.
—Nietzsche

P ICK UP a typical—perhaps a better than average—book or
article on film and, as likely as not, you will come upon a
sentence like the following, one that describes Marnie's initial
interview at Mark Rutland's home, "where the camera tells a
story (Mark's dawning suspicions of her) that is quite different
from the story the dialogue is telling (Marnie's qualifications for
the job). Here we have the essence of Hitchcock's cinema."[1] Like
other statements about essences, this one contains a measure of
hyperbole but also enumerates some basics. There are, indeed,
two (or more) channels of communication at work in the scene
described, and dramatic irony is generated by discrepancies in
the information received. We enjoy the spectacle of a patholog-
ical liar running on about herself under a skeptic's amused observation. But how are we to understand the statement that our
perception of the latter comes from "the camera tell[ing] a
story"?

The expression seems familiar and commonsensical, roughly
of the same purport as the one that follows it, about "the story
the dialogue is telling." We use similar expressions casually to
refer to the meanings we discover in daily experience—some
detail or other "tells the story," someone's face "has a story
written all over it," "there's a whole story in that remark." But
these expressions are quickly recognized as metaphoric, part of
the creative activity in language usage that expresses the speaker

1

more than it describes the object in question. We are tacitly aware that some of Marnie's dialogue lines consist of (false) narrative statements about her past (the story she is telling); that the dialogue as a whole is not telling a story (the story of *Marnie*) but acting part of it out; and that the film is a dramatic action in a virtual present, though containing reports and reenactments of past events. Yet there is reason to believe that a good many people who see, think about, and write on films take literally the claim that "the camera tells a story."

There is, no doubt, a virtue in using a metaphor when it sharply conveys an idea; moreover, people will continue to use even vague metaphors as shorthand references to complex processes. But under closer scrutiny, this camera-as-storyteller formula conveys myriad questionable notions of how films communicate, of what it is we experience when we see a film, and of what a narrative is. Everyone is aware that films convey visual and aural images of actors and actresses (some of whom are also active in the theater), who have been helped to prepare for performance by teams of makeup artists, costumers, set designers, lighting technicians, propmen, and the like—many of whom have also worked in theatrical productions using substantially the same skills. The moviegoer is also pragmatically, if not vividly, aware that a film runs its course in time, with a duration comparable to that required for performing a play. One knows that many directors and scenarists are active in both media, that they compose and work from scripts that include dialogue lines and instructions for execution (these differ considerably in detail but not in kind), and that some films are little more than photographed theatrical performances. (These are often panned as "uncinematic," although no one would deny that they are films.) In short, while we are aware that there are distinct differences between film and theater, differences that may lead us to choose between them for an evening's entertainment, there are nonetheless gross similarities that should lead us to think of both as mimetic spectacles.

The distinction between spectacles and narratives goes back to the earliest thinking about dramatic and literary art, to Plato's and Aristotle's distinctions—they are not quite the same ones—between *mimesis*, performance or "imitation" of an action, and *diegesis*, storytelling by the statements of a narrator.[2] From this standpoint, cinema, like drama, dance, opera, mime, and other presentations of action, is mimesis and not diegesis. (The word "diegesis" has been used freely in film studies to refer to story content, irrespective of narration, and need not be abandoned if understood in this limited sense.) While films are different from other performances in ways that make for a distinctive kind of mimesis, it is a desire to see an action taking place before our very eyes that brings us to the movies in the first place. Is there some latent embarrassment in the idea of imitated action— a survival of Plato's disdain for impersonation—that leads some to claim that cinema is not mimetic but diegetic, not a performing but a narrative art?[3]

Perhaps an answer lies in narrowing in on that peculiar locution, with its personifying figure of speech (prosopopoeia), that "the *camera* tells a story." We do not ordinarily say that a director tells a story—except in special cases, to be discussed— even though *mise en scène* decisions like lighting changes and staging cues for actor movement or nonverbal reaction may govern our attention as firmly as camera work or subsequent editing. Nor do we pretend that a film's sound equipment tells a story, though cinematic sound is a resource almost as powerful and elaborately coded as photographic technique. But the director commands camera movement, distance and angle, montage, and other visual resources beyond the staging and sound, and it is this control, especially in marked or self-conscious instances, that provides suggestions of a narrational activity.

There are other forces at work in cinema experience to encourage the belief that we are being told a story when we are witnessing a visual and aural spectacle. A psychoanalytic school of film theorists, led by Jean-Louis Baudry and Christian Metz,[4] has described the effect of the darkened viewing place, the phantasmal flow of screen images, and the powerful evocation of elemental desires and fears as reproducing the conditions of dreaming. Cinematic technology by its very nature—the projection system at least as strongly as the filming equipment— manipulates the audience into unconscious identification not only with the characters but also with the process of screening- viewing (Metz's secondary and primary identifications, respectively). If this account of the moviegoer's imagination is to be believed, film projection induces psychological projection, so that we identify with the image-making apparatus—the "camera"—and feel ourselves to be generating both the images and the story, much the way we generate our dreams.

Other aspects of the moviegoing experience may encourage not so much the impression of ourselves as source of what we see but the equally mystified sense that filmgoing is storytelling time. Just as the audience's regressive tendencies are implicated by the Baudry-Metz account of its illusory identifications, so too one hears resonances of the childhood reception of fables in many an account of moviegoing. There seems to be wide participation in the belief that when we see a drama enacted in the movies, we are being told a story, presumably by an unseen but potent storyteller. Though the aura conveyed by the traditional storyteller has declined in modern culture—in the age of "mechanical reproduction," for which cinema is Walter Benjamin's prime example—audiences and critics have not entirely lost their taste for it. That aura is not so much mystical as personal, a feeling that when one receives a story there must be an individual who imparts it, endowing it with personal authority—in a testamentary as well as an originating role.

The feeling that a film is being narrated—that there is a narrator somewhere behind it, or behind us, producing it all for our benefit—may, then, be induced by elements of cinema far removed from those that would ordinarily be called "narration." The sense of an apparently personal source is an effect of cinematic projection, in both the above senses, but may have little to do with *what* we see and hear, as distinct from the process of filming, showing, and experiencing it. Just as Michel Foucault, Roland Barthes, and others in their wake have taught us to perceive the "author"-effect, the "reality"-effect, and other mystifications of literary texts, we may gain some advantage from (at least temporarily) freeing our minds of such ghostly presences as the "narrator"-effect.[5]

In an effort to locate the source of the "narrator"-effect in a cinematic narrator, film theorists have run through a variety of options. To appreciate the exhaustiveness of this quest, we may avail ourselves of a narratologist's model of the story communication process[6] (see Fig. 1). It will become clear that the variety of concepts in the collective effort to find a place for the cinematic narrator gravitates around the three positions to the left.

Narrative text

Real $\Rightarrow$	Implied $\Rightarrow$ (Narrator) $\Rightarrow$ (Narratee) $\Rightarrow$ Implied	$\Rightarrow$ Real
author	author reader	reader

Fig. 1. The story communication process.

The authorial and even anthropomorphic nature of the supposed cinematic narrator is nicely framed in the term employed by certain French (and, lately, American) critics for the hypothetical source of all film narratives: the *grand imagier* or great image-maker. The term is redolent of the transcendental but also carries more homely suggestions of a kind of showman or magician of light and sound. Often this vague presence is given a human touch by association with an actual filmmaker, especially one who has achieved an aura of wizardry. We hear not only of Hitchcock's camera as narrator but of Hitchcock the "enunciator," who tells his films in ways more subtle than but akin to his television introductions, insisting on his presence by inserting shots of himself, surrogate characters, and other authorial markings within them.[7] To identify the cinematic narrator with the real author or filmmaker risks, however, not only an elementary mistake in narratology but a return to the late and unlamented *auteur* theory. The approach has its devotees but is the least favored among the cinematic narrator gambits.

More cautious students of narrative are content to limit such a factor to an ideal position in a communication sequence. Acknowledging that the ultimate source of a film is the historical person (usually plural) who creates it, these theoreticians are equally aware that in cinema an actual narrator who reports events in language is possible but optional. Yet since an audience can receive a narrative even without a verbal narrator, some believe that an implied figure must be posited as the theoretical source.[8] In the line of transmission, this hypothetical giver of narrative would occupy a position between the real author and

5

the active narrator of story events. But these theoreticians caution that such a figure exists only as immanent in the text, not standing outside and producing it. While the dangers of anthropomorphism are still present here, narratologists have been on their guard against taking this presumptive and derivative placeholder as a real person or productive agent.

In the literary sphere, the equivalent phenomenon is the "implied author" posited by Wayne Booth.[9] As Booth and his successors repeatedly state, this is not an entity but a construct, which follows from rather than precedes the existence of literary texts. That is, given such a text, what kind of author is implied by it—what can we imagine the author of such a text to be, now that it has been created by the real author? Such an approach can be helpful in formulating the created persona of novelistic narrators, and may resolve questions about authorial execution as distinct from intention. It can even lead to a literary equivalent of cinema's "narrator"-effect, the image of the author as fount of wisdom, friend, and guide.

Yet it is doubtful that the implied author can serve as a model for the hypothetical narrator or theoretical source of film narratives. While the real author precedes, and the implied filmmaker may be thought to follow from, our experience of a film, a cinematic narrator would have to accompany the sounds and images. Narration is, in practice as in theory, an ongoing process of providing story information; the order of its discourse is distinct from that of the story, and it is an activity extended in time (or in the literary text's spatial equivalent of succession). But an implied filmmaker acting as narrator would be difficult to imagine in the act of formulating each shot as a narrative statement. We may theorize a narrative source at the origin of the stream of images, as a kind of signature of responsibility or gesture of commencement, but to suppose its continuing action as each image appears is to yield too blithely to the "narrator"-effect.

A third approach to the cinematic narrator would bridge the gap between implied source and active force by placing it further along in the communication chain. This narrator would narrate not by showing or telling but by standing at the point of view from which action is to be seen. Here the camera position and movement, montage, and other choices by the director seem to indicate a favored position to see—or to have the audience see—the action from a particular perspective, the equivalent of the consciousness or "point of view" that marks literary narrators. Since literary narration is focalized (to use the narratologists' term) from a number of perspectives, including the narrator's and the characters', there is a complex relationship between the questions Who says? and Who sees? for the rendering of a fictional scene. But even in the absence of a narrator who says, some theoreticians would establish an impersonal being who sees—who stands before each visual shot—as the cinematic narrator.

We shall return to the important narratological distinction between narration and focalization, who says and who sees, so as to question whether a narrator can function as a perspectival reference point in the absence of language. But the idea of a purely visual narrator cannot be confronted without considering its strongest formulation, in which it resembles that synthetic construct, the literary narrator's perspective. Since most fictional narrators incorporate their characters' points of view, a cinematic narrator too might be expected to synthesize the viewpoints of the film characters, as they are given in the shot/reverse shot series, "subjective camera" tracking shots, and other indications of character perspective.

In one such formulation, the visual narrator stands in a triangular relation: it is a "narrating agency or authority" that induces correct spectatorial perspectives by ordering and subtly criticizing the characters' points of view.[10] The difficulties of triangulated theories of character-, spectator-, and narrator-perspective are to be seen in the shifting terms employed for this variable focalizer: "implied narrator," "absent narrator," "effaced" author, who is "nowhere visible in the same manner as the characters," but is "visible only through the materialization of the scene and in certain masked traces of his action." Like the New Critical literary author, based on traditional ideas of a divine creator's hidden presence in the creation, this narrator is everywhere and nowhere in the film text—only occasionally tipping its hand by a "masked" gesture. Yet in the absence of a narrating voice, the conviction of its presence requires renewed bolstering by faith—cinema's narrator-effect.

Yet what are we to make of all the camera movements and

angles, subjective views and "objective" perspectives, that are associated with film images and animate the spectator's viewing? Without succumbing to the temptation of positing an authorial, implied, or focalizing presence as narrator, other cinema theorists have described the representational and expressive codes that regulate usage of cinema's technical resources, fully aware of the historical emergence and prevalence of favored practices at various stages of film history.[11] There has thus developed a powerful and comprehensive terminology to describe the camera, montage, acting, *mise en scène*, and other coded systems by which images are presented and stories conveyed in films. A new temptation arises, however, to think of these coded practices, and the significant deviations from them, as a cinematic language, in which films could be said to communicate and be interpreted.

This is not the place to rehearse the difficulties that Christian Metz's and other doctrines of cinematic language encountered in the decades of their prominence. But a marked shift may be noted from the linguistic and semiotic structuralisms of the 1960s and early 1970s to the tendency of their successors in the 1980s to search for films' "enunciation" and "enunciator." Where the structural study of film codes was content to model the text, the psychoanalytic ambience of the later period (including Metz's second phase) has induced even non-Lacanian theorists to make this communicative process a personalized one. French cinema journals report continued efforts to deal with such questions as Who speaks a film? How does the image tell (*raconte*)? and Can there be stories without narrators? Despite efforts to distinguish the presumed speaker of a film text from the narrators who function within it, there is continual slippage in such theories between hypothetical enunciation and functional narration. Even when the verbal aspect of narration is duly recognized, elaborate steps are taken to give enunciation the characteristics of telling in the absence of language.[12] Witnessing the shifts from one predominant and largely unquestioned metaphoric usage to another, we may suspect that the terms primarily reflect the discourse economy of an interpretive community, rather than referring to a set of communicative events in cinema.[13]

○   ○   ○   ○

Meanwhile, a number of practices that might more obviously provoke interest under the rubric of narration have been neglected. As I shall try to show, plenty of narration takes place in films, even though films are not as a whole narrated. There is even a set of film practices designed to induce reception of a given film as a narrated one—to produce the impression of narration, the narration-effect. But this code of narrational practices in cinema has not been formulated, while more ambitious but ultimately frustrated designs for a total narration have been pursued. The present study attempts the less quixotic gesture.

Certain films make an effort to capture the auratic effects of a storyteller and marshal them for ends of their own. In these films storytelling observably takes place, either on-screen or on the soundtrack alone. These practices are neither natural nor naive but conventional; they are accepted as readily as they are because they have been made familiar by collective behavior. (I ascribe no sinister motives to the code-makers, as other students of "dominant" film practices tend to do.) This film code, involving visual and sound techniques, includes more traits than narrative language alone. It is executed with varying degrees of systematization and is perceived with varying degrees of saliency. Despite the tendency of all codes to become automatic or "naturalized," film narration can be conceptually bracketed and described as a system.

To take an example of this unwarranted neglect of the narration code: When we hear a voice on the soundtrack without seeing it matched with the lip movements of a character, we are aware of it as "voice-over"—but what does this pat phrase mean? Most members of today's audience recognize the difference between the voice of a character speaking of his or her past self as seen on-screen and that of a character temporarily not visible—and can distinguish both from a voice that is not that of a character. Yet the term "voice-over" is used, at least in English, to cover all of the above, though there is a world of difference between speech from outside and from within a story world. (In French, the term is "voice-off," the English phrase having somehow been imported to cover *both* cases.) Audiences are also aware that a character may be telling either his or her own or another character's story, and that these again are different from a voice without strong personality reporting the action. These situations beg to be called by names that respond to their differing qualities and functions, but criticism is impeded in making some useful descriptions because "voice-over" (or "voice-off") has been used for multiple purposes for so long.[14] Further, when we try to formulate voices that filmgoers have less experience with but do recognize—say, a voice that expresses the thoughts of a character seen to be silent on-screen, or a voice that seems to emanate from a prop or from visible sound equipment—we sense that critical terminology is somewhat laggard by comparison with the ordinary filmgoer's competence in distinguishing them. To lack a battery of terms may be considered a precious freedom from overspecialization, as long as these voices are placed and grasped correctly in the viewing, but the difficulty of talking about films with a limited vocabulary becomes evident when we see critical observers missing perceptions that are presumed to be available even to nonspecialist audiences.[15]

To vary an adage, it seems that the attention paid to the metaphoric forest of film narration has made it difficult to discern the most palpable of its trees: the verbal activity of storytelling (with its accompanying cinematic code) that takes place on the soundtrack and in the dramatic action of certain films. How does one go about discussing film narration as an observable set of storytelling activities? One potential impediment may be painlessly removed: limiting the study to storytelling acts will leave the boundaries of "narrative cinema" intact.[16] Narrative is not, after all, necessarily narrated; indeed, the word has become a great portmanteau that has replaced "myth"—and competes with the term "allegory"—as a reference to socially constructed ideas that often only loosely take the form of stories. Narratives as diachronically extended ideas, rather than as plot sequences, have already become the objects of study in the realm of film genre—ranchers and farmers, or community and individual, in the Western—in place of the once touted applications of Propp and other structuralists to the basic story patterns. While this loosening of terms is not beyond reproach, the fate of "narrative"

10

may allow space for liberation from certain verbal traps—like the reflex that every narrative must be narrated.[17]

Even when we keep to the more limited notion of "narrative" as synonymous with "story," a closer view indicates that narration is not inevitably paired with it. Here the unavoidable linkage is between *story* and *discourse*. Although it is variously framed in English, French, and Russian, the relation between a narrative content, message, or set of events and the signs in which it is encoded is as widely recognized as the relation of signified and signifier. This consensus assumes the variety (and translatability) of discourse according to the several media—the dramatic speeches, the dance steps, the film shots—in which stories are encoded. But narration is distinct from discourse in referring to *acts* that deliver signs of a story. And, as we have seen, certain media present story signs directly, as mimesis, while others encode them in narrational statements, as diegesis.

There is a further disparity between the narrational arts and the mimetic media in which stories are imparted. Narration, telling, is distinguished from mimesis, acting out, not only by the relative degree of visualization of its signs but by the special relation of signs to their sender in language. While in mimetic arts the sender (author, director) stands outside the discourse (although the sender may defamiliarize or "bare the device" by appearing on-stage or on-screen), linguistic discourse encodes the speaker in the statement by the grammatical structures necessary to its formulation. These "deictic indicators"—marks of person, tense, relative position in time and place, modality, and so on—mark each narrative statement as proceding from a distinct perspective, even when the style endows the narrator with the impersonal voice of history. It is the linguistic encoding of a speaker that allows diegetic arts to posit a narrator who narrates the discourse, though we know that narrator by the discourse alone.

There is considerable pressure on mimetic artists to endow their productions with personality, yet they must do so within the medium, the *mise en scène* itself, lacking a voice to mark each sign with the trace of its origin. (The dialogue of plays and films is, of course, linguistic, but it is part of the story and discourse, not the language of narration.) Of course, for much of its history dramatic art has been considered at an advantage in achieving a desired esthetic impersonality; it is only in our own time that an endemic distrust of objectivity has led, if not to a preference for "telling" over "showing," to an assimilation of mimetic arts like cinema to the norms of narration.

Gérard Genette's schema of narrative levels may be of help in marking out the scope of film narration, for it is so precise in relating narration to discourse and story in literature that the corresponding stages *and absence of stages* in cinematic practice become salient. His by now well-known terminology of extra-diegetic, intradiegetic, and metadiegetic levels distinguishes an initial narration that generates the text as a whole from the subsequent narrators of framed and intercalated tales.[18] In literature, each of these narrators is linked to a segment of text, whether by the markers of direct discourse for quotations of their own words, or by other codes linking statements to their source (indirect discourse, free indirect style, summary, etc.). Thus the text as a whole must be ascribed to a primary or extradiegetic narrator, whether this giver of narrative be conceived as an omniscient narrator, "author"-narrator, or other indefinite speaker, or characterized as a fictional being who becomes a personage in his or her own story ("first-person" narration).

The system's advantages have been variously exploited and its aporias (beyond the issues raised here) vigorously debated since its initial appearance. But its chief utility for cinema studies may lie, curiously enough, less in its perfect applicability to films than in making clear where film and fiction diverge. The relevance of Genette's diegetic levels to cinema stems from the fact that in the course of a film stories may be told; since they are not within a discourse that has been narrated but within an ongoing action, we would be required to call them intramimetic narrations. (The story they narrate and the enactment seen on the screen occur within mimesis too but exhibit signs of having been narrated; it is conceivable that they be called either metamimetic or metadiegetic, according to one's emphasis.) Some films, moreover, accompany their opening sounds and images with the words of a narrator who exudes the implication that this speaking is the source of what we see and hear; such titles, voice-overs, and introductory on-screen personages stand in a position corresponding to the extradiegetic narrator of fiction and might be called extramimetic.

Both the impersonal and the character voice-overs, as well as the on-screen narrators, described in the following chapters are extramimetic; the dramatized and mindscreen narrators and the written texts of other narrated films may be considered intramimetic narration. Since this adapted terminology is not only ungainly but also debatable in its turn, I shall make occasional use of Genette's original terms below, with the understanding that they refer to films only with qualifications. But the urgent lesson of closely applying Genette's narrative levels to cinema is that there is no extradiegetic narrator who speaks the film as a whole. There may be thought to be an opening voilà gesture in the act of turning on the apparatus, showing the image, or other equivalents of the theatrical moment of raising the curtain. But this is hardly a role to qualify the gesture as narration, or the image-shower as a "great image-maker."

o   o   o   o

"Narration" is, then, the activity of articulating a discourse that conveys a story—and not articulation in an abstract sense, but the interpersonal (social, pragmatic) situation in which the narrating act takes place. What film criticism has generally studied as "narration" will be discussed below (not as fully as one would like, since subordinate to other concerns) under the heading of "discourse." What film criticism has generally neglected (because of its heightened attention to hypothetical progenitors of the discourse), the perceptible activities of telling a story, will be discussed here as "narration."

This social and pragmatic aspect of narrative has recently begun to have its due measure of attention. A recent book by Ross Chambers remarks on the curious lack of previous awareness and the evident need for it: "It seems strange that literary criticism and theory have paid so little attention to the performative function of storytelling, preferring to limit themselves arbitrarily to the study of narrative structure and the discourse of narration. . . . There is plenty of evidence in the literary tradition that the creators, unlike contemporary theorists, have been aware of storytelling as an event that presupposes a situation and mobilizes social relationships so as to give it performative force."[19] Although my sense of "performative" is not Chambers's speech-act use of the term, I share his concern that the interpersonal engagement and behavioral work of storytelling be given their due, in film as well as in fiction.

Despite the omission of an extensive social-historical grounding for the narrational modes to be discussed, it is important to conceive of them as motivated behavior by fictional persons involved in or commenting on fictional but pragmatic situations. (I leave moot the question of real-world reference, as a characteristic either of the storyteller or of the story told: once involved in a work of art, all putatively real tellers and true tales acquire a measure of fictionality.) One philosopher urging a demystified view of narration supports this reorientation toward an interpersonal focus: "All phrases like 'A sentence S narrates about this or that' . . . are metaphorical in nature. It is always the sender of the sign as such, and hence a definite person, who narrates. . . . The receiver of the narrative also is a definite person who reads or hears the signs produced by the sender and uses them so, i.e., decodes them so that he knows that the sender narrates so-and-so by means of them."[20] Attention has been given to the receiver in narratology (the "narratee"), literary reader-response criticism, and cinematic psychoanalysis. Yet close observation might well be expended on the dynamics of recounting and receiving stories—on motives, tactics, and mutual responses. And the scope of inquiry should extend beyond the relatively detached cinema audience to the engaged characters who tell and receive tales in the course of an action—to the speakers and auditors within a film's dramatic world.

What has been underreported in film studies, as in other fields, is the personal interaction in which stories are heard and/ or seen being narrated. I call the varieties of these voice-over and on-screen actions *storytelling situations*, drawing on Genette's idea of narration as the "whole of the real or fictional situation in which [the producing narrative] action takes place."[21] To deal with the dramatic context and the *mise en scène* of such acts, I shall often refer to the *scene of narration*. "Situations" is more encompassing than "scenes," however, for even an unseen figure directly addressing the audience enters into an interpersonal, though partially veiled, relationship (see chap. 4) and often reveals or discovers much about him- or herself in the process. This is likeliest when he or she is a character in the story told, but it may also occur when an outside observer tells the tale—although many voice-overs take steps to render their account impersonal. When we consider the potent effects that storytelling has at a number of levels in social and psychological life, cinema's varieties of narrating seem to cry out for attention—not merely as means of communicating a film's story but as dramatic activities with potential consequences within and beyond the films in which they take place.

Since cinema must develop a set of presentational codes to signal its story data in the absence of narration, it has also developed a code to indicate that narration is taking place within a film—indeed, to convey the impression that a given film is narrated. *Narrated films*, like those that are not narrated, begin with sounds and images not marked by a declaration of their immediate source (the conventionally last of the opening credits, "directed by . . . ," refers to the film's production, not dissemination, phase). Voice-over films use one channel, the sound-tract, to make statements about events seen in the other, and although the voice does not literally produce the images, its simultaneous position and other cues lead us to take them as proceeding from the act of speaking. Other films, in the course of non-narrated action, introduce scenes in which one or more characters tell others a story (or stories), followed, in various sequential programs, by scenes of selected or expanded story events. We take the scenes that follow as *enactments* of the story-telling, a dramatic rendering of narration that has itself been dramatized. (I shall limit my use of the word to these metamimetic or metadiegetic narratives and refrain from applying it to the visualization of voice-overs, intertitles, etc., at the diegetic level.)

The relationships of these complex transmissions of the story are by no means generally understood: they have been addressed by film theoreticians as intersemiotic translations (from one sign system to another); or as multiple codings, as in mixed-media arts; or on the model of psychically "overdetermined," redundant but revealing expressions. If we stay close to the pragmatic activity that is involved in moviegoing, we find these layered presentations perspectivally embedded—one situation (storytelling) encompassing another (dramatic)—with each making sense only in the context of the other. We understand narrated films as colored by their narrators even when a mere opening and closing voice-over places a personal frame around the action—as in *My Favorite Year*, though perhaps not vividly in *The Name of the Rose*.

Audiences seem to have little difficulty—although innovative filmmakers give them reason to have some difficulty—either in relating certain scenes to others as the telling and the told, or in placing voice-overs as later renditions of earlier events. Members of the audience are competent, in varying degrees, to discriminate differences between the spoken data and the visualized events—and sometimes they protest against discrepancies that suggest they are being lied to by a character or manipulated by a filmmaker. Their overall success in grasping such arrangements suggests that they take them, tacitly and unselfconsciously, to be what is required for narrated films, even if they do not use the term. It also suggests that the arrangements constitute a code of narration specific to cinema, though drawing on literary narration for some of its language and tactics.

Among the features of the narration code, a number follow from the above account: (1) there are images or sounds of person(s) speaking or writing to person(s); (2) there are narrative statements, that is, assertions to the effect that an event or events occurred (sometimes these take the form of descriptions asserting that a state of affairs existed); (3) these narrating acts occur in varied relations (frequency, duration, span of content) to scenes of the narrated events—for example, the scenes may be far more extensive than the statements—yet even unspecified scenes and their rich visual data are taken as generated by narration; (4) there is a subcode of transitions between scenes of narration and enactments of their content, such that audiences recognize time and space shifts and other relations between storytelling and story worlds. (A simpler subcode orders temporal relations between voice-overs and the events they narrate.)

The narration code systematically exploits the narrator-effect that may be inherent in cinema, both at the level of the film as a whole and at that of the stories told within it. One may also posit that, along with an aura of authenticity derived from a visible person as source (perhaps less intense when the narrator is heard only), the story also carries an associated message that it and its narration are fictive—that is, artificially devised by the filmmaker(s)—even when a recognizable or otherwise authoritative person speaks the voice-over or appears on-screen to attest to the events portrayed. While the motivation ascribed to film practices has almost universally been connected to realism, empathy, and other forms of intensified conviction by the audience, the effect of storytelling situations is to encourage a sense of fictiveness along with personal participation. Narrated stories seen and to some degree believed are also perceived to be stories told, and thus marked as created by the thought and speech of men and women.

This sketch of a narration code merely generalizes the elaborate repertoire of means employed by narrated films, one that has developed over time and undergone many changes. Although historically generated, it may be described as a cumulative construct, and my opening chapter is designed to give a synchronic account of the system, both to set out the theoretical possibilities and to indicate how efforts of various kinds are related. The narration code is also a matter of institutional practices that respond to differing conditions of the industry, the audience, and the technology. My survey history of narrated films in chapters 2 and 3 makes scant pretense to exhaust the influences of politics, commerce, and the larger culture on the relatively small affairs of film narration. It will confine itself to a number of filmmaking trends that shifted efforts in this realm— as well as singling out individuals whose creativity or curiosity opened up new modes of approach.

To what end? One of the unintended consequences of an Occamite argument may be to clear the field even of its own concerns. By urging that films are narrated not by their very nature but by choice and conventions, I may have raised the suspicion that those that are narrated are only illusorily so. If narration is taken to be an optional resource, it risks being seen as superficially applied or spuriously added, a self-indulgence by certain filmmakers or part of a period style. What does narration add to a film that may be considered well worth the having?

A substantive reply must come from the representation of varied strategies and exemplary films that makes up this book, but a theoretical hint may arise when cinema's rhetorical functions are considered in the abstract. Seymour Chatman has argued persuasively that narrative films are not normally assertive or descriptive: "It requires special effort for films to assert a property or relation. The dominant mode is presentational, not assertive. . . . In its essential visual mode, film does not describe at all but merely presents; or better, it *depicts*, in the original etymological sense of that word: renders in pictorial form."[22] Although Chatman does not develop the implication, we may employ his idea that the camera depicts but does not describe as an indication that films describe only when they are narrated. Narration is the "special effort" by which films complement their visual and sonic depictions with perspectivally oriented statements—the expressed attitudes and judgments of truth by a narrator.[23]

The difficulty of distinguishing the sources of an image's affective burdens remains to haunt any theory that would connect optical point of view to audience reception in the absence of a firm basis in language. Narration in sounds and images, in "light" and nonlinguistic sound, becomes particularly questionable when we try to pinpoint it as subjective in origin and to locate the precise position at which it stands in the discourse. The strong realist tradition in film theory would avoid such quandaries by taking the image at its face value, as a literal transcription of the world and even, in flashbacks deriving from a narration, as "actual occurrences." (I shall pursue this issue in chap. 7.) But it is not necessary to argue the literalness of cinematic depiction in order to stand in proper awe of the task of disambiguating cinematic subjectivity in the film text alone, not to speak of the mare's nest of spectatorial subjectivity.

Normally devoid of narratological theory but, as I shall suggest in a concluding chapter, often attentive to the problems and solutions of subjective narration in modern fiction, filmmakers have frequently availed themselves of the resource of storytelling to convey all or part of their dramas from a particular perspective. The degree to which they have been able to convince the realist that what he or she sees is something other than "actual occurrences" has varied, as much with the skill of the filmmaker as with the suggestibility of the viewer. The extent to which spoken or written narration has imposed the perspective of an impersonal authority or a character—and either encumbered it with or disencumbered it from that of the filmmaker, according to his intentions—must be judged from the detailed cases to be examined. But there is no gainsaying that when a character and even, under certain conditions, a commentator report a past event, they convey by the same linguistic act not only a grammatical position but an existential one—the responsibility entailed in intentional acts. A narrated story becomes indelibly "my story," his or her story, or even *its* story, when we have an impersonal voice-over speaking in the stance of Time or History—though these are not the last word in determining the audience's response.

Flowing from the general awareness that cinema is a synthetic medium, which can incorporate almost any other art or rhetorical function, is an implication that verbal reports by individuals of their views of past events are perfectly at home there. Cinema is a mimetic art that, like theater, is hospitable to narration:[24] it can incorporate storytelling as an explicit portion of its discourse and even make it part of its story content—as itself a significant event. In films that do so, narration is not merely an aid to communication but manifests and illuminates an eminently human sphere of action, well worth scrutinizing in its conduct and consequences.

1

Storytelling Situations:
Working Definitions

W HILE EVERY MOVIEGOER recognizes voice-over as a narrational act, and most are aware of early storytelling scenes
as framing narration, there are few established terms beyond
these and signs of hesitancy in devising new ones to talk about
narrated films. Flashbacks too are recognized and named as
such, but while audiences are tacitly aware of both the visual
and the verbal cues by which time shifts are signaled, there is
less attention to the differing effects of one or the other code on
the story represented—a situation that an enlarged repertoire
of descriptive terms might help to rectify.[1]

Despite the natural resistance to additional nomenclature in
an already crowded theoretical field, I am proposing a new set
of terms for the variety of narrational practices in films. These
names, descriptive and not categorical, have been developed
inductively from observations of storytelling activities in a body
of over 250 films. As in every effort to generalize from a limited
range of data, while responding to the observable differences in
detail, compromises have proved necessary. Despite my empir-
ical impulses, an arrangement has emerged that perhaps gives
the impression of a taxonomy. The appearance of a system in
what follows will be justified only by its capacity to provide an
overview of widely varied practices and by its convenience for
distinguishing and relating them in specific films (see Fig. 2).

The storytelling that will be analyzed in this book is that of
fiction films, distinguished as such not by the nontruthfulness
but by the invention—the made-up-ness—of their stories.[2]
Without claiming that this fictiveness represents the essential,

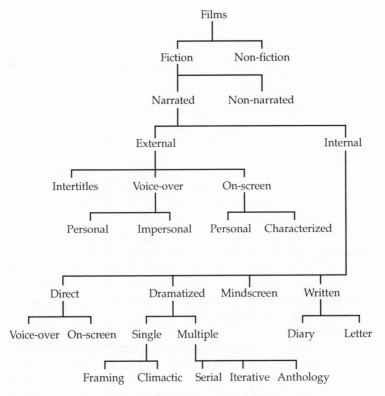

Fig. 2. Varieties of narrated film.

or even the most desirable, kind of cinema, I have looked to this body of films for my subject matter, making only occasional comparative reference to narrative documentaries (i.e., films with purportedly noninvented stories) and experimental films that eschew stories. To expand a conflated set of distinctions: We have to do with films *with stories* rather than those without them, and films with *fictional* stories rather than those with purportedly nonfictional ones.

Let us recall, according to the argument just concluded (indeed, opened), that while films in general are not narrated but mimetically performed, some films employ coded signals to give the impression that their images and sounds proceed from a narrator. In this restricted sense, fiction films may be classed as *narrated* or non-narrated, the latter being presentations of dramatic action that do not make special efforts to suggest that they are narrated. Since narrated films are only provisionally so, they might be referred to as "'narrated' films" (quotation marks of "as if"), but this seems excessively fussy. Despite the failure of the term to express the rationale for calling a set of (by definition, non-narrated) films "narrated," it may be useful in highlighting their aspiration to mark themselves out against the norm of films in general.

Non-narrated films constitute, according to my observations on a body of about fifteen hundred items, approximately five out of six fiction films in the sound era.[3] We are dealing, then, with the relatively narrow category of *narrated fiction films*. Yet the techniques to be discussed appear in isolated scenes or sporadic usage in a much larger number of films, so that the interest of these phenomena goes beyond any definitive corpus. Indeed, the decision to classify a film as narrated must be a selection from this larger number, based on observation of its total working and judgment of its effect.[4]

Within this limited grouping, a broad division may be discerned between films narrated from a source outside the world of their story and others narrated by a participant in that world, that is, by a character. I shall call these *externally narrated* and *internally narrated* films, with corresponding external and internal narrators (plainer than Genette's "heterodiegetic" and "homodiegetic" narrators). As we soon discover, a number of storytelling situations offer examples under both these heads; for example, voice-overs may be either external or internal to their story world. Both commentators and characters recount the past, and even pseudo-documentary voice-overs in fiction films may occur within or outside the "diegetic world." Thus the newsreel of *Citizen Kane* would count as internal narration, but the satirical main narrator of *Zelig* would not. The newspaper headlines and excerpts in both films are, however, internal narrations (see chap. 6).

External narrators, since they exist in a fictional realm distinct from that of the stories they tell, do not ordinarily address the characters (although there exist flamboyant floutings of this logic, in the manner of novelistic narrators' addresses to their creations; Genette would call them metalepses). They directly address the real recipients, the moviegoers, and thus—if every narrator may be said to have a narratee—the external narratee is the audience. Internal narrators have no qualms about metalepsis and more often address their stories to the audience (usually in voice-over) than to other characters in the course of the action. The latter may be thought of as internal narratees, but their salient mark is highlighted by the word "auditor," especially in its secondary meaning, "a person appointed to examine accounts." Since crossovers may occur, the distinction between audience and auditor as cinematic narratees is related to but not fully symmetrical with that between external and internal narrators.[5]

External narration may be seen only, heard only, or both seen and heard; thus we have the silent film's *intertitles*, the noncharacter *voice-over*, and the less familiar *on-screen* external narrator. When it is the director who performs the voice-over— or another filmmaker, like the producer Mark Hellinger narrating *The Naked City*—that individual's current degree of notoriety may make him or her an identifiable source, comparable to those novelists who, by purporting to speak in their own person rather than constructing an "omniscient" persona, have been called "'author'-narrators."[6] We may wish to call the resulting modes of external voice-over *personal* and, where no source is nameable, *impersonal* narration, with the understanding that these are relative terms that depend on audience recognition and may vary at different stages in the history of a film's reception. (There may have been a time when moviegoers did not recognize the voice of Orson Welles, and that time may come again.) Most external voice-overs are, of course, performed by impersonal professional announcers, not only in the realm of documentaries but also among fiction films that emulate their techniques.[7]

On-screen external narrators are inevitably personal and almost always the filmmaker; even if they have not previously established their "image" with the audience, their proprietary stance would give them away. But there is a further range of practical moves. The filmmaker may address the audience in a flourish of in propria persona self-presentation, itself highly fictive—as do Jean Cocteau in *The Testament of Orpheus* and Jean Renoir in *The Testament of Dr. Cordelier*.[8] Or the filmmaker may speak to the audience while playing the role of a character, as do Robert Montgomery in *The Lady in the Lake* and Woody Allen in *Annie Hall*. The salient distinction in this mode is, then, between *personal* and *characterized* narration.

In the latter case, we are on the borderlines of internal narration, for the on-screen narration is made by the filmmaker while acting as a character. The audience's awareness of the filmmaker's personal presence while performing that role gives this form of on-screen appearance a special piquancy. There is a note of ironic doubleness or even triplication here: we are aware of a historical person at work both as director and as actor, as well as of the character that person plays. In Allen's films, such ambiguities are extended in the character's commentative asides to the audience. These are redolent less of the rhetorical metalepsis found in novels than of the longstanding theatrical tradition of stepping out of character.[9] At this juncture between external and internal narration, inventive filmmakers delight in exploiting the ambiguities of on-screen storytelling as such.

Turning to internal narrations, we find some of the same dichotomies but also a new range of possibilities. As noted above, most internal narrators address not another character but the audience, in autobiographical or reminiscental voice-overs. Since they communicate not with a member of their fictional world but with the ultimate receiver, the audience, I shall call such internal narrations *direct*. The character—or, in a few flamboyantly campy films, characters—may do so *on-screen* but, just as in the similar dichotomy within external narration, *voice-over* is by far the more prominent mode. It is tempting to call encompassing internal narrators "first-person," since they employ the pronoun liberally even when their tale is primarily about others, but the disadvantages of the term have already led to its disuse in literary studies (even external and "omniscient" narrators can and do say "I"!). If any pronoun is marked in direct narration, it is the second-person, yet even this is not invariably expressed.

On-screen internal narration has been elaborated by inventive practitioners into a poetics all its own.[10] Direct address may

24

adopt the conventions of soliloquy, a character talking to him-
or herself (Billy Wilder's *The Seven Year Itch*); it may be performed
by a figure external to the story who is characterized in his or
her own scene (the lecturer of Ingmar Bergman's *The Devil's Eye*),
or by a character serving as the transmitter of another character's
narration (Bergman's *Hour of the Wolf*); by the asides of a character participating in ongoing action (Federico Fellini's *Amarcord*)
or by a number of such metaleptic characters (Richard Lester's
How I Won the War); in extended autobiographical accounts (Merzak Allouache's *Omar Gatlato*) or in brief anecdotes (Fellini's *And
the Ship Sails On*). A dichotomy presupposed in all these variations lies between on-screen narrating from a reserved position
(whether a bare backdrop or a studiolike space) and that from
a story-world setting. When a character addresses the audience
from the story world, a greater metaleptic shock is offered.[11]

Character narrators who are seen as well as heard are more
likely to address not the audience but another character. Since
they do so as part of the dramatic action, we may call this *dramatized* narration. The story or stories they tell may also be acted
out, though not necessarily: witness the success of *My Dinner
with Andre*. If the story is shown, we may—as noted in the
Introduction—call the visualized events *enactments*. If not
shown, we have a storytelling situation one might call *dry narration* (Hitchcock's *Under Capricorn* has an especially dry example)—with the proviso that the alternative not be thought of as
wet. Since cinema finds it hard to resist the opportunity of enactment, other considerations do more to determine the form
and force of dramatized storytelling. These concern whether the
storytellers are one or several; where, in the course of the film,
they tell their tales; the extent (or span) of the story they singly
or collectively tell; and the degree of overlap in their reports.

Any narrational mode can be engaged in, in a given film,
by more than one narrator—there are instances of films with
several direct on-screen narrators—but I shall reserve the terms
single and *multiple* for a distinction within *dramatized* narration.
Dramatized storytelling may occur at any point in a film, but a
curious polarity develops among single dramatized narrations:
either they are found at the film's outset and close, as a scene
of narration that frames the enacted story; or they occur in the

course of the ongoing action, in a series of storytelling scenes, reaching a climactic moment of revelation in the drama. Situations of the former type are already well known as "frame" or *framing* narration,[12] while those of the latter might be called *climactic* narration.[13]

Other distinctions present themselves when narrations are multiplied. Such films may have narrators who, each in his own way, tell the whole story (more precisely, whose narrative span extends from the story's beginning to its end), substituting alternative elements (the game and, to a degree, the film *Clue* are paradigmatic). Or the narrators may severally recount segments of the story, the sum of their efforts constituting the whole. Let us call these *iterative* and *serial* narration, respectively—although I have considered calling them *Rashomon*- and *Citizen Kane*–narration after their canonical examples.[14]

Another option of multiple dramatized narration is the reciting of a variety of related or digressive stories in the course of a film (i.e., neither one story *n* times, nor segments *x-y-z* of one story, but *n* stories). We may consider this as *anthology* narration, although the adjective risks confusion with what are commonly called "anthology films" (by more than one director).[15] It is used mainly to present a variety of examples, not only of a theme but of character, as in Bergman's *Secrets of Women*, so that the framing situation becomes at least as important as the individual tales. There are also films that resemble their literary sources by delivering a wide assortment of narrations. At times the source calls for narrations to be embedded one within the other, for example, Wojciech Has's *Manuscript Found at Saragossa*. Other multiple narrations of disparate tales may proceed from a single character, as in Raúl Ruiz's *The Hypothesis of the Stolen Painting*. These latter two remarkable films stretch the rubric of anthology narration, but because of their rarity they do not form new subclasses—as yet.

Another broad alternative to direct and dramatized narration exists within the sphere of internally narrated films. Instead of directly addressing the audience or speaking dramatically to another character, the character-narrator may write the story down. Without stipulating minimal conditions for *written* narration, we may expect that at least part of the text as well as acts of producing it will be shown. Two broad categories of such writings come immediately to mind: *letter* narration and *diary* narration. (A more expository type, *memoir* narration—e.g., Robert Hamer's *Kind Hearts and Coronets*—is also possible, though rare.) Beyond the differing spans of their segmentations of the story, a more basic difference between them exists: diaries by their nature have no immediate addressee—although qualifications are suggested in chapter 7—while letters do. Thus letter narrations tend toward personal interaction—we shall study a case in which this is true with a vengeance—whereas diary narrations tend to be introspective commentaries, recalling the musings of interior monologues. The trait such films share, distinguishing them from direct and dramatized narrations, is to insert images of the written page between narrator and audience, thereby mediating the narrational process by an independent entity, a visible text—with what consequences we shall see.

Internal narrators may tell their stories to other characters in speech or writing, yet what if they cannot or will not do so but only rehearse them mentally to themselves? One additional option for communicating a story to a cinema audience involves the premise that its narrator does not speak or write but thinks the story through. In order to transmit these mental activities and their story contents to the audience, filmmakers have devised an elaborate code for what I shall be calling *mindscreen* narration. It is provisionally positioned in the accompanying diagram between dramatized and written narration because it shares traits of both these modes. The mindscreen narrator is seen engaged in a dramatic situation, although he or she does not tell the story aloud; and the tale may, although uninscribed, use the style of diaries or letters—either as a self-assessment or as if told to an intimate friend. The subject requires careful exposition and will be developed in a chapter of its own.

To summarize, I offer a diagrammatic arrangement not in the expectation of exhausting the subject matter staked out here, but to suggest how these empirically derived alternatives may be seen as related to each other. The value of these, as of all terminological tools, will be measured by their efficacy in description and analysis, to be determined from what follows. I have skimped on theorizing the main—that is, most frequently employed—situations, preferring to develop them by extended illustrations of how they work in specific films. But a word of explanation is due on the choice of situations to be dealt with and those that will be mentioned only in passing.

The chapters to follow describe voice-overs, both external and internal; (single) dramatized narrations, both framing and climactic; multiple narrations both iterative and serial; letter and diary narrations, among the written variety; and one (and a half, or *manqué*) instance of mindscreen narration. These chapters are designed to answer the implicit question What difference does it (the situation under discussion) make? I have therefore chosen, in most cases, to work on some important and fairly familiar films, where a consensus of interpretation is, if not stabilized, at least presumable as a starting point. Other situations will be neglected, for practical reasons that vary from case to case.[16] But a fuller review would be welcome, and one may hope to encourage further attention to the subject.

Any overtones of generic codification that may have been sounded in the present chapter must also be dispelled. These situations are not laid up in heaven, as a philosophical idealist might put it, but have emerged in the course of filmmaking practice. Cinema's history, like history at large, is not as neatly organized as a logical schema; certain situations have come into existence or have been widely practiced at various times and under differing conditions. Before entering into close analysis of narration in specific films, a brief review of the emergence of the main storytelling situations is in order. While nothing like a systematic history of narrated films can be offered here, the following chapters will suggest how various influences played shaping roles—influences from the development of technology, from broad cultural trends, and from the creative drives of individual filmmakers.

2

From Silence to Sound:
Texts and Voices

A LL HISTORIES of the cinema include an account of that momentous 1895 exhibition by the Lumière brothers at a Paris café, when the only movie audience that can be called truly naive was treated to the "cinema-effect." Beguiled by the idea of an audience cringing in terror at the moving image of a train's approach, the histories avoid mentioning another element of the situation, conducive to a "narrator-effect."[1] The early projections of what we would now call documentary footage (and even of the fiction film "The Sprinkler Sprinkled" and the home movie of "Baby's Lunch") must have included not only a viva-voce introduction to the new technology but also narration to guide the audience in these new categories of experience.

The words used on that occasion have probably been lost forever,[2] but we may be sure that one of the Lumières or their surrogate told the assembly that they were to witness a certain kind of spectacle. Codes for transmitting and receiving film genres and sequences had not yet been established, and so a supplementary means of communication would be called for: an announcer or narrator, of the kind described above as "external." Like any supplement, this could be tactically suspended for surprise effect and that, apparently, was the game plan for "Arrival of a Train at the Station." While some films in the early silent era, particularly short and farcical ones, were to be shown without announcers or intertitles, cinema from the first had to reckon with the near-impossibility of dramatizing stories of any complexity without language. Just as silent films seized increasingly on dialogue title cards, they also explored the possibilities of a narrated cinema.[3]

The polar impulses toward letting the story speak for itself and letting the audience know the facts and form attitudes would continue to condition cinematic practice throughout the silent era, and may even be detected at work in films down to the present. On the one side were marshaled tendencies akin to those in other fields—like the well-known aversion to "intrusive" narrators in literature—tendencies toward dramatic immediacy and formal economy. On the other side were ranged all the practical reasons for conveying by whatever available means the necessary information on which context, motive, and suspense are based.

Above and beyond the pragmatics of communication, there were independent reasons for using narrational intertitles in silent films. External narration, it was soon recognized, could advance from being a mere necessity to something of an asset. Before tracing developments in storytelling by title cards, we may witness a parallel phenomenon in the oral field. While the early "live" performances by the Lumières' announcers soon gave way to projected texts that made up part of the film and freed it of the need for verbal, if not for musical, accompanists, such was not the case in all corners of the world. Ever remarkable for quickly appropriating technology while ignoring a number of the assumptions governing its use elsewhere, Japan developed the oral narrator and retained this figure as a cinematic institution even beyond the silent era.[4]

Noël Burch has described the cultural situation in which Japanese screenings were accompanied by a version of the traditional storyteller of popular theater, the *benshi*.[5] To summarize the main points of his account: The *benshi* were theatrical performers, present in the movie house; they were no mere adjuncts to the main event, for people went to hear their favorites, the "stars" of their time; they supplied not only narrative information and commentary but also dialogue, in the absence of intertitles; they conceived of themselves as the true sources of the story and "fought bitterly against the introduction of new narrative structures such as the flashback." Although Burch is content to take this as evidence for his argument that early Japanese cinema maintained a refreshing freedom from the dominant—and manipulatively covert—narrative codes of Western cinema, we may be struck by other implications. Filmmakers, from the outset of their history, have shown an interest in delivering not only dialogue and other data of the story world but also interpretive and expressive statements about that world. And this the *benshi* provided in abundance.

It was intertitles, however, that became the prevailing narrational instrument in Western cinema. Nondialogue intertitles state time, place, and context, make introductions, transitions, and conclusions, summarize characters' mental and moral states, motives, and so on. Going beyond these primary, though by no means self-evident, narrational functions are others of a more subtle influence. Although far less personal than the *benshi*'s delivery, the intertitles' all-knowing fiats induce a narrator-effect even when an individual source is not stated. Certain directors, like D. W. Griffith, Cecil B. De Mille, and Abel Gance, went on to sign one of the title cards in a given film, thus assuming authority for the others by marking a personal presence among them. Although less loquacious than the "intrusive" narrators of literary epics and novels—although some directors approach them in this respect—the authorial presence in such films is of a kind resembling the "author"-narrator. When texts are presented in handwritten versions or in idiosyncratic styles, intertitles work toward endowing the film with the aura of the traditional storyteller. Although these textual markings passed from the scene with the coming of sound, filmmakers down to the present have devised equivalent means of making their presence felt in the narration as well as in the discourse of their films.

As the conventions of silent cinema expanded in range and recognition value, narration by intertitles became necessary in fewer situations. Flashbacks motivated by a character's visible act of remembering no longer required time shifts by the narrator (recall the *benshi*'s chagrin at their introduction); metaphoric and other implications of juxtaposed elements of the *mise en scène* no longer needed to be spelled out to audiences familiar with parallel montage. But if narrators and narration were less often necessary, they became, in the hands of certain filmmakers, even more desirable than before—to judge by the lavish use and careful execution of intertitles in the 1920s. Despite the spread of cinematic codes of story presentation, the trend was toward more rather than less narration—with a few exceptions soon to be discussed.

The first idea of silent-film narration that today springs to mind is likely to be of lengthy and saccharine intertitles in a dated literary style. Their rhetoric is, however, anything but uniform in manner or effect, and this body of prose bears closer inspection before being relegated to the realm of camp. To focus on Griffith's titles for illustrations may suggest an unrepresentative sample, but I do so to suggest the wide range of his narrational practices, almost as wide as that of the industry at large.[6] The titles of *Intolerance* (1916) have always drawn attention for their imposing content—historical, metaphysical, and political by turns—but they also bear watching for their rhetorical agility, as well as for their occasional heavy-footedness.[7]

The introductory statements propose not only the stories to be exhibited and an interpretive model—"the same human passions, same joys and sorrows"[8]—but comment on the discourse itself, in the best self-referential manner. The film's local and larger forms are specified, each story juxtaposing "hatred and intolerance against love and charity—and turning from one to another as the common theme unfolds." The intertitles that follow are mainly declarative sentences in the present tense, according to the prevailing conventions for accompaniments to ongoing action, but frequent departures from the norm provide not only stylistic variety but a number of local accomplishments. Certain narrative statements are made in the past tense in order to quote a canonical source and draw on its authoritative tone, for example, "There was a marriage at Cana. —John 2:1." Elsewhere, statements take an exclamatory rather than a declarative form (even without the implied punctuation mark), for example, "Equally intolerant hypocrites of another age." Others are stipulative but exotic, such as "In the Temple of Love. The sacred dance in memory of the resurrection of Tammuz." At times, narrational authority is given over to a character, as when Catherine de' Medici rallies support for the St. Bartholomew massacre: "Remember, gentlemen, the Michelade at Nîmes when thousands of our faith perished at the hands of the Huguenots!"

(an internal narration that is then enacted in brief flashback shots). Toward the close, narration and commentary run together as their afflatus grows: "Cyrus moves upon Babylon, in his hand the sword of war, most potent weapon forged in the flames of intolerance." And throughout there are the footnotes, further gestures to make the narration seem authentic, such as "Note: the ceremony [of the Cana wedding] out of Sayce, Hastings, etc."

We can only conclude that Griffith, with all his other laurels, must be considered our classic *benshi*. But he has close runners-up, in the persons of the De Mille of *The Ten Commandments* (1923) and the Gance of *Napoleon* (1927). They are almost equal virtuosos in rhetorical flexibility and range of emphasis, as well as being equally memorable by dint of sheer wordiness. We remember them as personal narrators, moreover, because their intertitles have distinctive styles—homiletic and pseudo-biblical in *The Ten Commandments*, frenetic and Hugoesque in *Napoleon* (e.g., "And a man, the defiant sport of the ocean, his Tricolor sail opening to the wind of the Revolution, was being triumphantly carried to the Heights of History"). To compare this distinctive film storytelling with a similar one in fiction: These narrators resemble that variant of the omniscient narrator, the "author"-narrator, a fictive construct designed to impress the reader with the notion that it is the real author who speaks (*"moi qui vous parle,"* as Thackeray insists).[9]

The honors for constructing the most personal, or "author"-like, of silent-film narrators are best accorded to Josef von Sternberg. At the beginning of his first film (with director credit), *The Salvation Hunters* (1925), we read, "Dedicated to the derelicts of the earth. . . . Our aim has been to photograph a thought—A thought that guides humans who crawl close to the earth . . ."— and much more in the same vein. Long descriptions introduce each of the main characters, while another is lavished on a harbor dredge. The film closes with asseverations that this has been a drama "not [of] environment but faith," and that the heroic couple are indeed "Children of the Sun." It is easy to sniff at rhetoric of this order, but we should not be too quick to label it "uncinematic."[10] It is a personal style as marked by a specific literary tendency—turn-of-the-century American Naturalism—

as the Idealist or Romantic styles of Griffith or Gance. One might conclude of Sternberg's, as of these other, intertitles not that they represent excessive literariness in filmmaking but that they are marked by anachronistic literary tastes. The cultural lag indicated by prose of this order, employed during the breakthrough decade of modern experimental fiction, is one of the shaping factors in the history of film narration; together with innovations more consonant with modernism, it will be considered more fully in a concluding discussion.

During the same years that directors of the heroic stamp were expressing themselves at some length in intertitles, other films were being designed to eliminate narration altogether. The most important experiments of this kind were F. W. Murnau's *The Last Laugh (Der Letzte Mann:* 1924) and Dimitri Kirsanoff's *Ménilmontant* (1926).[11] Both explored the possibility of presenting a story without any intertitles at all—that is, not only without narrational statements but without dialogue cards. Since the characters are shown in speech situations, the omission of texts supplying their words must be considered an alternative convention, not the unmediated realism their creators may have thought they were achieving.

The results of these experiments have been variously appreciated. *The Last Laugh* is widely acknowledged as a vivid adaptation of Expressionist techniques to an unpromising subject (a pompous doorman's decline after being demoted to washroom attendant). Here the omission of intertitles can work, by dint of sharp limitations in the complexity of the subject matter, not only in plot but in characterization. At the point where a sharp twist in the denouement is stipulated, Murnau and his scenarist breach their implied contract and add a narrational intertitle, explaining the improbable plot turn and indulging in some heavy irony about the story and their practice.[12]

In contrast with *The Last Laugh, Ménilmontant* aims at a fairly complex structure, involving action in two generations and with two central figures, orphaned working-class sisters. It is only in retrospect that the opening murder of their parents—in a highly imaginative montage of frenzied activity—comes to be "placed" when it is partly repeated as a memory flashback. The main action—both girls' seduction by a sleek rogue, their near-undoing but eventual survival and reconciliation—works by combining elements of familiar enough tales, while the characterization borders on stereotyping. The demonstration effected by these films, then, was that narration and even dialogue might be dispensed with, at least in elementary or conventional stories dealing with simple (read: lower-class) characters, but only by losing nuances of plot and character that even filmmakers as visually oriented as Murnau would find it hard to forgo.

Between the extremes represented by these wordy and wordless films, most silents struck a pragmatic balance in supplying story information without unduly interrupting the flow of dramatic action. But certain films adopted strategies for storytelling that, indifferent to trends in the style of intertitles, explored new strategies of film narration. In retrospect, we discover most of the situations outlined in the preceding chapter already employed in the silent era. One implication to be drawn from the evidence to follow is that the choices involved in film narration depend neither on sound nor on its absence—nor on other technical resources—but are constant potentialities of the medium, exploited at various times and places according to manifold imperatives and not merely to meet the needs of communication.

This account of intertitles has so far concerned their most frequent appearance, as a form of external narration (indeed, their positioning in the schema of situations in chap. 1 was restricted, for practical reasons, to that role). But as new kinds of films were added to cinema's repertoire, an expanded range of uses for intertitles was explored. Internal narration—either as a primary narrative directed, like external intertitles, to the audience, or as a character's recitation given in dialogue cards—was not foreclosed to silent films. An instance of the former, pervading an entire film in a way comparable to the first-person voice-overs of the sound era, was the pseudo-documentary *Grass* (1925). Ostensibly a Flaherty-style documentary on a primitive people, the migratory tribes of Central Asia, the film emerges as a fictionalized narrative of the exploits of its creators, Merian C. Cooper and Ernest B. Schoedsack (exhibiting the flamboyance that would express itself in another form in their *King*

Kong). Not only were the anthropological data distorted to stage scenes for spectacular photography, but the reportage—anticipating the "New Journalism" of the 1960s—focuses as much on the observers as on the observed. Given this emphasis on the dashing young adventurers in exotic lands, it is entirely appropriate that *Grass* be narrated in the first-person plural. The fictiveness of this self-presentation is suggested by the fact that the titles were written by a specialist, Terry Ramsaye, and their artificiality has not escaped censure.[13] The narration of *Grass* shares in the mixture of bold and false steps that attends any ground-breaking enterprise, but its achievement in expanding the rhetoric of intertitles cannot be gainsaid.

This use of intertitles remained rare, perhaps because it depended on emulating the emergent externally narrated documentary, while the more accessible channel for internal narrators lay in dramatic situations. The classic instance of framing narration, Robert Wiene's *The Cabinet of Dr. Caligari* (1920), will receive due attention in a chapter to follow, but other examples of almost equal merit were produced in the same decade and should be acknowledged. In E. A. Dupont's *Variety* (1925), a convict approaches the warden's desk—we see only his bowed back and his number tagging it—and narrates the story of how he came to such a pass, the story that the film then enacts. There is a return to the framing situation at the close, expressing the predictable ironies and homilies. We recognize here the prototype of confessional situations in many a *film noir*, for *Variety's* story is a variant of the pattern of infatuation, jealousy, and betrayal in such works as *The Postman Always Rings Twice* (Tay Garnett: 1946)—also recited by the fall guy in prison, in this case to a priest before execution.

Another framing narration, one in which the storytelling situation reaches a dramatic development of its own, occurs in Alexander Dovzhenko's *Zvenigora* (1928). In the opening scenes, set in the contemporary Ukraine, an old peasant tells his grandson tales of the national past, and these are enacted with a derring-do appropriate to the storyteller's folkish style. (By a curious fillip, the old man is shown in action in his archaic tales, as if to suggest that his enthusiastic imagination has placed him there and that the enactments express his subjective perspective.) This innocent pastime has political consequences, however (and not unexpectedly, given the tense situation in the post-Revolution Ukraine). The grandson, Pavlo, is so caught up in the nostalgic narratives that he becomes fair game for exploitation by counterrevolutionary nationalists and ultimately must be "corrected." Not only does *Zvenigora* employ an evolved form of framing narration; it is also a film about—and, in some measure, warning against—the power of storytelling as an influence on the imagination.

The other broad type of dramatized narration, in which a character's recitation of a tale constitutes the climactic action, is also to be found in this period. Jacques Feyder's *The Kiss* (1929), better known as a Greta Garbo launching vehicle and as a fine director's Hollywood debacle,[14] is nonetheless a clear indication of growing interest in narration and its possibilities. After a creaky plot unfolds in stylish Art Deco settings, the heroine tells her lover what really happened on the fatal night for whose events she has just been tried. ("I have something to tell you," she says, and we can savor the line's frisson, having heard the later Garbo speak!) Her storytelling generates a dual drama, one enacting her self-justifying account of an accidental death, the other enlarging the present complications as the lover learns that she is shielding another man—his rival, at that. Not content to turn the scene of narration into the dramatic climax, Feyder opened another door in the history of cinema by showing scenes that turn out to be enactments of lies, anticipating the much discussed case of Hitchcock's *Stage Fright*. As the heroine embellishes her tale, the flashback's *mise en scène* reveals the spurious details; for example, the hands of a clock waver as she fumbles for an alibi time. The mismatched inputs of *The Kiss* do not allow it to make high claims as a film, but in Feyder's hands it became a proving ground for narrational techniques that later cinema would further explore.

The silent film that most fully develops the dramatic power and potential complexity of storytelling is Victor Sjöström's *The Phantom Chariot* (1921). In the framing situation, the ne'er-do-well protagonist, David Holm, tells his drinking companions about—and we see the enactment of—a now dead friend's dire warnings against his dissolute way of life. This warning is couched in the legend of Death's practice of recruiting lost souls to drive his coach until they are replaced on the following New Year's Eve. After Holm appears to have been killed in a brawl, his friend George (now Death's coachman) recruits him—in a memorable superimposition—as his own replacement. On their rounds, George provides Holm with images of a happy family life, contrasted with what turn out to be recollections of his sordid life story. But the storytelling goes beyond the past and brings Holm up to the minute on his family's dissolution. Since his wife's murder-suicide plan is contemporaneous with the telling, narration shifts from a retrospective to a climactic and functional role—no longer recapitulating a past action but intimating a present drama. Holm wakes to find himself not dead at all and intervenes to prevent his family's miserable end, incited by the coachman's and his own storytelling.

So complex is *The Phantom Chariot*'s narrational structure that it seems to receive a different summary from each of its commentators down to the present.[15] The variance may be due in part to the existence of differing versions, for the film was re-edited after early audiences indicated difficulty in following the frequent flashbacks and multiple narrational levels. Yet Sjöström's effort to film both scenes of narration and their enactments as mindscreen events flowing from an unconscious mental state—and to let storytelling serve a crucial role in present action—indicates that the potentialities of this resource were early on apparent to the more adventurous filmmakers.[16]

Besides their first steps in the realm of direct and dramatized narration, silent filmmakers were also attuned to the possibilities offered by written narration. Although silent filmmakers do not, to my knowledge, extensively employ letters or diaries to tell stories, two films organized by other kinds of writing suggest that the idea was already being scouted. Although the later example represents the clearer structure, the one dating from the preceding decade turns out to represent the more challenging use of writing.

In Paul Leni's *Waxworks* (1924), a candidate for a job in a Madame Tussaud–type gallery is asked to write stories, presumably for an impresario's spiel, about the famous figures on display. The scene of narration includes not only the gallery operator and his fetching daughter but the aspiring writer in the throes of composition. Each of the stories, compounded of history and fantasy, is then enacted in highly imaginative scenes. An additional source of the film's charm stems from its use of the actor and actress who play the writer and the daughter for the protagonists' roles in the stories—always narrowly escaping the clutches of Harun al-Rashid, Ivan the Terrible, and Jack the Ripper. The implication of this casting, as related to the storytelling situation, is that the writer has projected himself and his beloved onto the hero and heroine of his tales. As in *Zvenigora* and other narrated films of this decade, we are called upon to attend not merely to the dramatic event and the consequences of storytelling but also to its psychological components. As in the folktale film, the subjectivity evident in the storyteller's behavior in the scene of narration becomes legible in the enactments of his narratives.

The more complex instance of early written narration is Mauritz Stiller's *Thomas Graal's Best Film* (a.k.a. *Wanted—An Actress:* 1917). Action begins with a scenarist dictating a film script to an attractive typist and making advances to her, which she flees. He then is shown writing the scenario alone and, after much head scratching and inept typing, submitting it to his producer with the proviso that the typist be found to play the lead. When this condition is eventually fulfilled, she is shown reading the script—"The Little Adventuress: A Cinema Play"—and visualizing its scenes. Some of the enactments of her reading are repeats of scenes previously shown when the scenarist was composing them (an early anticipation of what I have called iterative narration).

As if this interplay of narrating and action were not thick enough, *Thomas Graal's Best Film* approaches a postmodernist disruption of narrative levels as it draws toward resolution. The typist/actress turns out to be a poor little rich girl who has fled her stuffy home and invented a tale of coming out of poverty, and it is this phony story that has inspired the scenarist's writing. The "cinema play" is allowed to stand, even after the heroine reveals her posh origins to the writer in the course of their engagement. Thus the film, playing on the fictiveness of scenarios and the personal inputs of their creators, stands as a prototype of films-about-filmmaking, of which Fellini's *8½* and Godard's *Contempt* are the culminating examples. As in *Waxworks*, such films foreground the scenarist's inspiration by his erotic object, with the result that not only his scenario but the film as a whole becomes caught up in a *mise en abîme* construction.

o o o o

With the coming of sound, there was a period of understandable hesitancy to explore narration while making more basic adjustments to a new technology. But by the end of the 1930s, experiments had accumulated, a number of less rewarding options had been run through, and the means were in place for further development, even for a grand synthesis.

Taking the line of least resistance to the problem of sound narration appeared to involve recycling silent techniques, but this invited a certain measure of redundancy. Silent films had often declared themselves to be transformed literary artifacts by composing intertitles in the language, and often with the visual appearance, of a book. When adaptations of great novels were made in the 1930s, they continued to pay tribute to, and gain prestige from, their sources by embellishing themselves with bookish trappings. In Jack Conway's *A Tale of Two Cities* (1935), for example, literary iconography includes an opening shot of a volume of the novel and frequent intertitles noting historical events and dates (the first reads, "The Period"). But the new resource of voice-over could not be ignored. When the culminating line in the novel—itself an echo of another text—is reached, the voice of the self-sacrificing hero accompanies an image of the biblical scripture he quotes: "I am the resurrection and the life. . . ." At a later stage, in Robert Stevenson's *Jane Eyre* (1944), this doubling of voice and text becomes an active relation: as the heroine's voice reads from the novel over a printed page on the screen, successive lines are lighted up as they are spoken. The technique may today suggest a programed instruction course, but it is designed to show that the "pages speak," that the novel "comes to life" as a film.

In the midst of these doublings of texts and voices, other adaptations dropped the iconography of the book and allowed sound alone to perform its function. In Orson Welles's *The Magnificent Ambersons* (1942), the filmmaker's already familiar voice reads from Booth Tarkington's novel, initially over a dark screen and then over shots resembling book illustrations of a Currier-and-Ives small-town America. Later excerpts from the novel are freed of all textual associations, so that action accompanies and seems to proceed from the voice-over's somber resonances. The book is dimly placed at the origins of the story, but the voice that articulates it becomes by the close the effective authority for the denouement. Here, as in other branches of his practice, Welles took the resources of filmmaking well beyond their initial conventions; by declaring the text as sonorously and portentously as it does, his voice makes the filmmaker himself appear the narrative source.

Other adaptations extended the doubling of printed texts and voice-overs in an effort to establish textuality in their *mise en scène*. Many of the French adaptations of this period—in the style that New Wave filmmakers were to scorn as "films of quality"—show a desire to transpose to cinema not only a novel's story but also its narrational form. Jean Delannoy's version of André Gide's *La Symphonie Pastorale* (1946) repeatedly foregrounds diary entries that recall the novel's form. And Jean Renoir's version of an Octave Mirbeau novel, *The Diary of a Chambermaid* (1946), dramatizes the diary's role as a place of safe haven in the protagonist's vulnerable life, making the book a tangible object and showing the act of writing in shots of her pen moving across the page (to be called writing closeups when we consider their extensive use in the soon to follow *Diary of a Country Priest*).

Adaptation was not the only cinema enterprise of this period that encouraged employment of film narration. This was also the era of the so-called biopics, in which benefactors of humanity from every age and clime were brought to the screen. In exploiting their stories, films had to dabble in the art of biography and its narrational rhetoric. Most were content to historicize their subjects with factual intertitles rather than external voice-overs, while romanticizing them with florid plot inventions. More frankly fictional biographies of the time assigned characters other than the protagonist to tell the story, usually by voice-over as in Albert Lewin's *The Picture of Dorian Gray* (1945). In Frank Capra's *It's a Wonderful Life* (1946), the biographical activity is expanded into a voice-over dialogue by unseen spirits in a vaguely visualized heaven, thus bordering on dramatized (need we speak of divine?) narration.

In the wake of the biographical tendency, autobiography became a temporarily flourishing subgenre. On occasion, a historical figure was allowed to tell his story in dramatic action: in Michael Curtiz's *Yankee Doodle Dandy* (1942), the entertainer George M. Cohan presents himself to no less an auditor than President Roosevelt. A number of dramatically narrated fictional autobiographies also appeared during these years, from Josef von Sternberg's *The Devil Is a Woman* (1935) to Preston Sturges's *The Great McGinty* (1940) and Ernst Lubitsch's *Heaven Can Wait* (1943)—often, as in the latter two cases, the confessions of a roguish anti-hero.

A smaller number of films go beyond anecdotal storytelling to present their protagonists' lives as an effect of writing. Sacha Guitry made a fresh approach to the rogue's story by having him compose it as a memoir in *The Story of a Cheat* (1936). The protagonist is seen writing in a Paris bistro and the enacted scenes of his life follow; the film's special narrational trait, derived from René Clair films of the period, is that they are done in pantomime, with the narrational voice-over supplying a steady commentary. By positioning the scene of writing and the narrating voice in this way, Guitry has convinced some that the film has a novel-like subjective perspective: a film "told entirely from the point [of view] of the leading character"—even a *"film 'à la première personne' (et quelle personne!).''*[17] Yet it is written autobiography, rather than the novel, that supplies the model for such single-perspective narratives.

In the following decade, the autobiographical subgenre acquired added doses of black humor—the stuff of many a British comedy of the time—in generating a film that makes writing a full-fledged participant in both story and discourse. Robert Hamer's *Kind Hearts and Coronets* (1949) provides, along with other virtues, an extensive autobiographical narration as its protagonist prepares for imminent death by composing his memoirs in a prison cell. The scene of writing is intercalated with enactments of his multiple-murder program, and we return to that scene when he concludes the tally—just as he is reprieved! A zoom in to the manuscript lying on the table indicates wordlessly that the autobiographical text has become a full confession, that writing will be the agency of the master criminal's undoing. While neatly serving the purposes of comic framing for a mordant plot, the storytelling strategy turns the visible text into an important element of the story—demonstrating the potentially mortal consequences of autobiographical and other narrational acts.

Other modes of written narration were being explored at about the same date as these memoiristic texts. The films to be discussed below as exemplary uses of letters and diaries, *Letter from an Unknown Woman* and *Diary of a Country Priest*, date from these early postwar years. But the success of the exemplary films served as no guarantee of high achievement, and films that casually invoke written and other modes of narration are at least as numerous as those singled out here. While fictional adaptations, biographies, and autobiographies were a constant presence during these decades,[18] it was not from literature but from another medium that fresh stimuli in film narration were to come.

A number of historians have described the influx of radio's narrational methods into cinema: not only the storytelling mode of mystery serials that helped shape *film noir*, but also the news broadcasting style that (with an intermediate step through movie newsreels) played a role in the new genre of semi- (or pseudo-) documentary films. Especially in the *film noir* sphere, "radio was the cinema's major role-model for first-person narration. . . . [It] simply illustrated to one and all the spellbinding power of the human voice." As for the semi-documentary genre, "The style of *The March of Time*'s narration was so distinctive and so effective that in many people's minds it is still synonymous with cinematic narration."[19] While the pull toward identification with an intimate storyteller was distinct from the effects generated by an impersonal "voice of history," the conjoint effect of these radio-derived voices was to further a decisive shift away from the book-oriented idea of a film's narrational source.

Central to this development was the transcontinental passage of East Coast radio, along with theatrical, techniques in the portmanteau of Orson Welles.[20] In his "Mercury Theater of the Air" he had exploited not only the power of his own distinctive voice but also that of his characters to convey unseen actions by narration. We are often reminded of the pseudo-documentary style of the famous Martian-invasion broadcast, but should also recognize that the multiple narration of Conrad's *Heart of Darkness* was an equally distinctive event on the airwaves. Although it was an external voice that was foregrounded in *The Magnificent Ambersons*, it was the multiple characters' collective portrait of the protagonist that was crucial to the success of *Citizen Kane*. Welles introduced to Hollywood not merely the multiplication of dramatized narratives but the more fundamental notion of a film structured as a medley of voices.[21]

This broader exploration of technique marks the relation of *Citizen Kane* to the family-resemblance category known as *film noir*—a relationship that goes beyond matters of tenebrous lighting, corrosive views of American values, or other debatable generic traits.[22] We tend to think of such films as narrated by the jaded voice-over of a private detective, a personal anecdote tinged with his sardonic point of view. Yet as often as not these films are dramatically narrated in the course of police investigations or trials, and some of them share with *Kane* the inclination to build up a gallery of idiosyncratic narrators. As early as H. Bruce Humberstone's *I Wake up Screaming* (1941), in the year of *Kane*'s release, the program of multiple dramatized narration moved toward synthesizing these fragmentary reports in a collective portrait. At a succession of police grillings, witnesses and suspects are called upon to describe their relations with the murder victim, and the corresponding enactments flesh out not only the story but the absent character. Both of the climactic confessions remain unenacted, yet despite their being dry narrations the scenes of storytelling assume a power of their own (particularly that of the obsessed detective, an early exposé of morally dubious authority). Combining elements of serial narration (fragments of the plot being gradually pieced together) and of iterative narration (a series of partially overlapping accounts by men who have been involved with the victim), *I Wake up Screaming* early establishes the *film noir* tendency to expand the immediate case in a widening skein of corruption.

Even the *film noir* narrated by a single protagonist could achieve considerable complexity. In Edward Dmytryk's *Murder My Sweet* (1944), police grillings are the occasion for dramatized storytelling by the archetypal private eye, Philip Marlowe. But these scenes of narration are intercalated with enactments marked by extensive voice-overs, and the latter often convey subjective states quite different in quality from the factual reports and bantering repartee of the former. For Marlowe loses consciousness on three occasions—once knocked out, once slugged and then drugged, and once blinded by a gunshot flash—so that, especially in the hallucinatory montage sequence on the second occasion, his voice-over expresses psychological impairment that sharply contrasts with his cool and collected dramatized recitations. The fact that movie audiences seem to have had little difficulty in following even the more complicated of these transitions indicates that the coding of narrations and enactments was developing apace.

While dramatized narration, either as a single or a multiple series of investigative testimonies, remained the dominant option for *film noir*, a number of such films enriched the resources of voice-over. In Otto Preminger's *Laura* (1944), the voice-over is gradually revealed as an unreliable narrator,[23] who not only turns out to be the murderer but whose status as a source comes to seem questionable. "I shall never forget the weekend Laura died," the narrator begins; by the close, we have learned not only that Laura has not died but that the narrator himself has, as we see in the final scene. We sense here a groping toward a mode that might be called narration from beyond the grave, which came into its own a few years later in *Sunset Boulevard* (see chap. 4). Another expansion of the voice-over code was an experiment in present-tense narration, John Farrow's *The Big Clock* (1948), in which the protagonist delivers a running commentary as he goes about his desperate, time-constrained project—at times immediately communicating his mental states. When the film performs an elegant time loop by returning to its opening scene at the close, we are led to understand the entire narration and its enactment as an instantaneous mental review of his situation by the hero at the decisive moment of his career. At such points, *film noir* narration verges on the psychological and formal innovations that would animate art cinema a decade later.[24]

The employment of voice-over in that other phenomenon of the 1940s, the semi- (or pseudo-) documentary film, was at least as intensive as in *film noir*, but neither as varied nor as exploratory. Louis de Rochement's awareness of the potentialities latent in his *March of Time* format for endowing fictionalized versions of contemporary events with a look of authenticity quickly seized upon its voice-over narrator as an inducement to belief.[25] The result was to extend to feature films the stern masculine voice subsequently to be denounced as authoritarian, enjoyed as camp, or satirized in a series of films from *Citizen Kane* to Woody Allen's *Zelig* (see chap. 6).

Henry Hathaway's *The House on 92nd Street* (1945) was the first and in some ways the best of this genre, but its narration makes a bulbous pill to swallow, with its war-fever threats of national security breaches and its aura of sanctity for the forces of law and order. What may remain rewarding for the more relaxed moviegoer of today, however, is the connection established between voice-over narration and the investigative process, especially as the latter becomes a process of filmmaking. Not only do this and its brother films insert documentary footage of the espionage background ("These are actual films taken by the F.B.I."), but there are staged scenes of the surveillance operation at work—in *House*, the filming of a Nazi spy nest through a trick mirror. The narration delivers more than a dreary historical report, self-consciously foregrounding the process not only of investigating but of documenting events. Indeed, these scenes of covert filmmaking are as explicit about the material conditions of cinema production as any avant-garde theorist could desire.

Subsequent pseudo-documentaries turned not only to a fresh set of political targets, as in William Wellman's *The Iron Curtain* (1948), but also to other kinds of sensational story material. Elia Kazan's *Boomerang* (1947) adapted the documentary style to a domestic crime case and in the process reduced the lofty omniscience of the historical narrator to a more folksy, and more garrulous, style (e.g., "Some wag once remarked that after New York it's all Connecticut"—while the camera pans over the small-town locale). A happier modulation was effected in Hathaway's *Call Northside 777* (1948), in which the narrator begins by providing historical perspective ("In the year 1871 a great fire nearly destroyed Chicago . . ."), but eventually develops a more intimate relation to its subject. As its investigative-reporter hero pursues his quest to overturn a typical "wrong-man" conviction, the voice-over follows his steps in steady increments: "MacNeill divided the district back of the [stock] yards into blocks and sections, and for days and nights systematically combed every beer parlor and saloon." Pseudo-documentary narration proved capable of closely attaching itself to an individual as more than a mere case study by taking pains to record his experience in concrete and precise detail, matching that of its *mise en scène*.

o   o   o   o

The opening years of the new decade saw the elaboration not only of previous strategies but of their psychic and moral implications. The multiple storytelling in many a crime film, in which numerous testimonies constitute a system of data collection, now came to serve a different enterprise, in which the multiplicity of stories represents a problem of interpretation. A transitional film in this regard was Dmytryk's *Crossfire* (1947), where the formula of *film noir* police investigations probed a state of mind along with a series of events. Three versions of an anti-Semitic murder are recounted and partially enacted (one of them an ancillary account, to be sure); including the murderer's among them allows the film to follow the workings of the unreliable narrator's mentality. It must have come as an intriguing suggestion to more than one filmmaker that this system of multiple versions could be used to explore the labyrinth of human communication, the conscious and unconscious distortions of the psyche, and the ambiguities of narration itself.

The year 1950 is usually thought of as the watershed of problematic narration, with the appearance of Akira Kurosawa's *Rashomon*, where successive versions of the same story called into question not only narrators and stories but the nature of human truth (see chap. 6). We might as readily recall that year for the emergence of other modes of multiple narration, working toward similar ends. Joseph L. Mankiewicz's *All about Eve* (1950)

47

adopted the *Citizen Kane* model of serial narration to trace the career of another American success figure, but with results almost as ambiguous as those of *Rashomon*'s iterative narration. Several of her "closest friends" rehearse the stages of a gamine's rise to stardom; all seem to agree on her reprehensibility and their own exploitation by her. But the self-characterizations of these narrators—particularly the most informative, the critic Addison DeWitt—enmesh all concerned in a mutually parasitic world, so that the film's title comes to refer to those around Eve, her narrators, as much as it does to her. An important element of this relativizing process is the curious occasion of the story-tellings: they are unspoken narrations by the friends as they sit at an awards banquet—a situation that foregrounds the subjective origins of each account. *All about Eve* may be seen as an early follow-up on the mental storytelling previously explored in such films as *Daybreak* and *Brief Encounter* (see chap. 8), elaborating it into multiple mindscreen narration with even more complex results. But the subjectivity of storytelling was only vaguely suggested in the ensuing collective portraits of Hollywood figures (Vincente Minnelli's *The Bad and the Beautiful:* 1952) and communications moguls (José Ferrer's *The Great Man:* 1957).

An alternative possibility, that multiple narration could lead not from consensus to ambiguity but from appearances to inner truth, was indicated in this period by Andrzej Munk's *Man on the Track* (1956). Here the storytelling program calls for a series of reports to an inquiry committee investigating a fatal railroad accident. The climactic incident is narrated and enacted three times over, each time at the close of differing characterizations of the dead locomotive driver. This mixture of serial and iterative narration develops nuances of character equal to those of *Rashomon* or *Eve*, as it gradually shifts from the superficial view to the hidden qualities of a craggy personality. In place of the "great man" debunked, we get the ultimately penetrating tale of a mistrusted traditionalist who emerges as a quiet hero.

In tandem with the elaboration and refinement of the multiply narrated film, the 1950s witnessed a virtual takeover by the autobiographical narrative done in first-person voice-over.[26] Nineteen fifty was, we recall, the year not only of *Rashomon* and *Eve* but also of *Sunset Boulevard*, which has joined them in the movie pantheon. The film's striking depiction of its Hollywood milieu rests on a thorough mastery of the fictional autobiography, as Joe Gillis frames his great adventure not only with details of his early life but with his death and postmortal perspective (more on this in chap. 4). Even without these extraordinary aspects, however, Billy Wilder's film may be seen as advancing a widespread enterprise.

Jean Renoir's *The River* (1951) showed the great director experimenting in a number of cinematic elements, color and locale prominent among them, but not least in shifting his focus to an individual's perspective on a social milieu (already begun in *The Diary of a Chambermaid*). The voice-over narration, scripted by Rumer Godden from her semi-autobiographical novel, beautifully articulates the nostalgic—indeed, elegiac—tone of the film's larger discourse. As in comparable literary narration in the hands of a Katherine Mansfield or an Elizabeth Bowen, the retrospective stance ("This is the story of my first love") carries with it a sense of the narrator's present emotional life ("I can still see the little lights"). By attuning his use of color, acting style, and montage tempo to this narrational chord, Renoir was able to convey a dual temporal perspective in the look and "feel" of the film as a whole.

Much the same can be said for Mikio Naruse's *Mother* (1952), but here the autobiographical reflections of a woman on her adolescence carry less an elegiac than a celebratory tone. As the voice-over introduces shots of her family in characteristic behavior, we see a young girl engaged in matutinal chores ("This is me") and watch a man come out of a wash-house drying himself ("And this is Pa"). This disarming naiveté is maintained throughout the film as it follows the family's business fortunes, the heroine's first romance, the father's death—all very matter-of-fact but with a hint of continuing significance in the present ("I'll never forget this day," she says at one point, but it is clear that she will never forget any of it). It is not for all tastes, to be sure, but only a heart of stone would fail to respond to such scenes as that in which Tashiko watches her widowed mother wrestling with her little nephew, reasserting the life of the family and its young.

Other autobiographical narrations of this period are not,

however, done in voice-over, or not entirely so. Luis Buñuel's *Adventures of Robinson Crusoe* (1952) takes up the novel's invitation to adopt the resources of written narration and makes the most of them. In the established manner of adapting the classics, the opening shot shows the printed pages being turned, but the ensuing action foregrounds the handwritten text and the activity of journal keeping. In dramatizing the autobiographer's devotion to recording and evaluating his experiences, Buñuel manages to give a fairly dispassionate rendition of a classic text and still insert indelible marks on his own metaphorically castaway status in Mexico during this period. The Buñuel etching tool does not score as deeply here as it does in his version of *Wuthering Heights*, but the scenes of writing help to make the film autobiographical for the filmmaker as well as the protagonist.

The film of the 1950s that most fully dramatizes the act of autobiographical narration is Sergei Bondarchuk's *Destiny of a Man* (1959). Its narrational situation—a soldier telling of long sufferings on his voyage home—is as old as the *Odyssey*; in this case, it is a World War II veteran who stops by the wayside to tell his story to a sympathetic listener. But this receptive bystander happens to be a look-alike for Mikhail Sholokhov (I have not been able to confirm the novelist's actual performance in the film, based though it is on his short story). The eventual return to the framing situation shows the soldier and his adopted orphan going off on their way, with the listener attentively looking after them. A closing title card gives the final lines of Sholokhov's text, along with his personal signature. Nothing is asserted, but we receive a sense of conviction on two accounts: the depth of the sufferings both of the protagonist and of the author, who bears witness to the authenticity of his fiction. By building Sholokhov into *Destiny's* narrational system, Bondarchuk showed that creators other than the director might be coded as a film's personal source, although his own presence in acting the role of the soldier also competes for attention.[27]

For the 1950s were the heyday of *auteur* theories of creation, and it is not surprising that filmmakers responded to the mystified images of themselves in the criticism of the time by playing a prominent role in narrating their films. Following the example of Welles, Jean Cocteau used his voice-over to telling effect in

Orpheus (1950; see chap. 4), and filmmakers under his influence, like Jean-Pierre Melville, soon followed suit (*Bob le Flambeur*: 1956). Even more overt was the on-screen appearance of the director to introduce his film, as with Hitchcock in *The Wrong Man* (1956) and Renoir in *The Testament of Dr. Cordelier* (1959).[28]

In these on-screen direct addresses, filmmakers were taking on a narrational role that had been played by characters before them and would be again with increasing frequency. The practice dates at least as far back as Sam Wood's *Our Town* (1940), where the town historian who discourses to the audience is taken over from Thornton Wilder's play. A more complicated use of internal on-screen narration was Robert Montgomery's *The Lady in the Lake* (1946)—famous, or infamous, for its extensive use of subjective camera techniques but worth attending to for its narrational methods. Montgomery appears on-camera in his role not as Philip Marlowe the hero-in-action, but as Philip Marlowe the emphatic narrator of his adventures. Although he appears "in character," Montgomery's dapper presence equally conveys the impression of a director's chat with his audience—that is, an external commentary as well as an internal expression of the private eye's view of life. The mixed signals of simultaneous speech by commentator, character, filmmaker, and actor remain challenging long after the subjective camera technique has become standardized.

Despite these exercises in metalepsis, it was still a shock to see Tom Ewell meditating aloud in the on-screen soliloquies of Wilder's *The Seven Year Itch* (1955). While framed in the grammar of talking-to-oneself rather than of direct address to the audience, these recitations were doubly effective: not only serving for access to the protagonist's mental processes (lust, anxiety, etc.), they also narrated his fantasy scenarios. Their enactment in a series of comic episodes—the onslaughts of desirous women, a grand seduction of Marilyn Monroe, his wife's tryst on a vacation hayride, her punishment of his infidelity—became an alternative narrative that ultimately outweighs the main action, both in the hero's mind and in the audience's. Although ambiguous as direct narration, the film showed that the time was right, even in a Hollywood "entertainment," for experimental narrational strategies.

Frank Tashlin was quick to take the hint, and in the next year he directed Ewell in a film that went Wilder's one better. Instead of the Ewell character alone before the camera, *The Girl Can't Help It* (1956) adds other characters' direct address, reaching a finale in which all three protagonists engage in multiple on-screen narration. This musically accompanied finale has affinities with the conventions of theatrical musicals, where everyone is called on-stage for a spectacular crescendo, but it was nonetheless a striking innovation in the cinema—partially justifying the New Wave's high estimation of the film and its director.[29]

From this point, on-screen direct narration was to become a familiar convention in the art cinema of the 1960s and after. Richard Lester's *How I Won the War* (1967) and Ingmar Bergman's *Hour of the Wolf* (1968); Arthur Penn's *Little Big Man* (1970) and Merzak Allouache's *Omar Gatlato* (1976); Federico Fellini's *And the Ship Sails On* (1983) and Agnès Varda's *Vagabond* (1985)—all may be considered representative of its usage in the following decades. The list suggests the powerful stimulus to further development in this narrational situation—as in others—that was generated by the experiments of the 1940s and 1950s. To introduce notions of evolution or progress would be as questionable in cinema history as in other histories.[30] Yet we may estimate that storytelling situations were as widely explored in the first decades of the sound era as they were subsequently to be problematized in the New Wave and art cinema to come.

3

New Wave; Art Cinema;
How It Is

NINETEEN FIFTY-NINE has usually been looked on as the precise moment when the New Wave began its powerful roll, broadening into the larger current of the 1960s known as art cinema and permanently changing the look of films in far-flung national cinemas. With the perspective of time, we may single out its specific innovations, including those in storytelling, though they may have been felt as part of a seamless whole during the movement's heyday. One has only to think of the opening moments of Alain Resnais's *Last Year at Marienbad* (1961), with its murmuring voice-over barely discernible amid lugubrious organ music—or the title cards for Jean-Luc Godard's *My Life to Live* (1962), dividing the film's segments of a life story as false-naively as those of a silent film—to grasp that established practices in narration, like those in story and discourse, were to be challenged, not discarded but renewed.

Where did this heightened attention to narration come from? Beyond the filmmakers' own absorption in cinema codes, there were the novelists who were enlisted to write its scenarios, some of whom went on to become filmmakers themselves. Marguerite Duras for Resnais's *Hiroshima Mon Amour* (1959), Alain Robbe-Grillet for *Marienbad*—both carried the experimental impulse of the "New Novel" into New Wave narration.[1] Along with Nathalie Sarraute, Michel Butor, and Claude Simon (whose Nobel Prize belatedly honors the school), Duras and Robbe-Grillet were engaged in extending the modernism of Joyce, Woolf, and Faulkner into new reaches of phenomenal, especially temporal, experience and its verbal processing. In its self-reflexive manner of putting in question every aspect of the traditional novel, the *nouveau roman* did not neglect the conventions of fictional narration. First-person narrators both ambiguous and highly unreliable (Sarraute's *Portrait of a Man Unknown*, Robbe-Grillet's *The Voyeur*); elaborations of diary and second-person narration (Butor's *Passing Time* and *Modification*); stream of consciousness with a shifting temporality and perspective (Simon's *The Flanders Road*)—all worked to place storytelling strategies at the center of attention.

Moving in the same direction and emerging at about the same time and place was another development in a neighboring field that had important consequences for filmmaking. *Cinéma vérité* (later called "direct cinema" by a school of documentarists with similar but subtly different emphases)[2] is sometimes considered an injection of social science "realism" into filmmaking, given its founding by the anthropologist Jean Rouch and the sociologist Edgar Morin. But "truth cinema" was never a simple matter of bringing the camera into the streets and filming life-as-it-is-lived without the intervention of the investigator. Rouch and Morin were fully aware of the methodological problems of observing and interpreting group and individual experience in their disciplines, and make appearances in their films, such as *Chronicle of a Summer* (1961), to plan and evaluate their projects. Not only do these frank interventions parallel the foregrounding of the narrational process that takes place in the New Novel and in New Wave films, but the substance of *cinéma vérité* films is itself a tissue of narrations by the interviewees. The "subjects," whether Africans or Parisians, are encouraged to tell about their lives and almost invariably deliver lively and skillful narratives. *Cinéma vérité* has been credited with bringing a number of vital influences into fiction films, and among these must be counted its vivid presentations of on-screen narrators. In speaking directly to the camera, they not only personally interact with their interviewers but intimately involve the movie audience in the drama of the storytelling situation.[3]

While no one could or would reduce the New Wave to a set of narrational strategies, some of its salient advances in cinematic expression will be found in that sphere. It is in this context that the career of Jean-Luc Godard is perhaps best construed. With all his striking inventions in camera work, montage, acting style, color, and sound, it may prove to be his sustained experiments in film narration that remain his lasting contribution.[4] Yet these verbal exercises are inseparable from Godardian semiotics—the stream of cultural signs drawn from advertising, politics, literature, what have you—that punctuates and even absorbs the ostensible subjects of his films. We are also frequently aware of a voice-over, evidently the director's, commenting, hectoring, and generally calling attention to itself. The semiological *mise en scène* and the omnipresent voice-over have each been acknowledged, but their connection in a unified story-discourse-narration has yet to be appreciated. Since these voice-overs are not only copious but as innovative, many of them, as his inventions in style and theme, it may be claimed that Godard's are among the most elaborately narrated films in cinema history.

While his second feature film, *Le Petit Soldat* (1960; released 1963), employed a standard first-person voice-over, it was in the fourth, *My Life to Live*, that a variety of cinematic resources were melded to create a synthetic mode of narration. The course of a prostitute's career, from innocence to experience and death, is structured here—in the manner of the Stations of the Cross— by a series of intertitles enumerating the stages of her progression. Some of these describe her state of mind and her actions ("Nana feels like giving up"); others sum up the stage of insight, or lack of it, to which she has come ("Pleasure is no fun"). Intersecting with these ironic tags, often resembling those in Brecht's plays, are others that draw on a wide range of textual resources. First of all comes a title card with an epigraph from Montaigne; later, as the heroine is shown watching Dreyer's Joan of Arc, we see a potent silent-film dialogue card ("We are here to prepare you for death"); and subsequently, a character's reading from a Poe story, with Godard performing the voice-over, is matched by the foregrounded image of the text. In the midst of these literate commentaries, an external voice-over of exaggerated dryness delivers a staccato question-and-answer recitation of the prostitute's working conditions (based on a judge's book on the subject)—the pseudo-documentary voice of history reduced to a baldly economic statement of the brute social facts.

While intertitles were used again and with similar effect in
The Soldiers (*Les Carabiniers:* 1963) and *A* [or *The*] *Married Woman*
(1964), Godard, never one to rest content with a good thing,
struck out on a new line of narrational experiment: external
voice-overs, almost invariably spoken by himself. *Band of Out-
siders* (1964) shows Godard overcoming the received theoretical
suspicion of narration, contenting himself at first with personal
remarks to the audience, like a bit of mild mockery for the late-
comers. After proposing to give the characters' subjective processes "in parentheses," the voice decides to "let the images
speak for themselves." But its narrational role develops in the
course of the film, as the voice parallels ongoing action, summarizes dialogues, and delivers lyrical commentaries.

What Godard had done for, or to, external narration he began
to do for internal voice-over in *Alphaville* (1965). Its opening voice
is, to be sure, redolent of traditional omniscient authority: "There
are times when reality becomes too complex for Oral Communication. But Legend gives it a form by which it pervades the
whole world."[5] But the scenario, evidently with some authori-
zation, assigns this gnomic wisdom to an internal source—one,
moreover, that grows to become an unreliable or at least adver-
sary figure, the supercomputer Alpha 60 (a predecessor of HAL
in *2001*). When the unseen computer engages in dramatic dialogue with the protagonist, telling of its quasi-omniscient control
of the futuristic dystopia, the distinction between external and
internal narration comes, indeed, to seem moot. Moreover, a
second character, the mock-detective-hero Lemmy Caution,
takes over as voice-over narrator, recounting his adventures in
conventional first-person summaries. One implication of this
multiplying and ambiguating of the voice-overs is that the contest
between protagonist and antagonist becomes not merely a struggle between man and machine but a competition for narrational
authority in the voice-over role. By the close, the "omniscient"
narrator is reduced to stating barren truths ("The world is a reality
. . . and I . . . for my misfortune . . . I am myself—Alpha 60":
p. 78) while the hero's rhetoric achieves broad judgmental scope
("Such people will serve as terrible examples to all those who
use the world as their theater, where technical power and its
religion become the Rules of the Game": p. 77).

Godard's next move in narration took up an inviting recourse for all experimenters: if you have run through your options, recombine them and observe the consequences. *Pierrot le Fou* (1965) employs almost the entire battery of narrational techniques: chapter-title inserts that incorporate literary tags and narrational matter ("Chapter Eight. A season in hell. . . . We crossed France");[6] voice-over and dramatized narrations by the protagonists, sometimes commenting on their own storytelling activities (MARIANNE: "Who are you speaking to?" / FERDINAND: "To the audience": p. 55); direct, on-screen addresses by a number of characters, including the hero's flip asides; diary narration, with writing closeups and to-the-camera as well as voice-over articulations; long autobiographical harangues by walk-on characters; even a spate of storytelling through mime by some lesser participants.

The mere listing, far from exhaustive, of *Pierrot*'s narrational gambits attests to the accomplished summation aimed at by Godard, but it may also hint at the rummaging among the ruins that tinges this, along with other aspects of the film. While increasingly self-critical investigation of cinema's resources proceeded in his other films of the late 1960s, it was in *Two or Three Things I Know about Her* (1967) that its corrosive tendency turned on storytelling itself. Not content merely to put external commentary, particularly his own, under scrutiny, Godard performed one of the few certifiable inventions in narrational technique, so as simultaneously to expand and to undermine its range. He placed a small receiver behind his lead actress's ear so that she could not only pick up directorial instructions but echo his hints and questions while playing her scenes.[7] External and internal, voice-over and dramatized, even sound and silent narration became strained, if not moot, distinctions.

The film opens with a documentary-like voice-over summarizing recent development controversies in Paris, then shifts to a shot of a woman on a high-rise balcony:

[*Godard's voice*]: This is Marina Vlady. She is an actress. . . .

MARINA: Yes, speak as if quoting truths. Old Brecht said that. That actors should quote. . . .

[*Godard's voice*]: This is Juliette Janson. She lives here. . . .

JULIETTE: . . . I have to manage. Robert, I believe, makes $225 a month.

(Pp. 24–30)

The breaking of narrative frames that we sense at work is accompanied by a mixing of narrational activities: stipulations for mimetic presentation are juxtaposed with first-person storytelling; bald statements of social (as well as filmmaking) facts alternate with interior monologues (for Juliette's self-reflections, even when spoken in ongoing action, are coded as unheard by other characters).

Just as the protagonist's opening account of herself is extended in voice-overs and interior monologues throughout the film, the external voice continues on in a number of modes. Its twenty-eight "commentaries"—so numbered and labeled by Alfred Guzzetti—extend the initial remarks on gross changes in the urban fabric to other cultural conditions of modern existence. As these include favorite subjects of semiotic interest, the commentaries develop a personal (and "authorial" first-person) style. Some concern the invasion of social processes into the work of filmmaking: "More and more there is an intermingling of image and language" (p. 190); others specifically address the problems of narration: "For example, how to give an account of events?" (p. 194).

This modulation from external commentary, through heard and unheard interaction of director and protagonist, to personal meditation makes *Two or Three Things* not only a narrated film but a sustained exploration of narration. As in *Pierrot*, there is an impulse toward providing a catalogue raisonné of storytelling situations: one prostitute's career is told in external voice-overs, another's in *cinéma vérité*–style direct address, while salesgirls speak toward the camera in the midst of ongoing action. The wide range of storytelling situations and the urgent interrogation of them turn narrating into no mere component but a condition of existence for full cinematic expression.

It is, like other basic elements of filmmaking, a condition by no means taken as innocent, even if fundamental. Godard's films of this period manifest, often declaratively, his increasing impatience with the medium as a means of personal expression and social truth—an impatience sometimes misconstrued as a rejection of the fiction film. For the director had learned how to make cinema with all the resources of the medium—as the New Wave's theory of the *caméra-stylo* had called for—but now seemed to find narrational virtuosity a mark of shame rather than of mastery (or shameful because masterful).

This inner crisis concerning the responsibility of the filmmaker explains, more tellingly than the political context, Godard's shift into other forms of cinema in his militant phase (1968–72).[8] The disappearance of the individual author into a collective entity—the so-called Dziga Vertov group, which became in the end a collaboration between Godard and the propagandist Jean-Pierre Gorin—represents one form of this concern. The increasingly extensive manifestoes of authorial ideology—both in lengthy and didactic voice-overs and directly on-screen (sometimes together with Gorin, as in *Vladimir and Rosa*: 1971)—may be considered another attempt at honest rather than covert manipulation.

Yet the impulse to amplify the narrational modes into bombastic ideological instruments sometimes resulted in genuine outbursts of cinematic imagination. The multiplication of choric voice-overs in *Wind from the East* (1970) reached toward a film on the model of an oratorio. The journalist and filmmaker protagonists of *All is Well* (*Tout Va Bien*: 1972) each deliver an autobiographical monologue in a studio setting, at times overtly responding to the unheard questions of an interviewer (an extension of the earphone technique in *Two or Three Things*, which, since it involves an unheard interlocutor, might be called "voice-under"). And just as the narrators in these films are free to comment on aspects of contemporary culture illustrated in still photos or documentary footage, there is even a film critically narrating the making of a film—*Here and Elsewhere* (1976), on the abandoned *Till Victory* (1970)—in which framing narration assumes the scale of an entire work incorporating and dissecting another. While the later phases of Godard's career show only sporadic flashes of the narrational inventiveness of his 1960s films, the potent intertitles of *Every Man for Himself* (1980) and his direct, on-screen discourses in *Carmen* (1983) indicate the continued scouring action of the New Wave, even in its recession.

To return to the beginning: While Godard was making his first full-length film, Alain Resnais achieved his own breakthrough with *Hiroshima Mon Amour*. While the importance neither of *Breathless* nor of *Hiroshima* can be reduced to their narration, we have only to recall the latter's initial impact to grasp narration's contributing role. The astonishing opening images of bodies connoting both eroticism and radioactive decay were accompanied by voice-overs (to be revealed as voice-offs), which soon adopted a narrative function (see chap. 5). The flash-cut memory image of wartime experience cried out for explanation, and dramatic suspense mounted toward the telling of that story. Eventually the unfolding drama reached its climax in an extended revisiting of the past, and narrational monologues became the focal points of cinematic experience. If any one film can be said to have put narration "on the map," as it were, that credit is due the creators of *Hiroshima*, Resnais and Duras.

If Resnais's first feature-length film made narration a force to conjure with, his second almost created a surfeit. *Last Year at Marienbad* (1961) begins with an internal voice-over on the soundtrack and seldom lapses from it during its entire length. Along with Chris Marker's shorter film *The Pier* (*La Jetée*: 1962), with its unbroken external narration, *Marienbad* may be called the most heavily narrated film of all time. Robbe-Grillet's scenario has received its share of both respect and abuse, and I shall add to neither sum. But it should be acknowledged, after due attention to prior instances, for bringing unreliable narration fully into play in cinema.[9]

Despite the novelist's often cited pronouncements on the experienced presentness of all screen images—in his metaphoric formula that films are always in the "present tense"[10]—*Marienbad* is a display of cinema's characteristic effort to assign a time to images, a process of inducing coherence by means of narration. It is not only the audience that is beguiled by the gap between the protagonist's assertions about past events and the temporally unmarked images that accompany them (as well as the differences between what he says on one occasion and another). The anxieties of receiving stories are fully dramatized in the heroine's harrowed experience, so that she stands as our surrogate. Nor is reception allowed to remain a distinct and innocent role, for the heroine is verbally seduced into supplying previously unspecified details of her purported physical seduction. As she gradually succumbs to the narrator's compelling language, they together demonstrate the power of narration to code images temporally and to induce belief in them—playing the roles of filmmaker and audience before our very eyes. In this, the cleverest of literalizations of a metaphor, the so-called seductive force of narrative is acted out as an elaborate sexual conquest. But the uneasy suggestion of the narrator's Plutonian (or are they Orphic?) traits is that the heroine's leavetaking is both an erotic liberation and a drawing toward death. Resnais and Robbe-Grillet made their film a monitory exercise in the miseries as well as the splendors of storytelling.

Resnais's subsequent ventures into narration and its discontents continue his sustained dealings with the themes of time and memory and the related drama of storytelling.[11] *Muriel* (1963) brings this drama even closer to home, portraying a group of characters' inept efforts to communicate their stories. Among these is a film: one of the characters reacts to his traumatic participation in the Algerian War by working on a personal documentary, excerpts from which we are shown. His limited success indicates that this is no certain route to truth or even to catharsis. *The War Is Over* (1966) was equally remarkable for developing a voice-over narrator of an original kind, an external speaker who addresses the protagonist in the second-person form. It recounts not only his past but his present activities as they transpire (and apparently even his actions yet to come), becoming at certain moments the voice of lyrical meditation on the Spanish exile's condition.[12] And in the decade following, *Providence* (1977) was structured as an extensive dramatized narration in which an insomniac novelist composes alternative versions of a work-in-progress. We must decode a spectrum of mental images, including enactments of his narrative, autobiographical events, and dreamlike hallucinations. Here the full range of mindscreen narration is explored—including what is told (to oneself), what is thoughtfully recalled, and what is semiconsciously imagined. Other Resnais films play on variants of the storytelling process,[13] but without substantially extending his already comprehensive survey. Though turning, in the twilight of his career, to a severely limited cinematic equivalent of theatrical mimesis (*Melo*: 1987), Resnais can look back on some of the most challenging episodes in storytelling devised by any filmmaker.

Another New Wave director, of almost equal inventiveness but narrower range, François Truffaut made himself the master of written narration.[14] While other directors steadily employ both novels and nonfictional texts as their sources, it was the largely self-educated Truffaut who exhibited endless curiosity and a near-reverence in bringing books to the screen. His first written narration, *The Wild Child* (1969), extensively foregrounds neither a diary nor a letter but the notes for a scientific report. Based on the accounts by Dr. J.-M. G. Itard of his study and education of a language-deprived child found in the forest, the film makes the act of writing up the case almost as dramatic as the struggle to inculcate symbolic thinking. Frequently shown in dramatic action (including writing closeups of page, hand, and quill) and read in voice-over by Truffaut, who also plays the role of Itard, this to-the-moment recording of the engagement between Enlightenment rationality and recalcitrant nature bears not only on broad humanistic themes but on the director's favorite and very personal theme—the "four hundred blows" unleashed by young people in the course of growing up. Numbered here among the blows given and received are those of language.

Truffaut's next period piece, *Two English Girls* (1971), was something of a tour de force, bringing together almost all the available narrational modes in an effort to duplicate the techniques of the film's literary source, an Henri-Pierre Roché novel.[15] Letters are shown being written and read: sometimes the text is delivered by voice-over, at others it is read aloud by the writer or reader—at one point in the manner of direct, on-screen narration. There is also the protagonist's novel, visually presented at the opening and near the close, to suggest its position as source. Beyond that, dramatized narration, interior monologue, and other gambits. After this bravura performance, one could welcome the forceful simplicity of dramatized narration in *Such a Gorgeous Kid Like Me* (1972), yet here too oral discourse gives way to writing. The titular character, in prison, tells her life story into a social researcher's tape recorder, and we watch the enactment of its picaresque scenes; but amusement turns to horror as we follow the sociologist's seduction-by-narrative, which ends with his imprisonment for one of her crimes. It seems scant consolation that he can authenticate by personal experience his treatise on female criminality—the manuscript that we see him working on in the film and that we recognize in its published form as the implicit source of what we have seen.

Truffaut's further exercises in written narration continue to probe the membranes separating story from storytelling. *The Story of Adèle H.* (1975) employs external, letter, and diary narration, in keeping with the heroine's highly literary (not merely deranged) romanticism, her effort to shape her life like one of her father's novels. *The Man Who Loved Women* (1977) exhibits another kind of literariness; it is framed by an observer-character's voice-over rendition of the protagonist's career, but we learn that she knows his story from his own narrative—the autobiographical novel he has submitted to her publishing firm. (We see him engaged in writing it and observe the varied responses to the manuscript at the publisher's.) One may hesitate whether to call this his narration or the editor's, whether it is voice-over narration, written, or a combination of the two. But the implication is clearly delivered that a mystified, lifelong pursuit of women requires articulation in writing, for this as for other Casanovas.

When, at the end of the decade, Truffaut returned to his longstanding autobiographical preoccupation and continued the Antoine Doinel saga with *Love on the Run* (1979), he also advanced his joint study of literary and cinematic storytelling. As in *The Man Who Loved Women*, the loves of a lifetime are not complete without textualization; here, Antoine has written an autobiographical novel that we must assume to be the fictional equivalent of the three (and a "half") previous installments of the film cycle. To flesh out this program, as it were, actresses from the prior films are recycled, visibly attesting to the passage of time and changed perspectives (the hero is, of course, rep-

resented by the appropriately maturing Jean-Pierre Léaud).
Thus, a character portrayed by Marie-France Pisier, who played
the heroine of "Antoine and Colette" (in *Love at Twenty:* 1962),
buys the novel out of natural curiosity and avidly looks up his
account of their youthful affair. Clips from the early film are
seen as she reads, accompanied by the novelist-hero's voice-
over. We gather that this is not merely a written narration but
a film that juxtaposes literary and cinematic representation, the
former carrying an uncanny sameness and difference from the
latter.

Not content with this frisson, *Love on the Run* extends into
the future the relations between present and past, between writing and cinema, when Antoine tells Colette the story of his new
novel, of which scenes are enacted with his voice-over. Many
other recombinations are considered, as when Colette meets his
ex-wife and they exchange stories about him, accompanied by
clips from the earlier films. A strong suggestion is left that narration and story are related neither as a present reflection on
past events, nor as a verbal translation of film images, but as
twin life-situations that reciprocally generate each other. Although Truffaut's last films exhibit only casual uses of storytelling situations, he had already done enough to demonstrate
his full participation in the New Wave's positioning of narration
at a central place in cinema.

o   o   o   o

While the New Wave was establishing Paris as the center of
the avant-garde in commercial filmmaking, beginning the process of breaking down the longstanding contradiction between
those terms, the more widely diffused impulse of what has been
called art cinema was coming to expression.[16] Although not exclusively European in reference, the term first calls to mind the
works of Antonioni, Fellini, and Bergman, which had as revi-
sionary an impact on film production and reception as that of
the New Wave. While Michelangelo Antonioni's films show few
instances of overt narration—*L'Avventura* may be described as
a film whose precipitating event is never spoken, much less
dramatized—and while Fellini's bursts of narration are not as
remarkable as his other cinematic innovations, Bergman's en-

terprises in storytelling were long sustained and cumulatively notable.[17]

Early Bergman exhibits the full range of dramatized narration—single (*Port of Call:* 1948), dual (*A Lesson in Love:* 1954), and multiple (*Secrets of Women:* 1952)—as characters rake over the debris of their lives. Written narration is well represented: by a newspaper report in *The Devil's Wanton* (1949), by a diary in *Summer Interlude* (1951). Perhaps most memorable of all is the intercalated tale of the clown with an errant wife in *The Naked Night* (1953).[18]

It was in the 1960s, however, that narration came to assume for Bergman something of a life of its own. Two films previously mentioned merit further acknowledgment for ingenuity in direct, on-screen narration. *The Devil's Eye* (1960) presents the spectacle of an authoritative lecture on Hell, complete with windy (but also witty) pedagogue, maps, and other paraphernalia, plus enacted scenes of the Devil, Don Juan, and their tribe. These scenes frame a comic fantasy set in the contemporary world— Don Juan's seduction of, and by, a modern young woman—but are returned to periodically for further commentary on the action. *The Devil's Eye* is remarkable as on-screen narration not only for its boldness in placing the external storyteller in a setting of his own, but also for using that setting's decor in a satirical dissection of a would-be eternal truth ("A woman's chastity is a sty in the devil's eye"). While the proverb is both illustrated and ironically undercut by the main action, the storytelling scene is filled with the trappings of genteel pedagogy that mark traditional wisdom as faintly absurd yet still worth considering.

An equal adroitness marks the internal on-screen narration of *Hour of the Wolf* (1968). An opening title card posits Bergman as a director with personal sources: "I had this story from Alma and from Borg's diary." The heroine is then seen emerging from their house and directly addressing the audience to tell her tale. In the course of the action, the diary becomes a key object of attention, although we do not see or hear its words. This multiplication of narrative authorities contributes to and partly explains the extreme ambiguity that the film generates. The essentially unviewable story of an artist's tormented mind is pieced together but hardly understood by the diarist, his sympathetic but overwhelmed wife, or the filmmaker himself—that is, by neither the primary, mediating, nor "author"-narrators. *Hour of the Wolf* confronts head-on the issues of how largely interior stories can be known, or be made known, in the cinema.[19]

As Bergman was reaching his apogee in the critical use of narration,[20] young directors entering the ranks of art cinema filmmaking were coming forward with equally incisive works. Bernardo Bertolucci's first film, *The Grim Reaper* (1962), employed the multiple narratives of *film noir* criminal investigations with sufficient ambiguity to invite comparison with *Rashomon* and *Citizen Kane*.[21] In *The Spider's Stratagem* (1969), this mode of filling in the past from fragmentary reports by the survivors is dramatized as a son's quest for the truth behind his father's heroic death, so that the revelations are by turns bewildering, personally implicative, and devastatingly negative.[22] And Bertolucci's most famous film, *Last Tango in Paris* (1972), although not on the whole a narrated one, features a climactic narration as memorable as any in cinema history—though its "dry" nonenactment must be energized by the power of Marlon Brando's performance.

In the early 1970s—perhaps in response to the striking acts of narration in the works of the new crop of art cinema filmmakers—Federico Fellini began a series of narrational experiments of his own.[23] In two films that freely mix autobiography and fiction, *The Clowns* (1970) and *Roma* (1972), he made equally free use of his personal voice-over and on-screen appearances. Taking another tack in autobiographical expression, *Amarcord* (1974) uses the direct addresses of a fictitious authority—a local historian or "histor," as his literary equivalent would be called— to introduce characters and incidents derived from Fellini's hometown milieu. A further variant of internal on-screen narration was employed in *And the Ship Sails On* (1983), in which a gossipy journalist delivers background stories on the other characters, his fellow passengers on an ocean voyage. Yet perhaps owing to his penchant for external and internal impresarios (including himself), Fellini's narrations do not develop in ways commensurate with his other cinematic resources.

Just as art cinema filmmakers were led to complicate their storytelling activities, several kindred spirits of the New Wave went on in the 1970s to pursue fresh modes of narration. Marguerite Duras, who wrote scenarios based on her novels for other directors in the 1960s, became a director in her own right, adapting her own novels and plays. A frequent element of this series of films, consistently probing the consciousness of their heroines, is their use of voice-over for lyrical, meditative, and ambiguously narrative purposes. In the best known, *India Song* (1975), the filmmaker joins with others to create a world of voices that seem personally knowledgeable about but independent of the world portrayed in dramatic action—leaving an open question as to which world is the more ghostly, the more beguilingly unreal.[24] If Godard's medley of voice-overs in *Wind from the East* had tended toward historical-oratorio declamation, Duras's unites the qualities of radio drama, stream-of-consciousness fiction, and poetry readings to generate a less public soundtrack of the mind.

An experiment of almost equal interest was Duras's on-screen narration in *Le Camion* ("The Truck": 1977). She sits at a table with the actor Gérard Depardieu—both of them simultaneously playing themselves and their roles—and explains the script of a film he is to star in. Scenes of the scenario, mainly consisting of a blue truck traversing the fields of France, are enacted—with the inevitable significant deviations between words and images. The ambiguity of Duras's and Depardieu's performance of the shadowy figures in the story comes to seem of less importance than their activities in the framing scenes, where storytelling and reception (particularly that of filmmaker and actor) become the main and more interesting action.

Another avant-garde filmmaker, Agnès Varda—her *Pointe Courte* (1954) is often called the first New Wave film—made a striking synthesis of narrational techniques in *One Sings, the Other Doesn't* (1977). She speaks the voice-over narration, in charmingly accented English for the export version; intertitles festoon the work in Godardian fashion; and the action, taking place over a span of decades, is summarized and carried forward by the twin heroines' exchange of letters and postcards. Something of this structure had already emerged in Truffaut's *Two English Girls* and would surface again in James Ivory's *Heat and Dust* (1982), placing *One Sings* at the center of a mini-boom in multiple-channel letter narration. Varda turned to extended internal voice-over in *Documenteur* (1981; the punning title is untranslatable), but it was in *Vagabond* (1985) that she took another firm stride—this time in multiple on-screen narration. Here a number of witnesses to the final stages of a dropout's demise recount, in a series of interview recollections reminiscent of *cinéma vérité*, the fragments of an ultimately unknowable life story.

Together with the new gambits of well-established art cinema filmmakers in the 1970s, the decade also witnessed the emergence of a number of innovative newcomers in the realm of film narration. Perhaps the most innovative but, by the same token, most vulnerable was Jean Eustache. As his career was too brief for more than a few sallies into narration, he will be remembered mainly for his three-and-a-half-hour saga of the Left Bank, *The Mother and the Whore* (1973). A string of dramatized but dry narrations, mainly by the *flâneur* protagonist (Léaud again), the film delivers not merely a slice of bohemian life but a hearty sample of its language, particularly the language of the raconteur. An equally extensive display of dramatized dry narration, by a string of storytellers, is Chantal Akerman's *The Rendez-vous of Anna* (1978). Other filmmakers of the Parisian milieu have, however, turned toward exploration of body and gesture,[25] and it may be that the long French dedication to the discourse of storytelling is drawing to a close.

While the New Wave found branching channels and fresh recruits for its exercises in narration, contemporaneous movements in other lands pursued their own agendas, but often with comparable results. In the so-called New German Cinema, the theoretician Alexander Kluge made a series of works—from *Yesterday Girl* (1966) to *Strongman Ferdinand* (1975)—that mixed Godarian (or Brechtian) intertitles, sardonic voice-overs by the director, and direct, on-screen autobiographical discourses by the characters.[26] While Volker Schlöndorff (*The Sudden Wealth of the Poor People of Kombach:* 1970) and Werner Herzog (*Aguirre, Wrath of God:* 1972) occasionally indulged in similar practices, it is only Rainer Werner Fassbinder who approaches Kluge as a narrational virtuoso. Fassbinder repeatedly drew on his personal presence to enhance his adaptations of classic texts: *Effi Briest* (1974) employs lengthy intertitles and external narration by the film-maker reading from Theodor Fontane's novel, while *Berlin Alexanderplatz* (1979–80) adds the director's on-screen appearance in a dream sequence. After Fassbinder's death, it is left to Wim Wenders to carry on the exploration of storytelling situations, as in the multiple dramatized narrations of *Paris, Texas* (1984) and the angelic monologues of *Wings of Desire* (1988; see chap. 8, n. 3).

Other "new cinemas" of the late 1960s and 1970s broke little new ground in narration. The folkloric dramatized storytelling in Japanese films, from Masaki Kobayashi's *Kwaidan* (1964) to Masahiro Shinoda's *Demon Pond* (1979), is mainly remarkable for its abundance (although the former does develop a sophisticated *mise en abîme* construction in its final episode). The extensive voice-overs in Nagisa Oshima's films—external and pseudo-documentary in *Death by Hanging* (1968), internal and temporally fluid in *The Ceremony* (1971)—do not go much beyond established norms in these techniques, for all their originality in subject matter.

It was a relatively isolated innovator in Spain who devised one of the few genuine novelties in narrational technique. After an experiment in placing an adult character within the *mise en scène* of a flashback to his childhood (*Cousin Angelica:* 1974), Carlos Saura found a novel means of moving between a narrator and her past self. In *Cria Cuervos* (released as *Cria!:* 1976), transitions between a child's fantasies of her dead mother's revisitations and the adult heroine looking back on her past are made by way of a camera pan, visibly rendering the continuity of past and present. It is a technique employed earlier by Alf Sjöberg in *Miss Julie* (1951) and by Antonioni in *The Passenger* (1975),[27] with similar effects, and it suggests that the flashback code can still find room to develop in future cinema.

The American filmmaker who most fully participates in the storytelling explorations of recent decades is Woody Allen. His basic narrational resource is his inimitable voice-over, a personal, "authorial" one even when the voice is ascribed to the character he plays (almost uniformly a version of his standard comic persona). Beyond the consistent voice, Allen's use of storytelling situations is among the most wide-ranging in cinema history.

Most striking, perhaps, are his personal and visible narrations, as in *Annie Hall* (1977), where the Allen character speaks not only in a studio setting, to give the broad contours of the story, but also in the midst of ongoing action. While the latter mode had been used before and falls under the rubric of direct, on-screen narration, Allen's delivery bears the marks of the theatrical (or comedian's) "aside"—used here to convey narrative information.[28] Not only does the Allen character punctuate the present action with his quips; in a manner akin to Saura's, he enters flashbacks of his childhood, even standing beside his boyish self to comment on his origins.

Allen has gone beyond the use of his personal presence to order a number of his films by multiple storytelling situations. *Broadway Danny Rose* (1984) is dramatically narrated by a group of comedians exchanging anecdotes about the eponymous hero. The lunching scene is frequently returned to for commentative kibitzing, while at the close, frame situation and main story fuse as the protagonists are seen ambling past the restaurant, while the parting quips of the comedian-narrators are heard in voice-over. There is also a nondramatized multiple narration, a series of internal voice-over monologues by the protagonists of *Hannah and Her Sisters* (1986). Structured like a set of short stories or character vignettes (intertitles are used for demarcation), the voice-over narration alternates among the sisters and husbands in a periodically foregathering family—although two of the husbands are given wider latitude in autobiographical expression. But the most complex of Allen's multiply narrated films is *Zelig*, and it will receive fuller attention in a chapter devoted to that mode.

o   o   o   o

Having traced careers that extend into the present decade, it may be time to take stock of current practices, although we are still too close to them to be able to chart their long-term drift or import. One generalization that may be accepted on all sides is that vigorous experimentation with storytelling situations ranks among the more stimulating aspects of current cinema. To go to the (first-run) movies today involves, as likely as not, an encounter with narration in one of its recognizable forms, but often with a new twist that attests to creative usage. To review recent instances in a number of modes:

External voice-over: Bertrand Tavernier's *A Sunday in the Country* (1984) makes a subtle variation in this well-worked vein by narrating not overt actions but psychological processes—a "psycho-narration"[29] consistent with the Proustian ambience the film establishes in its *mise en scène* and characterization.

Internal voice-over: The most popular mode of the day, as in Jerzy Skolimowski's *Moonlighting* (1982) and *The Lightship* (1986)—the latter closely echoing Conrad's autobiographical narrators reminiscing about their initiation into the moral world of the sea; there is even a recent instance of multiple internal voice-over, Jean Becker's *One Deadly Summer* (1983).

Dramatized narration (framing): Salieri's mad discourse in Milos Forman's *Amadeus* (1983) rivals *Caligari* as a classic employment of this mode, if only by demonstrating the power of unreliable narrators to generate distorted images of their antagonists (to be discussed in the Continuation below).

Dramatized narration (climactic): Hector Babenco's *Kiss of the Spider Woman* (1985) develops the form by establishing a narrator who delivers film scenarios, autobiographical episodes, and more in a prison cell, provoking his cellmate to emulate his reports and reveries, then allowing them to compose a joint fantasy that synthesizes their mental images and precipitates their emotional union.

Dramatized narration (multiple): The structure of slowly gathering testimony in Fons Rademakers's *The Assault* (1986) is that of many a crime investigation film, with the significant difference that these happen to be war crimes (the approach is also used in Constantin Costa-Gavras's films on neocolonialist crimes).

Dramatized narration (dry): Louis Malle's *My Dinner with Andre* (1981) represents the definitive exercise in storytelling without enactment, Andre's copious anecdotes depending for their charm entirely on his verbal powers and the low-key interaction between teller and listener.

71

External on-screen narration: Ross McElwee's *Sherman's March* (1986) places the filmmaker before the camera in the throes of planning a film about Civil War campaigns and enables him to discuss its transformation into a quest for his roots in the South.

Internal on-screen narration: Patricia Rozema's *I've Heard the Mermaids Singing* (1987) is narrated, almost from start to finish, by the heroine before a video camera (the monitor image being strongly foregrounded)—an indication of new narrational resources opening with the advent of video technology.

Multiple on-screen narration: When even a bubble of froth like Stanley Donen's *Blame It on Rio* (1983) establishes so elaborate a program, one senses narration's grave danger of becoming a mechanical exercise.

Written narration (letter): In tracing the correspondence of an American bibliophile and a London bookseller, David Jones's *84 Charing Cross Road* (1987) employs the entire manual of available techniques: voice-over, dramatized writing and reading scenes, mindscreen enactment, and so on.

Written narration (diary): Alain Cavalier's *Thérèse* (1986) is remarkable not only for its staging of a saint's life with a minimalist *mise en scène* but for placing her *cahier* at the center of the action, where it not only serves as the implied source of the story but acquires the aura of a sacred relic or canonical text (few other diaries being written in blood, as this one partly is).

This proliferation of storytelling techniques suggests that filmmakers and their audiences have become familiar with narrational situations once considered arty or murky. It does not, of course, guarantee that films tapping these resources have a higher probability of reaching dramatic depth or visual and aural power. Any of these modes can, as suggested above, quickly become formulaic or markedly derivative. By way of illustration: A number of recent adaptation films make a show of foregrounding the text of the novels on which they are based yet make scant effort to build that source into their dramatic development. Sydney Pollack's *Out of Africa* (1985) opens with a shot of the reminiscing novelist, Karen Blixen/Isak Dinesen, but subsequently contents itself with using the figure as a voiceover, adding only a summative intertitle at the close. Similarly, Jean-Jacques Annaud's *The Name of the Rose* (1985) opens with a voice-over narrator who speaks of writing his memoirs, but it never engages him in the process, preferring to close along the hackneyed lines of "I never saw him again. . . . I never learned her name."

There is no reason to fear, however, that familiarity will inevitably bring the use of narration into contempt, for a gifted filmmaker can often make of it something fresh and winning, even on an initial attempt. Leon Marr's first film, *Dancing in the Dark* (1986), makes striking use of written narration to tell a shattering story. The hospitalized protagonist is shown composing, guarding, and otherwise fetishizing the narrative of her almost catatonic and eventually blood-drenched marriage. Dramatic scenes of narration abound, coming almost to outweigh the enacted story. One scene of writing develops into a power struggle as she fends off her psychiatrist's attempts to see the manuscript, scores the page while resisting, then tries to wipe the mark away. An exceptionally precise technique is used to emphasize that the accompanying voice-over corresponds to the act of writing and is not merely a reading of the finished text; for example, we hear her exclaim, "And no match for me!!" and see her dot the exclamation points. At the close, she adds one more blue spiral notebook to the collection in her bedside drawer, indicating that they form parts of an ongoing narration whose outcome is no more predictable than—is perhaps identical to—her therapeutic process. It is a gesture that pays homage to one of the classic scenes of written narration, the gathered notebooks of *Diary of a Country Priest* (see chap. 7).

Where do we now stand in the longish story of film narration? The options have been thoroughly explored, some have been reduced to cliché by overuse, and even the more outlandish varieties have become fair game for exploitation. The situation represents a threat and a promise: the threat that the practice of film narration may become as ritualized as many gambits in cinematic story and discourse; the promise that imaginative film-makers will continue to discover further potentialities in narration—both within and beyond the modes we have been observing—to enrich their discourses and more deeply render their stories.

4

Voice-over Narration:
Orpheus and *Sunset Boulevard*

VOICE-OVER is well known to be the bread-and-butter narration or, in a more elegant metaphor, the zero-degree narration, yet if we pause to wonder where the voice may be coming from, it seems anything but a simple proceeding. Perhaps the beginning of wisdom in this matter is the reflection that voice-over is not the *technique* that adds vocal sound to images; that would be dubbing (or its more technical cognates). Voice-over is better considered as a storytelling *situation*, even though it lacks the visual element of dramatized and of other direct narrations. Voice-overs are, to be sure, not used exclusively for storytelling; there is no limiting the kinds of messages that might be delivered in this situation. But certain dubbed voices in cinema can, without undue prescription, be distinguished from voice-overs as communicative situations marked by other conditions of performance and observation. To distinguish and relate them, we may ask, Who speaks a voice-over, to whom, and under what conditions does a movie audience observe this communication?

An arrangement of the dubbed voices in films could be made in a fourfold schema based on two characteristics: whether or not the voice is heard by other characters, and whether or not the human source of the voice is seen by them at or about the time it speaks[1] (see Fig. 3). The resulting four classes would include *voice-off* (heard and seen), *interior monologue* (not heard by others even when the character is on-screen with them), the *acousmêtre*[2] (heard but not seen), and *voice-over* (neither heard nor seen by [other] characters). This classification, although

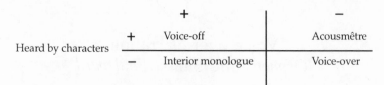

Fig. 3. Varieties of dubbed voices.

based on apparently secondary considerations (I shall consider the source of the voice in a moment, and the addressee in chap. 7), nevertheless responds to an intuitive or commonsense view that a voice-over speaker is not in a communicative situation with the characters, as are the other dubbed voices (the interior monologuist with him- or herself), but in a situation directly involving the audience; the speaker is presented not in but "over" the images.

When we consider the source or speaker of a voice-over, an immediate distinction presents itself: either a character or a non-character, that is, an internal or an external narrator.[3] But this easy dichotomy opens a Pandora's box of ambiguities and potentially fruitful associations. For an external narrator, to speak in voice-over is to declare authority as an ultimate source of the story and yet (except in cases where we recognize it as the filmmaker's or another individual's voice) to refrain from personal responsibility for the statements made. This is much in the manner of the novelistic "omniscient narrator," a purportedly neutral deliverer of the facts themselves that, upon inspection, turns out to be a coded system for inducing this impression. Like some omniscient narrators, external voice-overs may be marked by distinctive stylistic traits—the law-and-order toughness of the pseudo-documentaries, for example—and may thereby lose a measure of impersonality. Still, the authority figure is not ordinarily manifested as an individual with a personal viewpoint, even when expressing an ideology—thus remaining a voice *over*, in the sense of "above" the film. This implied claim of authority without personal commitment has, after decades of widespread use, irritated some in the present generation of film critics and contributed to its reduced use by filmmakers.[4]

For a character to speak in voice-over is an equally ambiguous stance, if not finally as elusive. The speaker declares himor herself without being seen speaking, and is relieved of this disembodiment only when the voice is related to a screen image. Even then, the internal voice-over remains shadowy, a voice that we must learn to associate with the figure seen in dramatic action. The correlation of commentative voice and character-in-action is fairly easy to grasp when the voice-over is the protagonist's, especially in personal anecdotes not far removed from the implied time of narration. But many voice-overs are reminiscences of considerably earlier experiences, and this structure requires our associating a mature speaker's voice with a much younger character. By an imaginative synthesis we have learned to perform, we take the mature voice and the youthful image to be the "same" person—a plausible enough view, but one that is not without its unsettling dubieties in some philosophical and artistic accounts of the continuity of individual existence.

The double status of characters who narrate their own stories is comparable not only to the literary autobiographer's but also to the novelistic first-person narrator's. Such storytellers necessarily exist in two time zones, that of the story they tell and that of their narrating activity. Unlike the sadder-but-wiser-man contrasts drawn in literature, however, the cinematic strategy for internal voice-overs—for example, *film noir* detectives delivering their anecdotal yarns—rarely requires that they describe their present circumstances. Rarely do we hear voice-overs indicate where or when or even how they are as they speak, and this abstemiousness—apparently for dramatic economy, for it keeps us focused on the main story—may actually generate an added element of mystery.

Despite the differences in their situations, the voice-over, both external and internal, has affinities with the heard-but-not-seen *acousmêtre*, which operates within the dramatic action, eerily present yet absent and thus mysterious and potentially threatening. Like the master criminal in Fritz Lang's *The Testament of Dr. Mabuse* (1933)—the prototype of all the tyrants and terrorists of later cinema who project their words but not their persons into the space of other characters—the voice-over is a mind controller of sorts, acting on the audience much as the

Mabuses do although, one hopes, more benignly. This heard-but-not-seen influence invites us into the storyteller's mental universe as he or she muses on the past, making our experience of the story an act of identification when we see the enacted scenes that correspond to the words. More overtly than in mind-screen flashbacks, coded as the mental images of a reminiscing character, voice-overs project a past by verbally inducing us to share an imaginative universe that is not our own. And this fiat can in turn be challenged as a shameful encouragement to the spectator's projection, "suture," and other self-mystifications by the dominant cinematic institutions.

Voice-over is, then, a resource that can be used for the cinematic equivalents of two very different options in novelistic narration, third-person "omniscience" and first-person retrospection—the apparently impersonal historian's view and the subjective confessions of personal experience. For all the similarities of their more insidious influences, "external" and "internal" are terms reflecting no merely formal distinction but two very different sets of claims to attention and authority. External voice-overs tend (or pretend) to deliver a historical statement or objective version—the story as it really happened. Internal voice-overs, on the contrary, recount the past as it later seems to a reminiscing participant; they mark it as memory and thereby associate their films with the widely branching genre of autobiography.[5] While both history and autobiography make claims of truth telling, and while both have been widely perceived to bear their measures of fictionality, their forms of expression produce markedly different audience effects.

Voice-over films of both kinds introduce echoes of repetition, but only the autobiographical type induces the uncanny sense of returning to the past once again. All historical and autobiographical narrative is, of course, verbal repetition of prior events, and their fictional versions—both historical and autobiographical novels—imitate this aim or claim by gestures that may be called pseudo-repetition (of events that are posited as prior). But the intensity of this sense of revisitation varies, in the cinematic domain as well as in the literary. Many external voice-overs make a point of introducing the audience to an event as if it were happening for the first time—on the model of the "you are there" formula of certain documentaries and pseudo-documentaries—whereas internal voice-overs sentimentalize in varying degrees their own revisitings of the past and invite us to share their nostalgia.

Other features of cinematic voice-over enhance this difference: the external speaker makes no claims to have been involved in the story; that is part of the speaker's assumption of neutrality or objectivity. But the internal voice-over posits for the speaker not only past involvement but also present attitudes—exultation, regret, and other feelings in various combinations. The external voice rarely conveys a hint of implicating the audience as personal interlocutors; in terms of the linguist Emile Benveniste's version of the story/discourse dichotomy, such utterance has the grammatical features of *histoire*, rather than the marks of personal communication notable in the *discours* of internal narrators.[6] To return to a point raised earlier: The external voice is invariably unsituated, yet while an internal voice-over is almost always so, it often arouses curiosity about the character's present condition, although that curiosity remains only partially satisfied. Indeed—such are the ironies of film narration—when a voice-over is ultimately revealed to be addressing another character, as in the 1946 version of *The Postman Always Rings Twice*, it may gain in dramatic force yet suffer a corresponding attenuation. When the scene of narration is visualized, we are no longer alone with the confiding voice, sharing its reflections in a private space of the mind, but are witnessing a ritualized confession in the public sphere.

The audience's impression of being personally addressed by internal narrators is, then, based on a delicate balance between their aural presence and their visible absence, if the oxymoron be permitted. No one worries about the present whereabouts of external speakers; they are as impervious to time and decay as their films themselves (that is to say, not entirely impervious). But internal voice-overs may inspire wonderings about . . . How *is* Philip Marlowe doing these days?—not simply because we have come to know and love him as a character but because his voice continues to resonate even though many years have elapsed since his acts of narration, and even more since his stories. Unlike the continuance in print of the words in first-

79

person novels, the voices of internal narrators generate the illusion of their speakers' presence—like other illusions of presence that have persisted throughout our phonocentric culture's history. There are even instances, as we shall see, when external narrators may invest us with similar notions of their continued presence.

The internal voice-over's present/absent mode of existence is, one suspects, not only a matter of cinematic technique or rhetorical traits but trenches on some of our most primitive responses to life and death. These voice-over characters—they were once fully alive in the story, as we see, but now have become a persistent echo of the past, as we hear. This trace of a past vitality, now reduced to verbal echoing and nostalgic repetition, may help to account for the aura of the uncanny that attaches to many an internal voice-over. It would be too much to say that they are all dead, these voices out of the dark, but our relation to them resembles what it might be like to hear communications from a spirit world. Some of the finest voice-over films give us a feeling of sharing the narrator's relieved detachment from the events narrated; the ironic voice of the dead protagonist in *Sunset Boulevard* is, as we shall see, a limit case along a well-filled continuum.

The temporal distance of internal voice-overs is not always so great and may vary widely even in a given film, as in Woody Allen's *Hannah and Her Sisters* (1986), where one speaker responds to the present with some urgency ("God, she's beautiful!") while another rehearses a series of incidents in his life story up to the present ("It's over"—after a diagnostic test). The former activity may, though conveying narrative data, be better considered as interior monologue, a practice intermittently engaged in by the sisters. For it is not only his lack of temporal distancing but his self-address while surrounded by others that characterizes this narrator, while the Allen character expostulates in a way that resembles a communication more than an internal process. The varied conditions of observing this and other self-communing narrators will be considered as storytelling situations of the mindscreen variety in a chapter of their own. Here it is worth recognizing that internal voice-overs may play on the borders between self-address and address to the audience, past-tense retrospection and up-to-the-moment immediacy, invisibility in the speaking role and on-screen presence.[7]

Having labored to distinguish internal voice-overs not only from interior monologues but also from external voice-overs, it may seem anticlimactic to conclude that the two voice-overs have more in common than either does with any of the other dubbings. Their deeper affinity shows itself when we consider films in which a noncharacter narrator acquires the verbal style not of an impersonal announcer but of an individual speaker who addresses us with some immediacy. There is no necessity for it, but most often this voice is recognizable as that of the filmmaker, whether in the freewheeling style of a Godard or in the categorical manner of a Chris Marker. An external voice-over may express—without (thus far) being labeled "authorial intrusion"—a filmmaker's personal view of the world and of the story, becoming as intimate in the process as a character's voice-over. These nonidentical twins, the personal external voice-over and the internal retrospective voice-over, share in the uncanny presence/absence that their invisibility to both characters and audience generates.

The two films I propose for close inspection illustrate high fulfillment at the extremes of external authority and internal intimacy, yet they also—like extremes in other spheres—meet. While an external narrator may go beyond the initial functions of introducing and linking to become a choric commentator in the film, a character narrator may get beyond anecdotalizing to become the farseeing articulator of the story's themes. When an authoritative voice achieves the timbre of personally bearing witness to a significant spectacle, when a character rises above personal involvement to acquire the afflatus of a universal perspective, the apparently absolute distinctions between external and internal, *histoire* and *discours*, give way. At this stage, the loose and baggy term "voice-over" comes to justify itself in relation to a univocal phenomenon after all.

o   o   o   o

We usually think of Orson Welles as the master of external narration, both in his own films—like *The Magnificent Ambersons*, mentioned above—and in those of others. But he was preceded and perhaps surpassed as a personal presence in voice-over films by another master of many arts, Jean Cocteau. Cocteau's first venture, *Blood of a Poet* (1930), remains perhaps the most individualistic film of any age, given its autobiographical theme, private symbolism, and surreal style. But it was only when he turned to the filming of his 1926 play *Orphée* that the possibilities of manifesting himself in the narration as well as in the *mise en scène* were fully exploited. While neither a collection of private symbols like *Blood of a Poet* nor a set of autobiographical anecdotes like the later *Testament of Orpheus* (1959),[8] *Orpheus* has proved the most distinctive of Cocteau's films, at least in part because of his presence in it as narrator.

Coming at the outset of the sound era, *Blood of a Poet* employs many of the signs of the author that silent films had already displayed, before initiating the expanded repertoire of such signs that marks the later films. At the outset, we have a title card with an epigraph or manifesto beginning, "Every poem is a coat of arms. It must be deciphered," and ending with a dedication to the painters who have inspired him.[9] The director himself is shown in the first figural shot; as the scenario describes it, "The author, masked except for his eyes, holding a plaster hand in his hand, . . . announces that the film is beginning, against a background of studio lamps" (p. 9). Later, we see a sample of his manuscript, with signature: "The surprises of photography, or how I was caught in a trap by my own film" (p. 17). The dramatic climax, the felling of a schoolboy (Cocteau's own avatar) by a snowball, becomes the occasion for his voice-over recital of his poem on the subject (pp. 45–46). With this mixture of sound and textuality, we are, as in the visual-verbal doublings in adaptation films of the period, in transition toward the predominance of voice.

Blood of a Poet is memorable for its epigrammatic pithiness, as in the final line, "The mortal tedium of immortality" (p. 60), but the voice-over is considerably more copious and varied than we may recall. Its narrational style begins with the calculated anachronism of delivering sequence divisions in the manner of silent-film intertitles ("First episode: the wounded hand, or the scars of the poet" [p. 9]), but it becomes more broadly parodic, as in the early shot of a falling chimney accompanied by the line, "While the cannons of Fontenoy thundered in the distance, a young man in a modest room . . ." (p. 9). In the course of the film, narration increases in length, duplicating the action yet— because of the ambiguity of what we see—not felt as redundant. The abundance of voice-over here is determined by the need to explain the extraordinary identifications and obscure proceedings, and must be regarded as a heavy compensation for a symbolism that had not reached cinematic communicability.[10]

Although *Blood of a Poet* makes full use of the author's voice and other forms of self-presentation, it is only a first approach to the making of a narrated film. When Cocteau turned to the adaptation of his play—incorporating many of its themes but radically departing from it in plot and *mise en scène*—he devised means of mingling dramatic action, narrative statement, and lyrical commentary. While the voice-overs of *Orpheus* are few— indeed, only seven in number—they play a crucial role in the film's workings. Beyond indelibly marking the decisive presence of its author, they endow the film with a prophetic dignity, the reverberations of an authority that may appropriately be called Orphic.

Self-manifestation begins with the opening titles, and in a variety of media: Cocteau's inimitable drawing and calligraphic style is used in the credits, putting forward beautiful images of the titular figure's head and lyre. The dedication to a friend is shown in the author's handwriting. An authorial voice-over then offers a summary of the Orpheus myth and proposes a modern treatment of it: "Where is our story taking place . . . and when? A privilege of a legend is to be without age . . . as you like it [*comme il vous plaira*]." Cocteau fully exploits the standard opening conventions to orient the audience toward a heightened receptiveness to symbolic generality. He does so by linking the film to some of the normally extraneous material of the dissemination process, which Genette has described for literary works as the *paratexte*.[11] With *Orpheus*, this paratext is extended in the notes appended to the published scenario, the interviews subsequently given, and the allusion to its title in a later film— perhaps even that film in its entirety.

The first scenes are also replete with personal intimations,

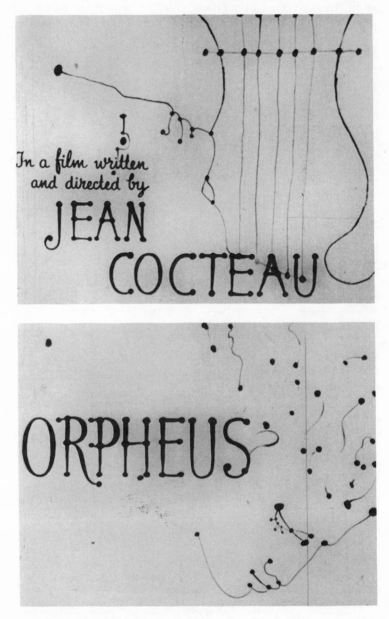

Orpheus: Two title frames—visible marks of the voice-over narrator

although they are not as overt: the mildly satirized ambience at the "Café des Poètes"—which, the scenario leaves no doubt, is to recall the Café de Flore near St.-Germain-des-Près[12]—and the Cocteauian quips ascribed to its habitués, as when the poet is challenged, "Astonish us!" (p. 107, although the translator chooses the weaker "Surprise us"). The opening parody of Left Bank literary culture—little mags, cult figures, militant women's groups, and the like—soon gives way to evocations of Cocteau's more universal themes.

As the story develops Orpheus's involvement with the Princess of Death at her château—with its mirror of passage to the other world, the "Zone," as it is called—the poet's fascination not only with mortality but with other forms of the irrational is dramatized. Orpheus seizes on his contact with the beyond as a source of poetic inspiration and takes to transcribing his car radio's droning chains of apparent nonsense. Cocteau's notes indicate that the poet makes a fundamental error in listening to sources of inspiration outside himself (p. 188). Yet what should be the medium for conveying these repetitive numbers, broken phrases, and gnomic sentences but the voice of Cocteau!—in this case performing as *acousmêtre*. Even the nonsense carries marks of personal authority; Cocteau later explained that the line "The bird sings with its fingers" comes from a letter to him from the poet Apollinaire. (It also becomes a bone of contention in the film when a rival poet's followers turn on Orpheus for his appropriation of the line.) The implication seems to be that when the poet draws on the nonlogical resources of his own mind, he taps into the stream of imaginative language that flows from poet to poet. Yet, the dramatic action affirms, he should still act as if he relied on himself alone.

At this point, even ordinary mirrors begin to provide passage to and from the other world, as the Princess passes through, in a series of superimpositions, and invades the conjugal bedroom of the poet's worldly life and love. To mark this as the beginning of the central action, Cocteau's voice-over intones, "That first night, the Death of Orpheus came to his room to watch him sleep" (p. 130). After a foray into town, represented by an elaborate montage of shots at various Parisian sites, the alternation between the ordinary and extra-ordinary worlds continues. The return of the supernatural—the Princess swathed in a hooded robe suggestive of ancient funerary figures—is marked by a voice-over of the same form as the preceding one: "And every night, the Death of Orpheus returned to the room" (p. 141). Here the narrator performs the role of supplying continuity by indicating habitual behavior—what Genette calls "iterative" or "frequentative" narration in his study of Proust, its stamping ground.[13]

The climax, Eurydice's death-by-motorcycle, executed by the Zone's twin black-leather-clad messengers, leads to conflict between the Princess and her assistant, the angelic Heurtebise (who has fallen in love with Eurydice), so that he becomes Orpheus's guide in his efforts to gain her return. There follows the most astonishing of the mirror passages, as Orpheus's rubber-gloved hands are shown approaching a mirroring surface and entering it—with the implication of the whole body passing through. (Cocteau explained in an interview the ingenious techniques of these and other shots, including the use of a vat of mercury!)[14] In the trashy chambers of the Zone, a stodgily bureaucratic tribunal adjudicates the messy love lives of the living and dead, allowing for Eurydice's return with an exaggeration of the myth's testing of Orpheus; here the condition of her remaining alive is that her husband *never* look at her again, not just during the return passage.

After some comic scurrying to keep her clear of Orpheus's sight, further complicated by the heightened attention given to mirrors, Eurydice becomes disenchanted with the grotesque arrangement, especially as Orpheus continues in seclusion at the oracular car radio. The voice-over returns with a more limited function, that of explaining motivation: "Eurydice felt she had lost Orpheus. She could not bear this situation. She wanted to free him, and there was only one way" (p. 173). The scene of her waking him up in order to be seen—and of the interruption of her project—is so swift and unexpected that it requires another voice-over to explain it: "A brief power failure prevented her from achieving her aim. She had to go on living. The next day . . ." (p. 174). As the final phrase suggests, Cocteau was well aware of the rudimentary narrational function of these explanatory voice-overs and plays upon their formal turns with his usual light touch.

A final pair of voice-overs is used for the denouement. When Orpheus is shot in an encounter with hypercritical avant-gardists including a women's group described as the "Bacchantes," Heurtebise guides him on another descent into the underworld. The author intervenes to explain its significance: "It is not the same journey as before. Heurtebise is taking Orpheus to a forbidden place. He no longer walks upright and still. Orpheus and his guide drag themselves along, at times swept along by a strange wind, at times struggling against it" (p. 180). These shots of painful movement through the Zone are among the most extraordinary of the many in the film that qualify for the epithet. In an interview explaining their elaborate technique— some of them were shot from above, with the actors crawling across a platform made to look like an upright arcade—Cocteau expresses satisfaction at having achieved the "movement of a dream"[15] but does not fully account for these shots. The voice-over, running in the same turgid rhythm, suggests a gathering urgency in these laborious movements: an approach to an ultimate test, a struggle to reach a reserved place for a final encounter.

The setting, amid ghastly illuminations of a ruined fortress, is the visual high point in a long succession of spectacular scenes. (It is also used for the coda, in which the Princess and Heurtebise are taken away for unspoken punishments.) But Orpheus's ultimate encounter turns out to be a test not so much of him as of his lover, the Princess herself, who disobeys the order of things by returning her beloved to his wife in the ordinary world ("their muddy waters," as Heurtebise puts it: p. 187). In order to underscore this deflection from one hero to another, Cocteau's voice-over again intones, "The Death of the Poet must sacrifice herself to make him immortal" (p. 182).

There are numerous possible objections to this dictum: it is by no means established that Orpheus gains immortality by the transaction, but only a return to life and wife. Another difficulty lies in its sentimental reversion to an old theatrical pattern, that of the femme fatale who graciously stands aside so that her lover can be happy with his more prosaic but nurturant love (as in contemporaneous "woman's films"). Perhaps a better choice for a conclusive dictum would have been a sentence in Cocteau's appended notes: "The poet must die several times in order to be reborn" (p. 188).

These objections aside, the final voice-over comes as a second climactic moment in the film. Cocteau's pithy pronouncement crowns the drama and distills its symbolic complexity into a single line of what can only be called poetry. In this film about poets, filled with both parodic jesting and high talk of the poetic vocation, it is at the finale that drama and narrative give way to lyrical utterance. This may not be sufficient to justify *Orpheus*'s exalted notion of the poet as hero, but it does give us a taste of the real thing. Cocteau's voice comes at the close to take on the tones of the poet as *vates*, abstracting from the dramatic situation a paradigmatic fate in an immortal line.

Voice-over narration moves in *Orpheus* from an initial, preparatory role, through a series of frequentative and explanatory functions, to a final, summative articulation of the film's larger themes. We find here a potential paradigm for external narration generally: though usually content to introduce or provide helpful continuity for what we see, it can and sometimes does rise to the more creative role of crystallizing in language a film's visual impact and dramatic import. Though *Orpheus* becomes immortal on the strength of its power to show—by its astonishing visual inventions—its Leonardo-like creator had no difficulty in tapping cinema's added power to tell.

Language becomes the supplement to action and, by a further turn, voiced language makes an even more impressive claim. Cocteau's imposition of his personal voice on the film comes to suggest that all that we hear and see—not merely the words but also the images—proceeds from the act of naming by the living voice of the filmmaker. This view of the power of sounded language to bring things into existence has a philosophic history almost as ancient as the Orpheus myth itself, with whose charming lyre and singing head it is genetically associated. The claim seems the more arcane now that deconstructionist philosophers have brought to light the obscure assumptions in which it is grounded.[16] Yet it retained its force in the French Symboliste tradition, in which Cocteau has his poetic roots, and when he turned to filmmaking the resource of voice-over facilitated its cinematic articulation. It is now no longer the poet who names things into being but the filmmaker's voice that makes them appear: so runs the illusion generated by these resonant authorial tones. Not content to devise a modern revisioning of an ancient myth in the dramatic action of his film, Cocteau uses voice-over to insinuate a new myth. The very act of projecting images in tandem with his own vocal accompaniment exploits the potential of the "narrator-effect" of our earlier speculations. It is now not the poet but the filmmaker who stand as the genius of narrative creation.

Even if we refuse Cocteau's voice-overs the credence accorded to poets and prophets, they go far to explain how *Orpheus* compels us to acknowledge the aura of the creator himself. More vividly than do his more overt, though still symbolically disguised, autobiographical films, this one allows the filmmaker to manifest himself. The voice-overs of *Blood of a Poet* always maintain a distance between a highly literary artist and his visual symbols, allowing him to comment on them as parts of already achieved works of art now reassembled. His on-screen appearance in *Testament of Orpheus* create another kind of distance; we now see the artist as subject matter, somewhat shorn of mystery and reduced to a comic, rococo, even faintly Chaplinesque image of the man. It is only with the distinctive yet exemplary *Orpheus* voice-overs that we sense the filmmaker's presence—neither external to the affair like a critical mythographer, nor internal to the story and posed for our inspection, but emerging at the junctures of sound and image. If, as I have suggested, the internal voice-over may instill an uncanny sense of receiving the disembodied echo of an absent other, there are also instances when external voice-over acquires a similar power over our imaginative responses. Cocteau's vocal presence/absence in *Orpheus* well qualifies him for the title of *acousmaître*.

o   o   o   o

In the year following *Orpheus*, a comparable fulfillment of internal voice-over's potentialities was made in Billy Wilder's *Sunset Boulevard* (1950; scenario by Wilder, Charles Brackett, and

D. M. Marshman, Jr.). Instead of the lofty tones of an external narrator, the protagonist imbues his story with the pungent flavor of his own personality, in a mixture of personal reminiscence and Hollywood gossip. Despite their gross differences in this and other qualities, certain strong similarities to *Orpheus* come to the fore: their house-of-death decor, seduction (of the male) theme, and larger-than-life femmes fatales. In this ambience, the all too human internal narrator of *Sunset Boulevard* can reach an expanded, even transcendent, relation to his story— becoming not only an exemplary case in the world he describes but, like the external voice-over, hovering somewhere "over" it.

This achievement may seem, at first blush, to be beyond the powers of a protagonist-narrator of less than heroic stature. Joe Gillis presents himself from the outset as a young man on the make—and not making it very successfully—until his encounter with and ultimate undoing by his femme fatale. Yet Joe shares at least one attribute with creative spirits like Orpheus and Cocteau: like them he is a professional writer (and like Cocteau a screenwriter too). While Joe's narration of *Sunset Boulevard* may lack the poetic and prophetic strains of *Orpheus*, it is a convincing expression of a temperament and an effective evocation of a social milieu. Indeed, by comparison with the stories Joe describes himself at work on, this narrative may be thought of as a treatment for his finest scenario, one he has not lived to complete.

We are faced in *Sunset Boulevard* by the phenomenon well known in fiction as a *mise en abîme* construction. While not as fully patterned as a novel about a novelist writing a novel about a novelist . . .—as in *The Counterfeiters* by André Gide, who devised the term—this is a filmed scenario about a scenarist who is at one stage shown writing a scenario. Nor is this a mere structural similarity, for the scenarist's life, including his vocation, becomes a subject of this film as surely as those of novelist and poet do in Gide and Cocteau. Without apology for the lesser genre, *Sunset Boulevard* may be considered the *Orpheus* of screenwriters—at least as the beginning of a mythic view of this modern form of mythmaking.

The narration generates, then, not only a slice of Hollywood lifestyle, especially as it involves writers, but a taste of what an anthropologist—describing the presence within folkways of their own interpretive paradigms—has called a "thick description." For this is a film in which a great but unemployed director, Erich von Stroheim, plays the role of a has-been director (we are not sure how great) who once guided the career of a now fallen star—played by Gloria Swanson, who had worked with Stroheim. It is also a film replete with the products and processes of filmmaking; from the inserted clips of Stroheim's *Queen Kelly*, starring Swanson, which her character Norma Desmond enjoys watching, to the bridge-party sequence in which relics of past greatness like Buster Keaton appear in almost mummified form, the sense of fallen glory is palpable. It is true that Cecil B. De Mille, on his set for *Samson and Delilah*—in production on the Paramount lot while *Sunset Boulevard* was being made—exudes continued vitality, yet with hindsight this sequence can be seen as anticipating the end of the line in historical-biblical spectaculars. In such a context, the fall of a screenwriter at the hands of a decadent diva becomes an exemplary fate and its narration is called on to aspire to mythic resonance.

The film's initial voice-over, "Yes, this is Sunset Boulevard, Los Angeles, California," is therefore not merely a typical insider's invitation to scandalmongering among the celebrities, but an individual's personal testimony to an entire social milieu. Without proposing anything like an autobiography of their own,[17] the film's three scenarists give us a sweeping overview of the vagaries of their profession. At this stage, Joe delivers a running patter of shoptalk, emphasizing a writer's insecure finances, his demeaning relations with studio bosses and personal agents, but also the youthful camaraderie at Schwab's drugstore and at the somewhat bohemian parties of that era. The film's best moments on the working life include scenes of the protagonist teaming up with an appealing young story editor to compose a script of their own. Here the film dramatizes the romance of the writer's workshop rather than the actor-director relations that occupy other films-about-filmmaking.[18]

Though it sheds considerable light on the surrounding milieu, Joe's autobiographical narrative is not an outwardly focused memoir but an inwardly turned confession. It is dramatically structured by the climactic phases of the life story: his degrading affair with Norma, his budding love for Betty Schaefer, and the debacle that follows their intersection. He gives only a sketch of his origins in the Midwest, his earlier career as a journalist, and his lack of success in Hollywood. Within its sharp limitations, his narration traces a passage from innocence to experience, from seduction and domination to the liberation of self-knowledge. It thus recapitulates a consistent pattern in autobiography and autobiographical fiction of the past two centuries.

We cannot immediately tell on a first viewing that the opening voice-overs, which accompany shots of police cars arriving at a murder scene, are spoken by the victim himself. But that impression may dawn on us well before the point when the narration comes full circle and the shots of a corpse floating in a pool are repeated. "The body of a young man"—left floating, as it were, by the third-person designation—is by then firmly attached to the narrating voice, and we recognize this as the rare autobiography that includes the life story's conclusion. Still, it comes as a shock to find the tale completing its fatal line of development, for the continuance of the narrating voice gives us the sense of continued life and hopeful outcomes. We must adjust now to the uneasy presence, if only the vocal presence, of the dead.

Like all illusions of presence, this one is difficult to explore without resort to psychoanalytic theories that are themselves not much more comprehensible than the phenomena they seek to explain. Yet ordinary narratological terms do not do justice to this situation, for Joe's voice-over goes beyond the usual ambiguities of narrators who speak without being seen. This voice encourages the illusion of presence-despite-absence by appealing to certain morbid but widespread attitudes toward the dead. Drawing on perhaps instinctual tendencies regarding ghostly visitants, *Sunset Boulevard* may be more of a horror film than we think when dismissing its lurid finale as Grand Guignol theatrics. For by that time we have been confirmed in the impression, if not that the dead can speak, at least that they may be superb narrators of their stories. One might wish to call this mortuary narration, but I shall follow others in describing it as narration from beyond the grave (Vernet: *d'outre-tombe*).

While not the first narration from beyond the grave—one

Sunset Boulevard: Narration from beyond the grave (JOE: "They
beached me like a harpooned baby whale.")

thinks of the ghosts on the chandeliers in Ophuls's *Tender Enemy*
and the ultimately-exposed-as-dead villain of *Laura*[19]—that of
Sunset Boulevard remains the most sardonic, if not macabre.
When Gillis is first seen, floating face-down in a pool in a special-
effects arrangement suggesting a shot through the water, he

speaks of himself with third-person detachment: "The poor dope: he always wanted a pool. Well, in the end he got himself a pool—only the price turned out to be a little high."[20] When the narration of the story that has led him there comes round to the same point and we see the shot again, the same jaded voice takes a new tack in its corrosive irony, reminding us, "Well, this is where you came in"—as if to complete our disengagement from the tawdry affair by reducing it to a movie.

The immediate effect of narration from beyond the grave is, then, a distancing one but, perhaps not surprisingly, it is of the comic variety. *Sunset Boulevard*'s black humor is largely derived from its mixture of intimacy and detachment, from that sense of the simultaneously familiar and unfamiliar that is not out of keeping with the macabre aspects of the uncanny. We are comfortable with this ghost as he tells us, in his easygoing, self-mocking way, not only of his life but of his death. The derisiveness of his tone ("the poor dope") serves him well in telling his story as if it were another's. But its frankness and muted self-pity also draw us to him as our likeness, our fellow in life's delusions and seductions.

This mixture of identification and estrangement effects—the mordant tone, the eerie otherworldliness, the sense of witnessing a common fate—was to have been considerably expanded in a scenario scene that may have been filmed before being discarded. After Joe's body has been picked up in the opening sequence, the second was to have played in the morgue:

> An attendant wheels the dead Gillis into the huge, bare windowless room. Along the walls are twenty or so sheet-covered corpses lying in an orderly row. . . . Beyond [Gillis] the feet of the other corpses stretch from under their sheets: men's feet, women's feet, children's, two or three negroes'—with a linen tag dangling from each left big toe.
>
> The attendant exits, switching off the light. For a moment the room is semi-dark, then as the music takes on a more astral phase, a curious glow emanates from the sheeted corpses. . . .

A MAN'S VOICE[:] Don't be scared. There's a lot of us here. It's all right.

GILLIS[:] I'm not scared.

. . . .

FAT MAN[:] How did you happen to die?

GILLIS[:] What difference does it make?

And we would have been off on the wings of narration, as the hero tells his story to his fellow corpses.

The rejection of this dramatized narration must have been based on a number of motives—some of them obvious matters of taste—but among them may have been a sound narrational one. The film's eventual return to the morgue could never have been as effective as its return to the illuminated body of the narrator, suspended as though in midair at the scene of the crime. For this shot brings Joe's story to its end at the same moment that its accompanying voice-over brings the narration round to its beginning. "Well, this is where you came in"[21] returns the tense structure of narration to its opening form ("this is Sunset Boulevard"). The voilà gesture of the demonstrative plus copula not only indicates a return to the present but also renews Joe in the position of commentator on ongoing action. Only a voice-over could shift seamlessly, not only from the past to the present but from Joe's visible residue as corpse to his continued, though invisible, function as narrator. For, though dead, he has a further role to play.

To appreciate the force of Joe's return to the present tense and the role of present-action commentator, it may be useful to review the wide range of forms his narration runs through in the course of the film. After his demonstrative gesture to indicate the scene, he turns to subtly differentiated past tenses to explain its significance. In his report of recently completed action—"You see, the body of a young man was found floating in the pool of her mansion . . ."—Joe's use of the passive voice suggests not only the completion of a process but his own submission to that end; these things have come to pass. The voice then addresses us in the second person and switches to the conditional and present perfect for its invitation: "Maybe you'd like to hear the facts, the whole truth. If so, you've come to the right party."

To begin his retrospective narrative, Joe shifts to the progressive form of the past tense, and the first-person pronoun, to recount habitual behavior: "I was living in an apartment house above Franklin and Ivard. Things were tough at the moment." This form is also used to describe the bizarre lifestyle at Norma's mansion, expressing unfolding discovery and portentous revelations; over a shot of rats in the empty pool, he says, "There was something else going on. . . . It was all very queer." The past progressive is again employed to describe Norma's intensifying delusions in her plan for a grand comeback: "She was still sleepwalking."[22]

At the climax, Joe's voice returns to the second person and the present tense ("Well, this is where you came in"), but it has time for another firm assertion of the closing of the past: "They beached me like a harpooned baby whale." This simple past might suggest considerable temporal distance, were we not aware that the events have only just transpired at the time the narrator speaks. The shift of perspective from a long retrospect on the developing affair to a brutally concise summary of its conclusion suggests the distance the narrator has come in his demystification. The murder and its discovery take place shortly before the time they are narrated, but the narrator now looks down at them from the detached perspective of the dead.

Having skewered, or "harpooned," the close of his affairs, Joe's narration of his own story is completed. Yet he has one more action to perform, for which his disembodied, aerial state may accord special advantages and which the voice-over storytelling mode effectively serves. He is now to be the narrator of Norma's story, at least of its closing stages. The denouement, despite having the somewhat tacked-on feel of a coda, lends the film a new dimension. By shifting the focus from Joe to Norma, *Sunset Boulevard* resembles those modern novels—of which Conrad's *Heart of Darkness* is paradigmatic—that begin as an ordinary man's personal reminiscences yet give way to a second and more awesome figure, who arrests our final attention. Joe has told his story of lost illusions and now takes on a new narrational function, as crucial as though much briefer than his initial one.

The narration now becomes spectatorial, as Joe bears witness to events as they unfold before his, and our, eyes. Its tenses shift accordingly, first to questions about the future that express his anxieties with to-the-moment immediacy: "What would they do to Norma? . . . Those headlines would kill her." There follows a return to the main narrational tense, the past progressive, as we see her descend the stairs in the full transformation of madness: "So they were turning after all, those cameras." Although it seems like a regression to Joe's backward-looking perspective on his story, the structure of this sentence is designed to correct a previous prediction, for Joe had described Norma ludicrously making herself ready for "those cameras that would never turn." And now we see them do so, although for the newsreels and not for a Hollywood spectacular.

Yet our sense of witnessing a present action is not allowed to remain unmodulated, for the narration shifts again as Norma embraces her ultimate companions, "those wonderful people out there in the dark." Joe concludes with a summative employment of the past perfect tense, using it to express a self-consciously artful metaphor: "The dream she had clung to so desperately had enfolded her." Here the voice takes on the character of a choric summation, as lapidary if not as poetic as Cocteau's final speech in *Orpheus*. The sentence achieves, by its doubled phrase structure, a resonance that conveys both Norma's fulfillment of a tragic destiny and Joe's attainment of dispassionate wisdom in contemplating it.

Most vividly in this choric closure, but in varying degrees throughout his narration, Joe's voice-over has been the intermediary not only for our knowledge of the story but also for our emotional reception of it. At the outset it establishes the detachment and even amusement with which we are to join the narrator in reviewing his past flaws and foibles. Near the climax of the main story, we are encouraged to sympathize with him in his plight and to identify with him as he makes a belated effort to assert his freedom. But at this final juncture, the voice-over encourages both engaged concern ("What would they do to Norma?") and a distanced, resigned sense of fated completion ("The dream she had clung to so desperately had enfolded her"). In his unassuming way, Joe has come to fulfill some of the functions of a tragic chorus, expressing irony, pity, fear, and submission to the way things are.[23]

To gain a sense of voice-over narration's role in *Sunset Boulevard*, we must acknowledge both the subtle modulations in its retrospective account and its final shift to a new rhetorical function. The protagonist has at first been the expositor of his own story, rehearsing it with bitter bemusement as a monitory case ("the poor dope"). He becomes at the close one who bears witness to Norma's story, watching it along with us and all "those wonderful people out there in the dark." As the voice of the dead joins us in anxiously anticipating the outcome, it drops its comfortable detachment and becomes, like us, vulnerably exposed to potential horrors and their realization.

By expressing in elevated prose his reactions to events of which he too is an awe-struck spectator, Joe stands in for us as a responsive surrogate. In becoming at the close a conduit for the spectacle of a figure with greater claims to tragic stature than his own, the voice-over performs one of the age-old roles of dramatic choruses: to be an articulate voice for the audience, otherwise condemned to remain silent in face of an appalling spectacle. While the normal functioning of internal voice-over is amply exemplified and even uncannily extended in *Sunset Boulevard*, the film reaches further, toward the rare status of cinematic tragedy, by transforming its narrator into a choric voice.

5

Dramatized Narration:
The Cabinet of Dr. Caligari
and *Hiroshima Mon Amour*

DRAMATIZED NARRATION—the term rings with an air of paradox, hinting at a combination of theater and fiction, of showing and telling, that may strike some as an impossible harmony and others as a tainted compromise. Yet like the Molière character who learned to his astonishment that he had been speaking prose all his life, we may reflect that dramatized narration has been going on for a long time. When the messenger informs Oedipus that he is no son of Corinth, for he himself had received him as a child from a shepherd of Laius's house, we are in the presence of dramatized narration as climactic as any to follow in the dramatic arts. From Sophocles to Ibsen's "continuous exposition" and beyond, storytelling in the theater has been not only a technical means of giving the characters temporal depth but a wellspring of significant action.[1] It is the basis of Aristotelian *anagnorisis*, the ultimate revelation of the true state of identity and relations—conceived as no mere culmination of suspense but as the fulfillment of an entire dramatic pattern. Though fiction films are not plays, they perform dramas, and in some of them a scene of storytelling generates the main action or fulfills its developmental design.

Generates or fulfills: the processes suggest two situations that I have called *framing* and *climactic* narration, scenes of storytelling that surround the main action, and storytelling throughout the action, reaching a climax in which a key episode is told. The words "framing" and "climactic" imply alternative structural relations of storytelling scenes to the larger drama, where

99

structure carries narrative significance. In the one case, the main action is posited as anterior to the act of telling, as already completed but brought to renewed life by teller and auditor—a (re)experience for which the enactment is a coded equivalent. In the other case, a dramatic action proceeds to the point when a story told can bring it to its turning—not necessarily its emotional peak or plot resolution, but the watershed moment we call the climax.

In life and art, a storyteller who can inspire in his or her auditors an imagined reenactment of events may no more than they remain unaffected by that achievement. Nor need the teller's response be entirely proportional to theirs: it may be the teller who most intensely (re)experiences the tale. Narrating, and not the narrative alone, has consequences. In such cases, past events lead to a present drama, that of expression and interactive reception. The storytelling scene, whether as frame or as climax, becomes a critical event, heightening as much as resolving the tension. For dramatized narration and its story do not stand in a mechanical relation of producer and product but in a dialectical one. Narrations renew stories, and that resurgence of the past may in turn change the storyteller's or the auditor's life.

Even in the more detached atmosphere of framing narration, the neat distinction between the frame and what is within it may blur. This overflow of story into action suggests that passive anecdotalizing is not a weaker vessel in dramatized narration but a potentially powerful form of cinematic storytelling. These generalized considerations may justify a renewed look at one of the most discussed films of all time, Robert Wiene's *The Cabinet of Dr. Caligari* (1920), where telling a story assumes the proportions of constructing a myth—with commensurate consequences for the mythmaker and his eventual audience.

Merely to place the director's name in a position of authority for this film becomes a tendentious move, given the continuing controversy over the production and its consequences. Lotte Eisner sums the situation this way:

> We know from the comments of one of the authors of
> the scenario—quoted by [Siegfried] Kracauer in *From*

Caligari to Hitler (1947)—that the prologue and epilogue were added as an afterthought in the face of objections from both authors. The result of these modifications was to falsify the action and ultimately to reduce it to the ravings of a madman. The film's authors, Carl Mayer and Hans Janowitz, had had the very different intention of unmasking the absurdity of asocial authority, represented by Dr. Caligari, the superintendant of a lunatic asylum and proprietor of a fairground side-show.[2]

Let's hear that again: The scenarists' original premise was that the villain combines with his "asocial" institutional authority a little moonlighting as a traveling carnival exhibitor. Their proposed scenario would presumably have unfolded as a conventional mystery, leading the investigator-hero to the local asylum the charlatan operates, where he has for some time succeeded in exploiting one of his patients, a catatonic, to perform on the road as freak somnambulist and nocturnal murderer. At the point of discovery, the hero must overcome the incredulity of the asylum's clinical staff but would have no great difficulty in doing so, though faced with physicians apparently oblivious to the gross malfeasance and prolonged absences of their chief.

The uplift of this scenario would derive from the audience's identification with the heroic Francis as he cleans up a nest of psychiatrists, bad and indifferent, who manipulate if they do not destroy us ordinary good folk. We would have been asked, then, to entertain a state of mind remarkably similar to that of patients suffering from certain mental disorders—not to put too fine a point on it, from paranoid delusions of a conspiracy by evil mind controllers to incarcerate the truly sane. There are still some viewers of the film who profess a preference for a story along these lines.[3] Yet an unframed *Caligari* would have had some hard explaining to do in resolving its données—not to speak of the additional complications of the contemplated parallel stories, with incidents drawn from the scenarists' war experiences of "Prussian authoritarianism."[4]

The evident difficulties that stand in the way of taking the main story as a realistic contemporary drama neutered by being ascribed to a psychotic incline us to think that *Caligari* was designed from an early stage as a fantasy. With or without its frame, it stands as an early instance of the monster film, in the vein of the already filmed Golem legend and the soon to be immortalized Nosferatu. The scenarists may well have aimed at promoting their anti-authoritarian convictions by means of fantasy, and the only deviation from their intentions becomes a reascription of the sources of their myth. Most viewers of the film are not greatly distressed by the eventual reduction of the hero to a psychotic and of the villain to a figment of his imagination, for a relatively simple reason. Irrespective of its present capacity to provide a good scare, *Caligari* offers striking images of mythic figures whose force and interest are not reduced when disclosed as products of a disturbed mind. In our psychiatrically sophisticated day, they may even be enhanced by that provenance.

Eisner adds to the scenarists' account (as relayed by Kracauer) an explanation that posits another creative hand: "Today we know [*sic*] that Fritz Lang . . . suggested to the production company that a good way of not scaring off the public would be to bring in a kind of *Rahmenhandlung* (framing-treatment), a prologue and epilogue in conventional settings supposed to take place in a lunatic asylum. Thus the main action, related in a conversation between two lunatics sitting in the asylum garden, became the elaborate invention of a fantastic world seen through the eyes of a madman."[5] This way of putting it makes the change a purely tactical commercial move, and reduces the frame to a gross imposition by denigrating the narrator as "lunatic" and "madman." Yet the claimed role of a Fritz Lang in the film's construction suggests that there may have been a more profound cinematic imagination at work than that of the credited participants—one capable of anticipating the film's eventual success neither as social exposé nor as genre film but as myth.

Though his original intention may have been to protect the audience and the profits (scaring, but not scaring away), the positive results of the producer's intervention may be judged to compensate for the scenarists' wounded sensibilities. Without its narrational frame, *Caligari* might have made an earnest polemic against mind controllers, or at best a fantasy of possession by dark powers like the almost contemporaneous *Nosferatu* (F. W. Murnau: 1922). With the addition of an unreliable but undiminished narrator, there is a basis for a drama concerning the social life of myths. Francis is no longer a hero of mystery detection but an exemplar of the mythmaking imagination. In thinking of *Caligari* as myth, we must try to determine the underlying fears or aspirations it, like myths in general, brings to expression.

An incidental benefit, also derived by a revised reading of Eisner's evidence, is that the framing narration provides the basis for a genuinely Expressionist work of art, exteriorizing in its set designs, acting style, and other forms of imagery the terrors of the inner life. Although Expressionism could operate in various media without necessarily grounding visual distortion in the protagonists' subjectivity, there is a strong current of psychological objectification in some of its finest productions. In order to grasp this relation of mind to its creations, we shall need to make more precise the relation between the sets of the frame and the main story than is indicated by Eisner's "conventional settings" and "fantastic world."

The film has been positioned in modern history as a cultural expression of German inclinations toward, as well as horrified repression of the desire for, a national *Führer*, a mind controller who can will an entire somnambulistic people into murderous action. According to Kracauer's *From Caligari to Hitler* thesis,[6] the provision of a framing action that justifies the asylum director's authority represents the filmmakers' accord with postwar Germany's submissiveness. This neatly places the scenarists' "revolutionary" exposé of tyrannical authority in the main story and "conformist" acceptance of control in the frame. Despite Kracauer's acknowledgment of a film-within-the-film that reflects the "double aspect of German life," *Caligari*'s thematics cannot be so neatly divided. Without pretending to make assertions about the depths of the Germanic mind, I believe the film bears a more complex relation to the cultural dynamics of its time. Indeed, a closer analysis suggests that a salutary process may be at work in *Caligari*: a critical purgation of racial illusions by demystifying the myth-encumbered narratives of an unreliable narrator.

Fully to describe *Caligari's* narrational structure, we must begin with the opening title card: "A tale of the modern reappearance of an 11th Century Myth involving the strange and mysterious influence of a mountebank monk over a somnambulist."[7] Whether this is an exact equivalent of the text that introduced the original release is now probably impossible to determine, but there must have been some form of external narration to lead the audience into so exotic a subject and setting.[8] I shall take up this intertitle again when discussing the film's dealings with myth, but at this stage it is necessary to acknowledge the existence of a double framing system. In addition to the dramatized narration performed in the garden storytelling scene, there is an external narrator to introduce the framing action and make narratological statements about the "tale" and the sources of its "myth." The drama we are introduced to is, then, not that of Caligari *redivivus* but that myth's unwholesome "reappearance" in the minds of our contemporaries.

Similar three-tiered systems have been observed in literature, and Genette's terms for them may be heuristically useful, although with appropriate modifications for mimetic works, as suggested in the Introduction. The opening title card is an extramimetic narration that frames and implicitly evokes the story world of an asylum, its staff and patients, and the storytelling behavior of one of them. In these terms Francis is an intramimetic narrator, and his storytelling in the garden and later activities in the asylum constitute the film's primary action. The yarn he spins, the story of a mad doctor's misdeeds and comeuppance— occupying most of the film, to be sure—is positioned as a metadiegetic narrative. Like many another such tale-within-a-tale, it is significant as a story told by a particular narrator, that is, symptomatically, for its thematic and symbolic contents tell us much about the kind of mind that produced it, and about the cultural resources on which that mind draws. Even without recourse to narratological terminology, we can say that *The Cabinet of Dr. Caligari* is a film about Francis's mythmaking process— not merely the delusional activity of a pathetic sufferer, but a creative transmutation of materials drawn from a collective consciousness.

Although it does not speak in anything like the sweeping way in which it begins, extramimetic narration is also present at the film's finale. The intertitles that deliver the dialogue of the closing scenes cannot be ascribed to Francis, as are those that accompany his tale of Caligari, since he is no longer narrating; these quotations can be made only by the opening narrator, who stands as the source of the framing scenes. In the final dialogue text, the asylum director—now seen as a benignant healer meditating in the pose we have seen his patient assume in emulation of him—closes the framing action with a diagnostic breakthrough: "At last I understand the nature of his madness. He thinks I am that mystic Caligari. Now I see how he can be brought back to sanity again" (p. 100). Although we may harbor doubts about the lasting efficacy of his ministrations to Francis, his words bring us back to the demystifying perspective we were invited to take by the opening narrative text.

While the good doctor may restrict his focus to the individual's delusions, we discover that the forms assumed by his peculiar narrative can be understood only in the context of his cultural milieu. Just as we learn to interpret the Caligari story as the fantasy of a disturbed mind, we must further contextualize that mind's choice of the Caligari legend as the "modern reappearance" of a collective myth. Neither context can reduce the force of the film's primary matter: the spectacle of the demonic magus figure and of the erotically charged, living-dead automaton (whose morbidity is signaled by his coffinlike "cabinet"). Yet it is possible for a work of art both to reproduce a myth and to teach us to read it, to convey a cultural community's ambiguous discourse and still provide cues by which audiences may reflect critically on the myth-mongers' unconscious investments. It is this achievement that marks *The Cabinet of Dr. Caligari's* true distinction.

The setting for storytelling is a garden, which is only toward the close identified as that of the asylum grounds. Its sparse *mise en scène* is vaguely naturalistic, though it is clearly that of a studio set; the mottled texture produced by old prints of the film accentuates the effect of Impressionist rather than of Expressionist visual style. (Another visual style is used in the closing frame sequence, but it maintains the distinction between reality

The Cabinet of Dr. Caligari: Scene of narration
(FRANCIS: "That is my fiancée.")

and fantasy spaces—with one exception to be discussed below.) The opening lines indicate that a multiple narration or story-telling contest is being entered in medias res: Francis's interlocutor sums up what may have been an autobiographical narrative by declaring that spirits "have driven me from hearth and home, from my wife and children" (p. 41).

After the "fiancée" Jane passes, Francis matches him with his own tale: "What she and I have experienced is yet more remarkable than the story you have told me" (p. 42). He then plunges into his narrative, which is illustrated at first by models and backcloth scenes reminiscent of folk artisanship. The painted townscape of Holstenwall, the *mise en scène* of the traveling fair—including the organ grinder's monkey and a dwarf whom even Caligari turns to stare at—the costuming and gestures of the mountebank, all are marked as products of a collective tradition, though filtered through the discourse of an individual, the dramatized narrator.

Another folkloric register is tapped with the scenes of the mountebank's tent, his cabinet, and its inhabitant. Caligari's pitch promises the thrill not merely of seeing the living dead awaken but of hearing secrets from beyond the grave: "Cesare knows every secret. Cesare knows the past and can see into the future" (p. 52). Alan accurately intuits the sphere of his significance, asking, "How long have I to live?" (p. 53). Francis's narrative thus moves familiarly amid the cult features of carnival, the unofficial mass culture to which recent literary historians have directed renewed attention. It is not, however, the primal sexual energy and potentially revolutionary satire of carnival that Francis taps but its delvings into the occult, the equivalents of voodoo—all those ritualistic efforts to gain power to deal with death.

When Francis's narrative turns into the streets and inner spaces of the town, the decor changes to the Expressionist style by which the film is universally recognized. We may surmise that this change in visual style marks a shift from the collective imagination, in which the narrator shares, to a more highly individualized world-view. Francis speaks in, and the visual techniques illustrate, two linguistic registers: that of the community, which includes the folklore of Caligari-type legends, and that of his private fantasy life, given to elaborate subjective distortions. What the Expressionist sets express is a particular narrator's angle of deviation from the cultural norm.

Beyond these visual renderings of his world-view, Francis's declaration of his own role in the story provides further data on his mental universe. "I will not rest until I have got to the bottom of these terrible events," he announces (p. 65), in keeping with a narrative design that casts him in the hero's role. But the terrible events, both past and to come, have a peculiar tendency to center on himself and those near him: it is his friend Alan who is the second Holstenwall victim of Cesare, the same friend who is his competitor for Jane. After they part on the fraternal note, "Whatever her choice, we shall always remain friends" (p. 55), Alan is struck down. Later, Jane visits the fair and is powerfully attracted by Caligari's invitations to view the somnambulist. After taking her peek, she is horrified by what she sees and runs away. But that very night, this skin-tight-black-suited, heavily rouged, and sinuously moving figure enters her bedroom and . . . instead of thrusting his long dagger into her steals her away, compelled by the force of his own erotic drives.

One need not labor the point. Francis's story includes a readily recognized set of sexual symbols, ordinarily restricted to the dreamwork but emerging, for those in his condition, as a conscious production in which the narrator devotedly believes. The potentially violent hostility toward his sexual rival, the ambivalent erotic impulses toward his beloved—whose own sexuality is brought to uncomfortable attention—and the anxieties of homoerotic feeling expressed in his images of Cesare require no great Freudian sophistication to discern. When we adduce other elements of Francis's imagined world—the stipulations that another male authority figure, Jane's father, is a doctor, that his archenemy is ultimately revealed to be of a profession even more threatening than that of mountebank, and that at the height of his discovery he himself achieves the power to make psychiatric diagnoses and commitments to which the asylum staff respond without hesitation—we can determine the limits of the narrator's vision even without a framing device to circumscribe it. It is not the frame that reveals Francis's unreliability but the style and substance of his narration itself.

"And since that day the madman has never left his cell" (p. 96). Thus Francis concludes his dramatized narration in the garden, and we return to the framing situation and its Impressionist decor. The ensuing sequence is a study in contrasts, as one after another of the characters in the enacted story is now shown in the frame milieu: Jane serene in her delusion of royal status, the somnambulist engrossed in examining a flower, the archfiend exuding benevolence as he moves among his patients. We have been, as the current term has it, demystified, not only in our reading of the story but in our relation to its narrator. Where before we may have empathized with his efforts to reveal authority as evil and the keeper of madmen mad, we now experience an almost comic relief in matching up the subjective with the objective versions of the characters. The pleasure is short-lived, however, when we observe Francis's distress in unsuccessfully denouncing the director and his subsequent strait-jacketing. The turn from private storytelling to social interaction marks not only the end of a good story but the loss of a skilled narrator, for Francis now is reduced to sputtering ineffectual explanations of the contretemps.

Two other aspects of the transformation call for further attention. The setting in the asylum courtyard, initially presented as part of Francis's narration, is now to be seen in a different light, no longer as the scene of action in a distorted imagination but as a neutral public space. This perspectival shift is made easy for the audience by the design of the studio set. The courtyard's decor is busy enough to accommodate both atmospheres: its Renaissance arches and geometrically divided pavement can provide a background either for menacing complexities or rational equipoise.

The closing sequence bears, however, an almost fatal mistake; although the final courtyard scene can be justified by its ambiguous decor, one must assume that at the end the filmmakers simply erred. Francis is placed in the cell where "Caligari" has been shown at the finale of his own story, with "two high windows in the rear wall of the cell, which is painted with amoeboid shapes" (p. 95). "Caligari's" cell is a product of Francis's narrative fantasy; the latter's cell should have been a neat, clinical one. But the filmmakers seem to have been tempted to draw out one last ironic reversal—on the order of "the biter bit"—and thus distorted the return to benevolent directorship and daylight reality at the close.[9]

What implications are we to draw from this conclusive (though marred) return to normalcy, rationality, and medical authority? It is tempting to side with the scenarists' esthetic objections that their original design has been distorted, so that we see a palimpsest with the underwriting showing through. The final scene nevertheless highlights by juxtaposition the doctor's hopes for the power of mind ("At last I understand. . . . Now I see") and the tangled web of the patient's mind, interwoven with his cellular space.

Having avoided the naive anti-authoritarianism of the original project, the film develops fresh political implications that anyone can approve. In the course of the main action, "Caligari's" arcane books, journal, and other documents are inspected, revealing his tainted sources and perverted intent. But these arcana of the Caligari legend are after all elements of Francis's discourse, so that he stands as their narrative source. It is he—in his own view, a typical young German—who seems to have a full stock of such legendary lore at his disposal. Even without a psychoanalytic interpretation of his fantasy-work, one can recognize in his story a process of displacing onto others the myths that populate his own imagination: it is not he who has revived the Caligari legend but the mad doctor! What we learn from the framing situation suggests that Francis represents an extreme case of a widespread tendency in his society: not merely the projection of his own destructive impulses onto others, but the specific use of myths of mind controllers to deflect the opprobrium that might fall on his own manipulation of others through myth.

Such a line of reading is encouraged by the film's multiple narrational structure, and it may be useful in hooking a larger fish. Films like *Caligari* are said to reflect a Germanic fascination with the demonic, enshrined deep in the folk imagination in legends of magus figures with occult powers to direct individuals and masses, robbing them of their already weak will.[10] "From Caligari to Hitler" is thus a formula for a social-psychological process: a nation that entertains legends and makes films about figures like Caligari will tend—Kracauer does not say exactly how—to fall under the sway of leaders like Hitler. As at other places in Kracauer's film criticism, this is a point that needs to be sharpened if it is to hit a worthwhile mark.

We recall the opening words of Francis's interlocutor in the garden: "Everywhere there are spirits. . . . They are all around us." What shape these spirits may take in the folk mind is suggested by an intertitle apparently omitted in the British version and thus from the published scenario; after one of the murders, a bystander says, "There is something frightful in our midst." Here we have the language of persecution heard so often during the rise of Hitlerism. The corporate fantasy of parasitic invaders of the body politic, an alien infection that must be removed by a final solution, was soon to be acted out in a collective psychodrama that turned myth into history. The question raised by such expressions when they appear in cinematic or other arts is whether they are an incitement to persecution of the Other or a revelation of the processes by which he is invented. To the question raised by Kracauer's thesis—Does *The Cabinet of Dr. Caligari*, as revised, no longer strike a blow against evil authority but encourage submission to it?—another alternative may be added: Or has it become a more profound reflection on the workings of the Germanic (and of the human) mind in relation to collective tradition, psychiatric and other scientific knowledge, and the aliens who often introduce such knowledge?[11]

When we come to ask, Whose imagination promulgates demonic myth in the film? we return to the source of the Caligari story, its narrator. It is Francis who has absorbed the legends of magi manipulating the innocent, of frightful aliens invading the folkish community, and of bookish intellectuals unmasked as charlatans and worse. *The Cabinet of Dr. Caligari* fulfills its opening declaration to tell of the "reappearance of . . . Myth" in modern life by focusing on Francis's mind. His is the subjectivity to which we are forced to attend, not only as he narrates in the frame story but also as we examine the contents of his imagination in the main story. Indeed, the very notions of "frame" and "main" come under stress when we grasp that the framing situation is not a blunting of the film's radical force but its most challenging psychosocial drama.

To shift attention to Francis as not simply an unreliable narrator but the generator of the film's fantastic world is not to dispel the powerful imaginative effect of *Caligari*. All its talk of demons, aliens, and evil doctors may be fantasy, but such fantasies proved capable of turning a nation upside down for twelve years, and a continent for six. With benefit of hindsight, we may discover in the film's focus on the narrator's myth-governed mind a prophetic demonstration of the way similar myths invaded an entire society's historical storytelling, with well-known consequences in political behavior. Without its framing narration, the film would have chimed in neatly with collective obsessions about demonic intruders and scientific controllers. With its framing narration, *Caligari* reflects the preoccupation of many an unhealthy mind with racial myths that play out their own destructive impulses. The film should work, then, much as does the good doctor who puzzles through the complex sources of his patients' symbolic stories. The capability of its own society or of later ones that witness the film to discriminate between health and illness, myth and reality, cannot, however, be guaranteed.

o o o o

As *Caligari* represents an early fulfillment in framing narration, *Hiroshima Mon Amour* marks a high point in climactic storytelling. The long night in which the heroine recounts her wartime love for a German soldier and its enduring place in her consciousness remains as etched in the viewer's memory as the story itself. The narrating of her story is no mere revelation of yet another wartime anguish (paralleling the atomic holocaust sequence) but, as the title suggests, the intersection of past and present action. It is the dramatic moment in which the protagonists' developing relationship is crystallized, when the heroine's life reaches a renewed crisis and the film takes a new tack toward its thematic resolution. For these reasons, which I shall attempt to substantiate, the act of narration that occupies the central place in *Hiroshima*—we get only brief visualizations of the story it recounts—is the climactic phase of the film's dramatic development.

Given the scene's saliency in the drama, it is only gradually that we reflect that storytelling has been taking place from the first scene of the film to, as we come to discover, the last. The opening voice-off dialogue of vaguely present but not visibly speaking lovers—famous for the incantatory repetitions that became a hallmark of scenarist Marguerite Duras's cinematic style—sets the film's pattern from the outset. The Japanese protagonist provokes narrative by his questions or statements; the Frenchwoman responds with lengthy and impassioned accounts of her recent actions, sufferings, and reflections:

HE: You saw nothing at Hiroshima. Nothing.

SHE: I saw *everything. Everything.* . . . The hospital, for instance, I saw it. I'm sure I did. . . . Four times at the museum in Hiroshima. I saw the people walking around. . . . I was hot at Peace Square. Ten thousand

112

degrees at Peace Square. I know it. . . . I saw the
newsreels. On the second day, History tells, I'm not
making it up, on the second day certain species of
animals rose again from the depths of the earth and
from the ashes. . . .

HE: You made it *all* up.[12]

These exchanges exemplify the film's often ironic stance toward
the narration in which it is so copious: the heroine is quick to
put her present experience into words—though she is equally
reluctant to express her past anguish—but his bitter hyperboles
express the difficulty of speaking, much less discovering, truth
either public or private. Yet the man's resentful negations serve
the same function here as do his later encouragements to share
her love story with him alone. Narration is provoked even as it
is denied.

The earlier love story begins to be told even at this initial
stage: "Like you, I too have tried with all my might not to forget.
Like you, I forgot. Like you, I wanted to have an inconsolable
memory, a memory of shadows and stone" (p. 23). Although
she does not proceed with her narrative at this point—only the
involuntary memory of her dead lover's arm is given, in a mindscreen flash-cut triggered by viewing the Japanese abed—the
film's dealings with memory and with narration itself are initi-
ated here. Beyond her question, "Why deny the obvious necessity for memory?" the film implies a further burden: *and the
obvious necessity of telling it.*

Bolstering the heroine's report of her Hiroshima experiences, other phases of the ongoing action sustain the narrational
imperative. After the couple make contact during the stagey
peace demonstration and renew their tryst at his home, the
pattern of provocation and storytelling continues:

HE: Was he French, the man you loved during the war?

SHE: No . . . he wasn't French. . . . Yes. It was at
Nevers. . . . At first we met in barns. Then among the
ruins. And then in rooms. Like anywhere else. . . .
And then he was dead.

(Pp. 47–48)

Beyond delivering the broad outlines of her story and the first shots of its French setting—their grainy tones conveying remoteness not only in time but in place—the scene at the Japanese home creates further interest in storytelling as a medium of relationship. The hero's motivation is different now from his bitter rejection of any outsider's capacity to know the horrors of nuclear war. He begins to grasp that her story is a means of knowing her: "It was there, I seem to have understood, that you were so young. . . . so young you still didn't belong to anyone in particular. I like that" (p. 51). Accompanying his sexual possessiveness is a measure of genuine intuition of another life: "It was there, I seem to have understood, that you must have begun to be what you are today" (p. 51). His encouragement of her narration becomes, then, not only a mode of wooing but a way of knowing; *Hiroshima*'s powerful eroticism is connected less with its images of bodies than with its transmission of stories.

Finally, the climactic scene: "*Night falls over Hiroshima, leaving long trails of light,*" as Duras's scenario describes it (p. 53). "I can't picture Nevers," the man begins ("*Shots of Nevers. The Loire*"). And so she begins at the beginning, in true storytelling fashion: "Nevers. Forty thousand inhabitants. Built like a capital—[but] a child can walk around it. . . . I was born in Nevers, . . . I grew up in Nevers. I learned how to read in Nevers. And it was there I became twenty" (p. 53). By the end of this autobiographical summary, we may sense the heroine's strong impulse to skip the painful events and come out at the end of the tale—for twenty is her age near its close.

The tale is replete with well-known narrational phenomena; to use another set of Genette's terms, they include ellipsis, summary, and *anachrony*, or time-scrambling (to use a more colloquial term).[13] While the indirections are fully motivated by the heroine's state of mind, it requires close attention to sort out the precise story she tells, given the distorted sequence of its delivery. Labeling her statements by letters and listing them in the order in which they are delivered, we find the following *narrational* series:

A. "You [i.e., the German lover conflated with the Japanese] are dead." (P. 54)

B. "How is it possible to bear such pain? The cellar is small."
(P. 54)

C. "They pretend I'm dead, dead a long way from Nevers.
That's what my father wants. Because I'm disgraced." (P. 55)

D. "I don't scream: I call you softly. . . . Even though you're
dead. Then one day, I scream. . . . That's when they put me in
the cellar. To punish me." (P. 57)

E. "One day, I'm twenty years old. It's in the cellar." (P. 58)

F. "At night, my mother takes me down into the garden.
She looks at my head." (P. 60)

G. "They shave my head carefully till they're finished."
(P. 60)

H. [HE:] "And then, one day, my love, you come out of
eternity."
[SHE:] "Yes, it takes a long time." (P. 62)

I. "Winter is over. . . . I'm beginning to forget you."
(Pp. 63–64)

J. "When I arrived at noon on the quay of the Loire, he
wasn't quite dead yet." (P. 64)

K. "I stayed near his body all that day and then all the next
night. . . . It was that night Nevers was liberated." (P. 65)

L. "And then one day . . . I had screamed again. So they
put me back in the cellar. . . . I think then is when I got over
my hate." (P. 66)

M. "I don't scream any more. . . . One night, a holiday,
they let me go out." (P. 66)

N. "Not long after that my mother tells me I have to leave
for Paris by night. . . . When I reach Paris two days later the
name of Hiroshima is in all the newspapers." (P. 67)

The *story* sequence, a series of past events that can be linked
in a temporal order, follows another track. Marking its key units
with numbers, we get: (1) the shooting; (2) her vigil; (3) his death;
(4) the head shaving; (5) seclusion in her bedroom (as seen in a
number of shots); (6) hysterical screaming and deeper seclusion
("That's when they put me in the cellar"); (7) renewed screaming

and seclusion ("I had screamed again. So they put me back in the cellar"); (8) gradual return to normalcy ("I got over my hate," "I'm beginning to forget you," "it takes a long time"); (9) end of seclusion and outdoor airings ("they let me go out," "my mother takes me down into the garden"); (10) her move to Paris.[14]

We find here the intriguing nonlinearity of impressionistically delivered narratives that highlights some of the finest modern fiction, from Conrad and Proust forward. In considering the heroine's *narration* as a treatment of her story, we see that she has recited events in a classic anachrony: A = 3, B = 6 and 7, C = 5, D = 6, E = during 6 or 7, F = 9, G = 4, H and I = 8, J = 1, K = 2, L = 7 and 8, M = 9, and N = 10. Her narration plunges into the time of confusion and anguish (in which the death and the cellar are focal points), moves on toward the healing phase, then braces itself to recite the most wrenching events (public humiliation, the long vigil). After a sharp echo of the time of madness, she returns to her recovery and delivers a summary conclusion.

Reviewing the *story*, however, as it is distributed over the course of her narration, yields a different emphasis. The story sequence runs: 1 = J, 2 = K, 3 = A, 4 = G, 5 = C, 6 = D, 7 = L, 8 = H, I, and L, 9 = F and M, and 10 = N. The story gets told, but by a meandering route that reveals tacit attitudes toward the subject matter. The hard facts of violence and personal loss (1 through 4) are deferred, apart from a brief acknowledgment of the lover's death. The middle stages of mourning, mental breakdown, and recovery (5 through 9) are distributed from nearly the beginning of narration till almost the end, with the implication that this psychic drama is what most preoccupies the heroine—an implication supported by other cues. And the isolated closing gesture suggests an indifference toward anything that could be called a resolution. From the evidence of the heroine's anachronic narration of her story, she seems mainly concerned to dwell on her mental anguish, enshrine the most bitter loss in a carefully reserved corner of her mind, and suspend the outcome with a superficial closural gesture, as though leaving the past in the limbo of unfinished business.

Yet the story's chief events are clear enough; only her repeated sequestrations must be eked out from the statements that, after an initial effort to hide the family shame (not an immediate incarceration), the family restrains her during two periods of violent mental distress. Even the historical chronology in which these events are located is fairly secure: the shooting, just before the local Liberation (July 1944); the passage of the seasons (winter is mentioned) during her healing process; the holiday when "they let me go out" (Easter or Whitsun); the trip to Paris, arriving during early reports of the Hiroshima bomb (August 1945).

Only two time elements remain ambiguous, and permanently so: the precise moment of the German's death ("The moment of his death actually escaped me": p. 65); and the turning point in her recovery, called by the Japanese "com[ing] out of eternity" (p. 62). Here we may apply to another of Genette's terms, *achrony*, not merely for labeling but for a firmer grasp of such phenomena: "events not provided with any temporal reference whatsoever, events that we cannot place at all in relation to the events surrounding them"; and again, "an event we must ultimately take to be dateless and ageless."[15] Although we can generally locate the events in question here (3 occurs sometime during 2, "coming out of eternity" is a euphemism for 8), the narrator insists on their position outside of clock time ("Oh! how long it took him to die": p. 65; "Yes, it takes a long time": p. 62). Her account of imperceptible change, coupled with a report of a sense of physical fusion ("I couldn't feel the slightest difference between his dead body and mine": p. 65), hints at a dissolution of the boundaries between life and death. The narrational phenomenon of achrony becomes something more than a stylistic feature, evoking a state of mind that dwells timelessly with the dead.

This third phase of a narrational process that begins with the heroine's allusive account in the hotel room and hesitantly develops at the Japanese protagonist's home may be considered the climax not only of their relations but of the drama of narration as well. It is, however, noteworthy that this is not a point of full revelation, of all things falling into place and time. The anachronies of the narrational process as a whole persist even within the concerted storytelling at the riverside café; certain gaps in the story as it is first alluded to are not dispelled but made permanent as achronies in the completed narrative. Some philosophers of language would claim that such fissures are endemic to all storytelling—that no one can ever tell the whole story, or tell it straight. I have suggested, without leaning heavily on psychoanalytic formulas, that the heroine's arrangement of story elements and her way of approaching highly charged events derive from and express a still disturbed, not to say distorted, view of her past. The special qualities of the individual case bear out but should not be reduced to broader generalizations about narrative language.

What does the heroine's narration accomplish if it is not the full disclosure expected of climaxes? To answer this, we must refer to the cinematic procedures that convey the storytelling scene and make transitions to the wartime story. While the earlier phases of the heroine's storytelling are cinematically unremarkable, despite the disturbing content of the nuclear holocaust stills, the main phase in the café by the Ota is one of the more powerful visual evocations in the film. Introduced by shots of sunset whose glowering light and dark masses are laden with apocalyptic associations, in contrast with the harsh chiaroscuro of the café atmosphere (recalling *film noir* lighting style), the sequence makes as much of the dramatic present as it does of the narrated past. As Duras's scenario describes the dual focus: "In the previous scene they had been overwhelmed by the thought that their final separation was only sixteen hours away. When we see them now they are almost happy. They don't notice the time passing. A miracle has occurred. What miracle? The resurrection of Nevers" (p. 53). While the religious metaphors of Duras's account may be vague, Resnais found cinematic ways of realizing the scenarist's broad intent, elevating the scene of this narration above previous and later ones.

Dramatized narration at the protagonist's home is conducted along the lines of conventional cinematic codes. The subjects discussed are illustrated by intercut images. For example: "HE: Was he French, the man you loved during the war? / (*At Nevers. A German crosses the square.*) / SHE: No, he wasn't French" (p. 47). The climactic visualization of the story is not only fuller but designed to integrate the narrating activity and the story narrated. The man's questions call up appropriate images in the heroine's mind and, following the conventions of mindscreen flashbacks, we assume the screen images to be hers. But they are often placed so as to emphasize *his* ongoing effort to visualize her and her milieu: "HE: I can't picture Nevers. / (*Shots of Nevers. The Loire.*)" (p. 53). This montage of grainy landscape and town-scape shots provides not merely narrative data but an exposition of her state of mind as *he* experiences it. Although her verbal responses cannot provide him with a visual equivalent of her mental images, it is the interaction of their imaginations that produces the "resurrection of Nevers." (We will observe a similar process at work in *Letter from an Unknown Woman*.)

By rapid intercutting, the two visual (and even aural) fields of past and present are emphatically fused:

SHE: . . . The *Marseillaise* passes above my head. It's
. . . deafening. . . .
(*She blocks her ears, in this café [at Hiroshima]. The café is suddenly very quiet. Shots of Nevers' cellars. [The young heroine's] bloody hands.*)

SHE: Hands become useless in cellars. They scrape . . .
they rub the skin off . . . against the walls. . . .
(*Somewhere at Nevers, bleeding hands. Hers, on the table are intact. [The young heroine] licks her own blood.*)

(P. 55)

The difference between the cinematic treatment of this drama-tized narration and that employed earlier corresponds to a distinction between two modes of recounting the past that we have observed before. Whereas most enactments of stories told in films are rendered by means comparable to "historical" language, even when the story is told in an interpersonal exchange, this climactic scene employs means suggestive of "discourse," person-to-person utterance. In the usual flashback, we witness the story of the past, aware of it as distinct from the present; in this instance, we experience a mixture of past and present, of story and narration. This central scene in *Hiroshima* may stand as an exemplar of the full sense of the term "dramatized narration," for it dramatizes both the story (in the enactment shots) and the narrating activity, accomplishing these feats at the same time.

It needs only a short step to see that a like process is at work in the heroine's consciousness, where the ultimate drama of *Hiroshima Mon Amour* takes place. The dialogue makes vivid the uncanny way in which, as she reexperiences her story of youth, she fuses or confuses her German and Japanese lovers. It is not simply memory that leads to this semidelusion, of which even the participants are aware, but narration. Memory alone would lead to sensory associations, of which the opening flash-cuts of the two lovers' hands are the type. It is the verbalizing process, strongly encouraged by the auditor, that leads the heroine to address him as if he were the other: "HE: When you are in the cellar, am I dead? / SHE: You are dead" (p. 54). There follows the eerie string of second-person utterances ("I call you. Even though you're dead" [p. 57], etc.) in which the fusion of past and present is played out.

Before turning to the final phases of *Hiroshima*'s narration, it may be useful to position the climactic scene in its larger context: the heroine's piecemeal narration of her life story, whose sum approximates an autobiography. As early as the opening sequence, there has been infilling of various phases: as the heroine describes her recent exposure to the nuclear holocaust, she also makes sketchy allusions to her sexual encounter with the Japanese (pp. 24–25), which are later complemented by his account of the affair (pp. 32–33). And we hear the initial mention of Nevers (p. 28), of her first learning about the Hiroshima bombing (p. 33), and of her Parisian acting career (p. 28).

A number of points about this opening sequence as a storytelling scene should be noted. In the terms employed by narratologists, it includes the first run-through of what is to become a "repeating" narration (Genette: "*narrating n times what happened once*"). Later, the German lover's death, her relegations to the cellar, and the process of forgetting will also be recounted in repeating narration. It is the mode that we come to accept as the film's and the heroine's distinctive narrative style, and which begins even at this early stage.

Further, it may be said of the opening narration that it is ample as to the immediate past, but intentionally elliptical on the intervening years; it leaves a large gap between the flashed image of death in Nevers and the trip to Hiroshima—a gap that will only gradually, and only partially, be filled by later narrations. Given the allusive opening narration and the scattered but persistent return to key phases of her life, it may be seen that autobiographical reflection occupies the heroine throughout *Hiroshima*, and that dramatized narration is a consistent, though anachronic, mode of dealing with her life story.

Beyond these implications for the film's narration, the opening sequence carries important burdens regarding the structure of her life story. Just as the climactic narration can be analyzed by ordering its story elements and its narrative statements, the same procedure can be applied to the dramatized narration of the film as a whole. The heroine's life may be divided as follows: 1 = childhood and youth (first eighteen years); 2 = love affair ("I was eighteen and he was twenty-three": p. 48); 3 = trauma and recovery (the period immediately before and after her twentieth birthday: p. 58); 4 = life in Paris, including acting career, marriage and motherhood; 5 = trip to Hiroshima. Marking the narrations in the hotel room, home, and café as A, B, and C respectively, we find these phases narrated in the following order: A = 5, with passing references to 1, 3 ("mad in Nevers": pp. 36f.), and 4 ("And then of course when I had children": pp. 37 and 38); B = 2 (with further reference to 4—"I'm a woman who's happy with her husband": p. 46); C = 3.

Hiroshima's characteristic narrative style, of which all viewers are broadly aware, emerges here with some saliency. The anachronic order we have examined in the decisive storytelling scene is also to be found in the larger narrational structure; and the permanent aporias we noted in the climactic tale are matched by the large ellipses within the life story. Except for cryptic mention of marriage, career, and occasional sexual flings, we learn little of the heroine's adult life—that is, her posttraumatic consciousness—up to the time of her trip to Hiroshima. (At least its duration is unambiguous: "Fourteen years have passed": p. 67.) We must look, then, to later scenes of narration to supply further information on an important phase of the story: how has the heroine's later life been shaped by her experience?

After her climactic narration, the heroine dismisses the Japanese and returns to her hotel, but has difficulty in remaining in her room. As she washes her face before a mirror, she conducts a dialogue with herself. Some of her utterances are dubbed and may be taken as unspoken thought, while others are spoken on-camera and resemble normal talking-to-oneself. Duras's text describes this twin stream as "interior dialogue" (p. 73):

> You think you know. And then, no. You don't. / In
> Nevers she had a German love when she was
> young. . . . / We'll go to Bavaria, my love, and there
> we'll marry. / She never went to Bavaria. (*Looking at*
> *herself in the mirror.*) / I dare those who have never gone
> to Bavaria to speak to her of love. / You were not yet
> quite dead. / I told our story. / I was unfaithful to you
> tonight with this stranger. / I told our story. / It was,
> you see, a story that could be told. / For fourteen years,
> I hadn't found . . . the taste of an impossible love
> again. / Since Nevers. / Look how I'm forgetting
> you. . . . / Look how I've forgotten you. / Look at me.

(P. 73)

In a narratological view, the most remarkable aspect of these memorable lines is their mixture of historical and discursive forms. After a self-addressing second-person present-tense statement about her state of mind, the speaker/thinker turns to the historic past to encapsulate her story, quotes from its dialogue ("We'll go to Bavaria"), and returns to the present to address her contemporaries ("I dare those . . ."). At about the midpoint of this series, she recounts recent events (her storytelling and unfaithfulness), generalizes negatively about fourteen years of the past (the period we have labeled 4), and returns to the present, addressing her German lover in the imperative mood.

The mixture of addressees and the wide temporal range of this "interior dialogue" may be regarded as typical of the stream of consciousness—Duras's writing clearly stands in that literary tradition. But this flexibility also testifies to the heroine's heightened self-consciousness, for she covers most of her life story with sweeping summations, vivid excerpts, and bold self-assertions and self-criticisms, inconclusive as some of them may

Hiroshima Mon Amour: Interior dialogue at the hotel
mirror; interior monologue on the night walk

seem. She comments, moreover, not only on past and present events but on her act of narration itself, which has now become part of her life story and may prove to be one of its crucial events.

For the "dialogue" opens a new phase of the film's dramatic action: the tense issue of how the heroine will deal with her traumatic memories now that they have been reawakened by her decisive narrative act. Her assertion "Look how I've forgotten you" is clearly incorrect—a practical, if not a linguistic, impossibility—and is immediately negated by her urgent call, "Look at me." The film's denouement will be played out in the ongoing dramatic present, yet acts of storytelling will not be entirely excluded, even at this late stage.

The heroine turns to what the text calls "interior monologue" (p. 77),[16] her dubbed voice unheard by the Japanese and others as she makes a night walk through Hiroshima. This mental speech too is a form of narration, with the unusual feature of being largely in the future tense:

> I always expected that one day you would descend on
> me. / I waited for you calmly, with infinite patience. /
> Take me. Deform me to your likeness. . . . / We're
> going to remain alone, my love. / The night will never
> end. / . . . / We'll have nothing else to do, nothing but
> to mourn the departed day. / And a time is going to
> come. / A time will come. When we'll no more know
> what thing it is that binds us. By slow degrees the
> word will fade from our memory. / Then it will
> disappear altogether.

> (P. 77)

Moving through the modes we have already observed—direct address, summary of the past, imperative—the monologue arrives at a set of stipulations of the future. It is not simply a wish or a vision that heroine utters here but a carefully nuanced set of declarative sentences predicting future events. She continues the narrative activity in which she has engaged throughout the film, but now extends its span to tell the future. This prophecy has two distinct stages: the first, in which the lovers will consciously love each other and retain their sense of time (mourning "the departed day"), and the second, in which they will lose all consciousness and thereby their love as well ("the word will fade from our memory").

With the opening of these large vistas on the heroine's life, it is hard to resist the impression that *Hiroshima Mon Amour* is an artistic demonstration of the psychoanalytic process known as the "life history." In this narrational exercise, the individual "brings back into the present the origins of his own person," expressing the "discourse of earlier days in its own archaic, even foreign language."[17] The Japanese clearly plays the role of provoker-of-narrative, like the analyst, and the experience certainly has some of the cathartic effects of a psychiatric "talking cure." Even without such theorization, the film stands squarely within the sustained exploration of time and memory that shapes the cinematic careers of both Resnais and Duras. Although both went on to make other, and splendid, films on these themes, *Hiroshima* has never been surpassed as a drama of memory, its discontents, and its inevitability.[18] Yet despite the film's demonstration of the "obvious necessity for memory" (p. 23), it is perhaps even more compelling in its sounding of a new theme: the obvious necessity for forgetting.

This note was struck earlier, in the heroine's "interior dialogue" ("Look how I'm forgetting you") but reaches a crescendo at the close ("I'll forget you! I'm forgetting you already! Look how I'm forgetting you!": p. 83). Despite the dubiousness of all predictions—we shall never know how much good her experiences in Hiroshima will do her—this outcome is less a matter of bravado than it sounds. We have seen that the heroine has converted her narrating into prophecy, and that she shows herself to be rather adept at its verbal forms. Some of *Hiroshima's* most memorable, though difficult, lines are those that, in place of memory, anticipate forgetting:

> Silly little girl. / Who dies of love at Nevers. / Little girl with shaven head, I bequeath you to oblivion. / Three-penny story. / As it was for [her dead lover], oblivion will begin with your eyes. / Just the same. / Then, as it was for him, it will encompass your voice. / Just the same. / Then, as it was for him, it will encompass you completely, little by little. / You will become a song.
>
> (P. 80)

Despite the singsong rhythm of these lines, we recognize that she is bringing her life story to its finale, crooning to herself of her own death. This song of death too counts as narration; it tells the final stages of her love affair. That these events will be a solo activity simply reinforces what many observers, and not only Freudians, have said of love, that it is ultimately narcissistic and fully intertwined with death.

The story of the past is one in which, following the romantic metaphor she herself employs, she "dies of love at Nevers." (But she also knows that she "didn't die at Nevers": p. 78.) The story of the future is one in which, building upon personal observation of the stages of her lover's dying, she imagines her own death. Unlike less knowledgeable persons, she narrates that death minutely: "Oblivion will begin with your eyes. . . . It will encompass your voice. . . . It will encompass you completely. . . . You will become a song." The accompanying shots, both those of the present Hiroshima and those of the past Nevers, are calculated to support this outcome. The setting of this interior monologue is a railway station, where she sits next to a gnarled old woman; the memory flashes of Nevers are those of a thorny forest and a massive church, the great Romanesque cathedral of Saint-Saveur. By her absorption in images of dessicated nature and funereal architecture, by her pursuit of her mental incantation while maintaining a silent and detached presence in the ordinary world, she has already come a fair way toward her prediction.

The memory process, the talking cure, may have done much to break down the precarious embalming the heroine has made of her past and to build a securer basis for her subsequent life. But the renewal of intimate contact with death that it entails also leads her to contemplate her life's larger scope. In the course of intensively remembering and narrating her life story, the heroine has become capable of narrating its close. It is a rare autobiography that contains passages on its subject's close.

This and not the final exchange of symbolic designations by the Frenchwoman and the Japanese—"Hi-ro-shi-ma. That's your name." "Your name is Nevers. Ne-vers-in France" (p. 83)—is the true fulfillment of the film's dramatic development. It is a film about many things—the personal dimensions of war and the correlations between experiences of loss in far-flung places, among them.[19] But its ongoing drama is largely that of the heroine's exposition of her life through narration. It is a drama, then, not only of her story's reenactment, but of her multiphased activity of storytelling. The finale is reached when her life history reaches its final term, her own death, and includes that term in its discourse. *Hiroshima Mon Amour* may or may not rank as the greatest narrated film of all time, but it surely stands among the finest dramatized narrations.

6

Multiple Narration:
Rashomon and *Zelig*

WHERE IS Rashomon, narratologically speaking? A gate on the outskirts of Kyoto, amid the civil wars of the twelfth century, as an opening superimposed title tells us. Its thematic position soon becomes apparent, for it stands at the juncture between city and country, between civilization and nature, between law and order and the unguarded places of passional crime. The gate's function is largely symbolic even within its historical setting, as there are no adjacent walls to keep out what is on the other side. In its open/closed state it admits those who care to pass and those who, seeking refuge in extremity, pause to stay. For civil society is itself in extremis, the smoke of war rising to suggest a breakdown for which the battered gate is a synecdochic figure. Yet this society's institutions still hold trials in an effort to achieve truth and justice. Thus the settings of *Rashomon* are three: the forest of passion and crime, the court of inquiry and testifying, and the gate of review and interpretation. By multiplying narratives within established locales of story, narration, and renarration, the film dramatizes the story-making, story-telling, story-deciphering career of mankind.

Three settings, four tales—in the usual description of the film. Three participants in a death (murder? suicide?), rape (forced? willing?), and theft testify (one of them putatively, through a medium) about the events and their motivation. An eyewitness to the proceedings first testifies to discovering the body, and later confesses to stealing a dagger (but not to the potential charge of murder). The woodcutter's version gains credibility by culminating in his confession, but the main par-

Rashomon: Narration at the gate—the priest, the commoner,
and the woodcutter

ticipants have also implicated themselves. The bandit acknowledges raping the wife, killing her husband in fair combat, and
stealing his horse and sword; the wife skirts a confession of
murder but describes her approach to it; and the samurai pro-
claims his ritual suicide after losing wife and honor. We are
disposed to believe the woodcutter, since his version exposes
the bandit's and the samurai's equal cowardice and clumsiness,
as well as the wife's bitchiness in provoking them to fight so as
to leave her with only one master. Cynicism breeds farce (her
word for the situation, according to the woodcutter): we smirk
at the final enactment of the kernel story, in which all are revealed in their cowardice, egoism, and mendacity.[1]

Despite this gesture of a definitive final version, the story
as presented in this film remains permanently unresolved, and
not because of multiple narration per se but because a necessary
item of information is withheld. The samurai dies either of a

sword wound or a dagger wound; the bandit and woodcutter attest the former, the wife and samurai the latter. The police investigation presumably revealed the cause of death, but we are given neither this information nor word of the verdict, although the bandit is sure to be punished. Perpetrators, outcomes, even the charges—murder or suicide, rape or adultery—are left in limbo. Though the stolen horse, bow, and arrows are exhibited in court, we never confirm the sword's fate, though the bandit says he sold it for drink. (The policeman says he was captured with a fine Korean sword, but that may be his own.) We see the dagger raised as the wife approaches her husband; we hear from him that someone pulled it out, but though the woodcutter confesses to stealing it, we never confirm how—or even *that*—he disposed of it.

The film's concealments cannot be laid at the door of its fictional source or considered an inadequately detailed adaptation of that source. As Donald Richie has pointed out, the two short stories of Ryunosuke Akutagawa provide only the setting at a ruined gate, the main narremes (including the stolen clothes in the film's final sequence), and the schema of a multiple narration (by seven witnesses, six of whom are retained in the film). Richie summarizes Akutagawa's radically skeptical—and ultimately (for the author) self-destroying—implication that "all truth is relative, with the corollary that there is thus no truth at all."[2] This nihilism is contrasted with Kurosawa's humanistic relativism or perspectivism: "Truth as it appears to others. . . . No one—priest, woodcutter, husband, bandit, medium—lied. They all told the story the way they saw it, the way they believed it, and they all told the truth" (p. 82). The humanistic or existential view[3] leads Richie to an accommodation with the ambiguities that he has himself carefully noted in the film: "In the telling and in the retelling, the people reveal not the action but themselves. This is why Kurosawa could leave the plot, insofar as there is one, dangling and unresolved. The fact that it *is* unresolved is itself one of the meanings of the film" (p. 83). This rationale for an unresolved plot will satisfy many viewers in our postmodernist age, but it adds further obscurities of its own: does irresolution result from the lack of plot ("insofar as there is one"), the characters' subjective distortions, or the filmmaker's design (with scenarist Shinobu Hashimoto)? Though these questions remain open, a way to an answer may lie in the passing phrase, "telling and retelling," for it is narration that lurks in the shadows within and around *Rashomon*.

Whatever its explanatory limits, Richie's essay makes one of the first narratological approaches to this, or to any, film— although he seems to have devised it pragmatically rather than in service to a theory. Recognizing that only the woodcutter's final narration is performed at Rashomon and that the other versions are previous depositions, reported by the woodcutter and priest to a third party called "the commoner," Richie sets up a table correlating the story events with their narrations and renarrations (unfortunately Richie refers to the former as "first-person stories" and to the latter as "third-person recountings": p. 76). This leads to a valuable description, if not a solution, of the "Great Rashomon Murder Mystery":

1. The discovery of the husband's body.		A lie told by the woodcutter.
2. Man and wife seen in the forest.		The truth told by the priest.
3. [The bandit's] capture.	Told by the police agent.	The truth told by the woodcutter or priest.
4. [The bandit's] version of the story.	Told by [the bandit].	A lie told by the woodcutter.
5. The wife's version.	Told by the wife.	The truth told by the priest.
6. The husband's version.	Told by the husband through the medium.	Accepted as true and told by the priest.
7. The woodcutter's version.		A lie told by the woodcutter.

(P. 79)

With all its benefits in arranging the data of *Rashomon*, this schema invites both local and more general tinkering. Why characterize the wife's version as a "truth told by the priest" (apparently because he considers it true), while the bandit's equally questionable tale has been transmitted faithfully yet is characterized as a "lie told by the woodcutter"? There must be a way of distinguishing the initial from the reporting speech act, so that lies, faithful reports of lies, distorted accounts of true statements, and so on may be noted. A formula with this purpose is used for the husband's version—"accepted as true and told by"—though the intent here is to indicate the priest's belief in the credibility of mediums. One might also wish to fine-tune the statements that the woodcutter's initial and final versions are both lies, since both contain numerous accurate details, while the second makes an obvious improvement on the first, if only in having a greater span. And other points need tightening; for example, narrations 1 and 2 (Richie's numbering, though placed next to story units, comes to be a narrational series) are initially made at the court inquiry and, like narrations 3 through 6, renarrated at the gate.

Despite these invitations to further refinement, Richie's arrangement of the elements of *Rashomon* is surely the best we have. Its chief advantage is to lay out the phases or layers of the film's transmission process, for the three columns represent the sequence of narrational activities that are shown in action. The left-hand column lists story-events (or purported events), the middle one their narration at the inquiry, and the right one their renarration at the gate (or their unique narration, in the case of the woodcutter's closing report). We may think of the columns as stories, narrations, and renarrations,[4] respectively, for which FOREST, COURT, and GATE may serve as visible signs.

The visibility of both story and storytelling is an important matter—and a source of perhaps unavoidable gaps—for any description of *Rashomon*, since these activities are shown, yet not fully shown, at each locus. Since Richie is not alone in omitting the visual evidence for these events, it is best to indicate whether the renarrations are dramatized or not, and whether their contents—both the story events and the court testimonies—are, in the terms I have proposed, enacted or "dry." (I shall return to this distinction.) Here, then, is a revised version of the Great Rashomon Narrational Process:

FOREST	COURT	GATE
The discovery (enacted)	Woodcutter tells (enacted)	Woodcutter retells (dramatized)
Entry into forest (enacted)	Priest tells (enacted)	Priest retells (not dramatized)
The capture (enacted)	Policeman tells (enacted)	Woodcutter or priest retells (not dramatized)
The bandit's version (enacted)	Bandit tells (enacted)	Woodcutter or priest retells (not dramatized)
The wife's version (enacted)	Wife tells (enacted)	Priest retells (dramatized)
The husband's version (enacted)	Medium tells (enacted)	Woodcutter or priest retells (not dramatized)
The woodcutter's version (enacted)		Woodcutter tells (dramatized)
The theft (dry)		Commoner tells (dramatized)

A number of explanations are called for. I have labeled the scenes of testifying at court as "enacted," that is, as events narrated at the gate; they might also have been labeled "dramatized," as scenes of narration in their own right. Some of the renarrations are dramatized; another is an implicit repetition by the original speaker (the priest's testimony), but certain reports of other speakers lack this implication; we may take the authority for these reports as the woodcutter and/or priest, but we cannot list them individually as sources. This anomalous situation would seem an instance of *ellipsis*, not in the story but in the narrational process. It may be accounted to the filmmaker's tactful decision not to visualize every stage slavishly, teaching us instead to supply what is implicit.

There are, however, other aporias in the film's elaborate system of transmission; if the renarration is subject to ellipsis, omissions also occur in the story enactment and in the narration. All six court testimonies are enacted, to be sure, but not all the forest scenes are narrated at court. One of these, the woodcutter's version, is the enactment of a narration made only at the gate. At a further stage of the tendency toward ellipsis, the final story unit—the woodcutter's theft of the dagger—lacks two stages of transmission: both initial narration at court and visual enactment when posited at the gate. Nor does the woodcutter verify the commoner's accusatory tale; he merely assents to it tacitly.[5] We begin to suffer the vertigo of finding every stage of the storytelling susceptible to the opening of permanent gaps, and not always for reasons that we can rationalize as the film-maker's tactful elision.

The multiplying of narration in *Rashomon*, not merely among several witnesses but among several stages or levels of trans-mission, points to a further complication. While we have been content to place the forest events in the position of *story*, the terminological quibble about the court testimonies—(enact-ments of the renarration, or narrations of the enacted story?)—reflects a valid audience perception. The court proceedings are events, and these acts of narration become phases of a larger story. (Since Watergate, such extensions are no longer merely fancy theoretics.) If one were asked to give the plot of *Rashomon*, an adequate account would have to include the actions at the gate and court, as well as those in the forest. Indeed, there are those who would claim that the latter are mere melodrama, distinguished only by their association with the impressive story of human deception and interpretation that takes place at court and gate.[6]

What implications are to be drawn from this arrangement of the story and its extension to the storytelling of *Rashomon*? We might focus on either the repetitions or the ellipses that occur at forest, court, and gate, but this is to extend a well-known truth in amateur narratology to multiple storytelling: just as one can never tell the whole story, more than one can never perform an integral narration. Though this may win immediate assent if applied to *Rashomon* as a whole, it will also be discovered at individual phases of the transmission process. We may contemplate a model case in which an enacted story event is both shown being narrated and dramatically renarrated. Only two instances of such full transmission are to be found in the film: the woodcutter's initial statement of his discoveries in the forest and the priest's report of the wife's testimony. We see the woodcutter begin his tale at the gate and conclude it at court, with the enactment between, and hear him report his act of narration in a voice-over: "Then the police called me to testify" (p. 30). Similarly, the priest characterizes the wife's tale: "Hers was a completely different story from the bandit's" (p. 89); we then see her begin and end her tale, with enactment between. Although the priest does not close his report of her narrating act, he is seen in the shot of her conclusion at the court (shot 254: in scenario, p. 99). Normal practice in the film may be judged to be elliptical, with the two instances of full display the deviation. No other events of the film's story are fully narrated and re-narrated, so that the same ambiguity that inhibits the clear resolution of its story also indelibly colors its system of narration.

The audience of *Rashomon*, narratologists in spite of ourselves, perhaps, are not the only ones who must deal with these churlish resistances to even relative truth. The priest and woodcutter are in a state of shock after hearing the conflicting testimony at court, but the commoner listens with an ear cocked not only to the statements they repeat but also to those they provide. The characters at the gate are our representatives in a number of respects, chief of which is their effort to interpret the conflicting statements and establish the true story. Another respect in which they stand in for us lies in their attention to the form and manner of narration. They make a running commentary not only on the story but on the tellings of it, thus furnishing the film with some of the credentials of self-reflexive works of art.

Their interpretive positions are, moreover, differentiated and exemplary. At a climactic point in the narrational proceedings, the previous testimony is sweepingly impugned by the woodcutter: "It's a lie. They're all lies! [The bandit's] confession, the woman's story—they're lies!" (p. 88). We may take this as the film's own version of the skeptical position some have proposed for its interpretation: "All truth is relative . . . there is thus no truth at all." At this point, the priest and commoner express two further options: the relativistic humanist and the hedonist or estheticist positions: "PRIEST: That may be true. But it's because men are so weak. That's why they lie. That's why they must deceive themselves. / COMMONER: Not another sermon! . . . I don't mind a lie. Not if it's interesting. What kind of story did she tell?" (p. 89). These interpretive options—the skeptical, the relativist, and the esthetic—become a kind of choric triad in response to the ambiguity of human storytelling.

Punctuating the forest creatures' self-serving narrative performances, the woodcutter continues his "lies . . . all lies" incantation (p. 102); the priest warily reaffirms his humanist faith ("I must not believe that men are so sinful") while grasping at a transcendent source of truth, the reliability of mediums ("Dead men tell no lies"); and the commoner delivers a functional account of the human penchant for narrative: "Look, everyone wants to forget unpleasant things, so they make up stories. It's easier that way" (p. 103). In these choric interludes, the modes of interpreting narrative are inspected from a variety of viewpoints. It is thus not only multiple versions of the story that *Rashomon* presents, but also multiple ideologies of storytelling itself.

The final stage of the film's self-reflexive drama of interpretation occurs when the narrow difference between the woodcutter and the commoner—the absolute skeptic and the hedonistic esthete—become attenuated on the issue of self-interest. The woodcutter has maintained his negative mutterings with apparent detachment, but his outburst at the husband's/medium's tale reveals his personal involvement: "That's not true. There wasn't any dagger there—he was killed by a sword" (p. 124). The commoner is quick to note his slip—"Now it's getting interesting. You must have seen the whole thing"—but maintains the neutral spectatorship his position requires of him: "Well come on and tell us then. Yours seems the most interesting of all these stories."

The closing interactions of the woodcutter and commoner do not go far in adjudicating between their interpretive positions, for the revelation of the former's culpability in the main affair is quickly matched by the latter's flagrant exhibition of cupidity. When the commoner takes to stealing an abandoned child's garments, the amoralist position he has maintained is tarred with a rather crude brush. While the esthete is shown to be governed by purely acquisitive motives, the woodcutter's consistent skepticism of others is revealed as a coverup for his complicity in their debacle. By the same token, his version of the kernel story has much to recommend it but cannot be taken as a definitive account. As a lower-class satirist of his betters, he offers a version that is the most entertaining of them all. Yet the benefits of receiving a supposed outsider's viewpoint are annulled by his own involvement—his self-interest in covering up his criminal lapse. Though we may think we have left the main story behind, the vagaries of narration lead us back into it.

The renewed interest in the stolen dagger revives that irrepressible question of not who but what killed the samurai. *Rashomon*, we might agree, is a film of iterative narration in which a kernel story is narrated and enacted four times over. But these four versions are not wildly at variance; they break down into twin pairs. If the bandit and woodcutter are to be believed, the former killed the samurai in a swordfight after provocation by the wife. In the bandit's tale she brazenly urges combat after yielding to his sexual powers (p. 79), while in the woodcutter's version she is considerably more distraught after both men spurn her (pp. 137f.), but her motivations and the outcomes in these two versions are not far apart. As a synopsis printed with the scenario sums up the woodcutter's version, "She goads the two into fighting, a parody of the first fight scene described by the bandit himself" (p. 143).

If the wife and husband are to be believed, the dagger found its way to his chest. In her version, he scorned her after the rape or seduction; she approached him dagger in hand but fainted before the thrust—adding, in a "dry" phase of her narration at court, that she woke to find it lodged in him (p. 98). In his version, after she vainly provoked the bandit to kill him and ran away when scorned, the husband killed himself (pp. 117ff.). (It may be observed in passing that in all versions but hers, she is said to urge the men to fight.) Although the details and motivations cannot be fully reconciled, there is considerable congruence between these, as it were, domestic accounts, just as there was between the two martial accounts. In both these versions, she intended the husband's death (either when approaching with a dagger or when provoking the bandit to kill him), she did not (consciously) make the fatal thrust, and someone saw him with the dagger in his chest (she, in her narrative; the unknown thief, in the husband's).

Among the possibilities opened up by those two sets of tales, the most intriguing derive from the lone account of the theft. In the husband's version, the medium speaks his/her final words: "Then someone seemed to approach me. Softly, gently. Who could it have been? Then someone's hand grasped the dagger and drew it out" (p. 122). If this someone is the wife, the bottom line of her story remains consistent with his, and she is guilty only of omitting the distasteful retrieval of her precious knife. If it is the woodcutter, his tacit confession of theft is confirmed, while other troubling possibilities emerge. If the samurai is not killed in a duel, as the woodcutter has claimed, and it is his hand that draws the dagger from the corpse, how did it come there? The husband (or the medium) may have invented a death befitting a samurai by narrating his ritual suicide, when the truth may be that, while tied up, he was ignominiously killed by a peasant for the sake of the discarded weapon's value. If the woodcutter's tale of a death by swordplay is true, the married couple are both liars, yet both to some degree inculpate themselves—unaccountably, on his assumptions. But if their tales are true, at least in respect to the murder weapon, the woodcutter stands under suspicion of something more than theft.

A telling sign of the woodcutter's relation to the stories he and the others tell is a subtle but extended reaction shot. As the medium completes her tortured emission of the dead man's final words, we see the woodcutter in the courtyard, listening attentively but now increasingly agitated in facial and bodily gestures as he hears of someone approaching the corpse to pull the dagger out (shot 305: in scenario, p. 122). In the time-honored conventions of courtroom drama, such evidence is usually enough to convict a character—sufficient for the audience's confirmation of culpability, if not by a more exacting legal standard. But *Rashomon* is a murder mystery only at some remove, mediated as it is by the conventions of Japanese costume drama and by the exercises in modernist narrative form indicated above. Visual impressions, like narrative data, prove inadequate to resolve the "Great Rashomon Murder Mystery," and we are left with a multiplicity of parallel stories, undecidable interpretations of them, and permanent world-views on the nature of narration and truth.

A shift of primary focus from the purveyors to the receivers of narration has been a gradual but continual process throughout *Rashomon*. The process is interrupted, as it were, by the forest enactments of the iterative tales, but as these become nugatory, each in its turn, we are relieved by having somewhere else to turn. What the commoner says of the narration—that it is good to hear some storytelling to get through a rainy day (p. 17)— may be even more pertinent to the endless prospect of interpretation. As the four versions cancel each other out and leave us with our doubts about the forest events and court testimonies, the scene of commentary comes to seem a place in which we are fully at home. Hence the film's title: Rashomon is where we interpreters are placed, and left.

The closing actions at the gate—theft of the baby clothes by the commoner (the "common man," we call him, in postfeudal terms), tacit confession, and redemptive adoption of the baby by the woodcutter—may do something to condition our attitudes toward skeptical critics of various persuasions. There is little encouragement, however, to join the priest in reaffirming his faith in humanity (p. 165). The same irresolution felt at the levels of story and narration is carried over to that of interpretation, as we might have anticipated. The visual evidence missing from both story and narration scenes (what happened to the dagger?), the subtly varied data of the doubly paired narrations, the ultimately indecipherable commentaries of the renarration, all proclaim a lasting gap in stories and in their tellings.

Yet there is also visible display in *Rashomon* of a number of solid elements in the human condition of proliferating narrative and abiding irresolution. Returning to a shot first seen in the title sequence and again near the beginning of action (shot 24: in scenario, p. 19), the film's final image is "the great signboard of the gate" (shot 407). Like a Grecian urn, this artifact covered with symbolic figures seems to tell us all we know on earth and all we need to know. Under that sign, human figures are very small: both in the tilt down to the men in the earlier scene and in the penultimate, backward-tracking shot that keeps the wood-cutter and baby in the foreground but finally reveals the priest, "small, standing under the gate" (p. 169). Like the closing shots of *Citizen Kane*, which present images of packing crates and puzzles, an inscrutable inscription ("Rosebud"), and a house of mystery surrounded by "No Trespassing" signs, *Rashomon* dis-plays an architectural mass and a linguistic symbol to close the scene of narrative interpretation.

Yet the gate is not the only place of narration to be indelibly visualized by the film. It is, after all, only the scene of renar-ration, secondary to the space of initial narrative utterance, the court. Literally a court, paved with white gravel and backed by an earth-toned clay wall, the magistrate's courtyard strongly resembles the rock gardens of religious buildings in Japan. When the priest and woodcutter are seen, as they often are, sitting like small mounds in the background while others testify toward the camera, as if to the unseen magistrate, they may call to mind the stones of Ryoanji, that famous Kyoto temple. There we are invited to contemplate a group of stones, thought to be arranged in cosmic, geographical, and other referential forms, according to one's taste and inclination. In this film, it is the narrators and receivers of narrative who are the objects of contemplation, the ambiguous forms that we are invited to scrutinize. Their pres-ence in the court frames them in a social interaction and an esthetic drama. But their monolithic shape also offers an abstract image of human beings as narrative creatures—an image as in-triguing, powerful, and ultimately open as that of the gate and its sign.

○   ○   ○   ○

That *Rashomon* ends in ambiguity was to be anticipated, given its structure of *iterative* narration; could we expect that any story told four times over would remain a single story, much less a coherent one? At best one might discover patterns of self-reference in the commentaries, yielding insight into the narration as a process. To the extent that iterative narration itself becomes the subject of a film, it may present an arresting drama of men and women living with the imperatives, constraints, and rewards of storytelling. How is it, then, with *serial* narration?

In comparing the closing images of *Rashomon* with those of *Citizen Kane*, I have suggested a like suspension of meanings in open visual forms. Yet *Kane* is not as serenely agnostic in its view of truth, for its serial narration does not open quite so many yawning gaps as those of *Rashomon*. The four main (and one subsidiary) narrators interviewed by a news reporter give a fairly consistent account of the protagonist at successive stages of his life, and even the public image of the man purveyed by the newsreel conveys similar contradictions and grotesqueries in his character. Serial narration invites a parceling out of the territory for reports by the most favored witness at each phase of a story. Yet this linearity permits synchronic integration: a sense of fullness is derived from the arrangement of personal perspectives around the central subject, each somewhat at an angle to the others yet conspiring to build up a rounded view. (Thus several Kane-narrators urge the reporter on to others whom they trust to adumbrate their own views.) Even the paired iterative sequences—Bernstein's and Leland's accounts of Kane's entry into journalism, Susan's and Leland's accounts of her opera debut—do not undercut but flesh out the lived sense of those events. Though we never discover the essential truth promised by the Rosebud symbol, we come away with a fuller idea of the central character than is conveyed by most other films.[7]

Like *Rashomon*, *Citizen Kane* has had its imitators (as noted earlier), but another kind of offspring, a parody, was among the keenest in seizing on its special traits—the creation and analysis of character through multiple narration. Woody Allen's *Zelig* (1983) has, in the few years since its appearance, been accorded its measure of accolades, but its important position among narrated films needs to be secured. Though its recycling of *Kane's* multiple interviews and pseudo-newsreels is immediately evident, the film's systematic dealings with a classic also remain to be explored. Two archetypal American figures are erected in these constructs of public image-mongering and personal interviews: in the one, the captain of industry as power-seduced idealist and self-isolated egoist; in the other, the young man on the make whose malleability for every model of success derives from and reveals an absence of personal identity.[8] That Zelig matches Kane in the many-sidedness of his public image and the vacuity of his internal structure testifies to his status as a mythic figure: both are larger-than-life heroes, insistently demanding interpretation yet resisting all summaries of their significance.

As parody, *Zelig* helps itself to the full battery of narrational methods in its host text, then goes on to add a further array of film techniques that have come into play since *Kane*. It opens with a pseudo-documentary voice-over narrator, sporting a tony English accent as if to assume anthropological detachment in recounting the tribal customs of America's Jazz Age. His voice accompanies stock footage of ticker-tape parades, some of it repeated at the film's climax, after Zelig flies the Atlantic upside down. The generic reference is clearly to the pompous newsreel of *Kane*, itself a parody of the Hearst journalistic style, but not only is Hearst Metrotone News brought into play; Pathe, Universal, and even UFA Ton-Woche announcers and intertitle formats are also imitated in later sequences. Some of these clips are altered by process photography so as to insert Allen's phiz in old-time settings, while other documentary footage is intercut with grainily filmed reenactments, like the Hitler speech that Zelig breaks up by mugging to his fiancée in the audience. In addition to movie footage, newspaper photos of the period and imitations of them are employed, as in the mock-sensational reporting of the love-triangle deaths of Zelig's half-sister, her lover, and a bullfighter.

Zelig diverges from *Citizen Kane* when, instead of establishing a framing situation that would lead to dramatized narrations by those-who-knew-him-when, it develops the mode of direct, on-screen narration. Some of these interviews are close to those of *Kane*, but the interviewer is not in the shot or soundtrack. Speaking toward the camera, the female protagonist, her sister, and her cousin (the photographer for the inserted case-study film) address the interviewer/audience to give their recollections of the story, set some fifty years before (1928–c.1933). These autobiographical reflections are shot in color, using elderly actors who vaguely resemble those who play their youthful prototypes, thus adding, and mildly satirizing, historical authenticity.[9] Additional color interviews with elderly ex-journalists, who reminisce about reporting the sensational story, provide another kind of internal narration, by members of the story world who are mere witnesses. Into this camp also fall other interviews with fictional characters who recall their contacts with Zelig: a speakeasy waiter, a Parisian café proprietress (played by the historical person "Bricktop"), and an ex-stormtrooper.[10] Other interviews are filmed in black and white and set back in time: brief man-in-the-street opinion sampling that parodies broadcast news more closely than it does *cinéma vérité*.

A third kind of direct, on-screen narration, also shot in color to indicate a present-day perspective on the black-and-white past, is performed by a series of celebrity intellectuals: Susan Sontag, Irving Howe, Saul Bellow, Bruno Bettelheim, and the historian John Morton Blum, purporting to be the author of *Interpreting Zelig*. Since they are historical individuals commenting on fictional persons and events, there is some ambiguity in their status as external narrators. Their contributions lie, moreover, in the realm of cultural criticism rather than detailed storytelling, yet they fall under the rubric of *histors*, the voice of history personified in many a fictional work.

Additional parodies of film narration are laid on with a free hand, as in the fun-and-games tone assumed by the pseudo-documentary narrator when authentic newsreel clips are intercut with simulated shots to show Zelig cavorting at San Simeon with Hearst, Marion Davies, and other gossip-column figures—the prototypes of *Citizen Kane*. There is a tongue-in-cheek psychiatric case-study film of Zelig's treatment by his wife-to-be, for which the voice-over narrator switches to the style of training films, carefully specifying the technical preparations for filming "the famous White Room Sessions, a remarkable document in the history of psychotherapy" (p. 66). We even see two excerpts from an invented Hollywood movie based on the Zelig story, "The Changing Man" (1935); while not literally a narration, this *mise en abîme* construction accords with the above-mentioned tendency of multiple-narration films toward self-referentiality. To conclude the film, a scrolling intertitle recites the aftermath of Zelig's carrer, employing one of the most elementary of narrational techniques to complete the parodic repertoire.

As in literary parodies that follow the mode called anatomy or Menippean satire, to use the terminologies of Northrop Frye and Mikhail Bakhtin, respectively,[11] the film's sheer abundance of satiric targets plays a recognizable role. *Zelig* is truly a *satura*, a comic stew into which almost any shred of human folly or shard of semiotic silliness can be tossed—the intellectual pretentions and cultural illusions of our own day along with those of the 1920s. Some questions that may trouble the narratologist, enjoying the comedy along with everybody else, may be stated this way: Does *Zelig* parody so many narrational techniques, among its other targets, that it undermines film narration as such, or does it marshal them to tell its fable in a synthetic storytelling mode? And if the latter, can we read its accumulated narrative as a coherent myth of modern life? Or does the full exploiting of multiple narration create so zany a comic mishmash that it can never—need never—be resolved?

When so much of a film consists of storytelling situations, some effort to describe their relation to each other seems in order. To take the 1928–33 kernel story, those events are presented in some phases of the film by narrational data more or less contemporary with them. These include newsreel clips and shots of newspaper pages with photos, of both the genuine and fabricated sorts. We may consider this contemporaneous internal narration, consisting of reports and documents that themselves form part of the world of the story events, for example, the case-study film. Reflections about the story by the characters in the present day and by other elderly eyewitnesses constitute an intermediary level of transmission: internal narrations at a distance in time, comparable to retrospective voice-overs. Finally, there are the intellectual commentators, the pseudo-documentary general voice-over (not those of the newsreels), and the closing intertitle scroll: external narrations about historical events and their cultural significance.

As in *Rashomon*, we observe a multiplication of narrating acts not only by numerous participants but at several degrees of personal involvement and temporal distance. It would be excessively limiting to call this a sequence of narration and renarration. *Zelig* displays the manifold social process of storytelling—the extended dissemination of news, legends, and myths—of which *Rashomon*'s structure is a highly systematic instance. We may begin to suspect that *Zelig* is a film not so much about Zelig as it is about the making of tales about Zelig—about the explosion of mythmaking that is *"the* [Zelig] phenomenon"* (p. 3). Every viewer of the film is aware that it is a satire not only of behavior patterns in the Jazz Age but also of the languages used by the media, professional organs, and other institutions that define and transmit American behavior, then and now. It is a film *about* cultural codes, containing images and language illustrating and referring to a variety of symbol systems. More than a satire of a historical period, this is a comedy of semiotic dissemination.

Literary works that perform similar activities have been called "dialogical" in the narratology of Mikhail Bakhtin.[12] Such works are not merely texts about texts (i.e., writing that refers to prior communication) but also speech within speech, incorporating, either by direct quotation or by a rhetoric of subtle modification, the language that is their primary subject matter. In literature, the dialogical process includes the utterances of the narrator about those of the characters, the characters' use and abuse of each other's speech, and the author's inclusion of other writers' language, whether by way of parody, generic modeling, or other forms of intertextual relation.[13] While films are not texts in the same sense as literary works, they include dialogue, narration, and other utterances that can and do relate dialogically to each other and to other language systems.

In *Zelig*, the multiple modes and levels of narration described above provide a fertile field for many types of dialogical interaction. Most evidently, the external narrators report and comment on the language of Zelig's contemporaries. One example drawn from near the outset: The voice-over quotes an invented passage of F. Scott Fitzgerald's notebook "about a curious little man named Leon Selwyn, or Zelman, who 'seemed clearly to be an aristocrat and extolled the very rich as he chatted with socialites' " (p. 8). The narrator's citation characterizes Zelig but also indulges in literary parody, alluding to the famous exchange between Fitzgerald and Hemingway on the subject of "the very rich." Elsewhere we find characters referring to the language used within their cultural world. When a man-in-the-street interviewee says, "I wish I could be Leonard Zelig, the changing man, and be different people" (p. 30), he is clearly repeating—quoting without quotation marks, as it were—the newspaper cant of the day. And this sobriquet, "the changing man," will become the title of a fictional film, indicating the passage of artificial formulas into colloquial discourse and on to other media.

Other forms of speech-within-speech or language-about-language abound—largely of the parodic variety. The most frequent target, besides journalese, is medical jargon, including but not limited to the psychiatric. The succession of doctors spouting arcane formulas of one vintage or another continues the deflation of quackery that has been a staple of comedy since Aristophanes. But the film's accumulation of symbols is not limited to words; it includes the myriad cultural elements that would be found in an anthropologist's inventory: songs and dances, toys and bric-a-brac, cartoons, and other visuals. The Zelig craze documented in long montage sequences—the Chameleon flapper dance, the songs (including a modified recording by Fanny Brice), the vaudeville and circus exhibitions—represents an extended parody, not merely of the nine-days'-wonder enthusiasms of the flapper set but of an entire culture at a specific historical moment.

How can we relate the film's vigorous dialogical activity to its larger aims as cultural parody? Another concept of linguistic analysis introduced by Bakhtin is "heteroglossia," the capacity of a text to include and set in fruitful juxtaposition a variety of languages, professional or class registers, regional dialects, personal idiolects, and the like.[14] Aside from the journalistic code and medical jargon that are its chief butts of humor, other specialized languages in *Zelig* include the political rhetoric of his extremist detractors, ranging from Ku Klux Klan to Communist; legal terminology, as in the string of lawsuits brought against the protagonist; and even certain religious phraseology, in a

Legion of Decency–type broadcast that begins with "America is a . . . God-fearing country" and ends with a call to "lynch the little hebe" (pp. 108–9). Foreign languages abound: German, in the Hitler speech and Ton-Woche newsreel; Chinese, during one of Zelig's early transformations; Yiddish, when performed by his father's theatrical troupe in the course of a biographical summary of his antecedents; and French, during his European exploitation tour. Like its hero, the film is capable of acquiring and flaunting a kaleidoscope of languages in service to its panurgic parodism.

To what end? Since parody functions much as does parasitism, a simple answer might be: Absorption of its model or host. In this case, the conquest seems particularly appropriate, for *Citizen Kane* is itself a high example of the activities we have been tracing in *Zelig*. Not only does *Kane* locate itself in the newspaper milieu and present the hero's career reductively in headlines and newsreels, but it incorporates most of the cultural codes enumerated above: political rhetoric, legal jargon, religious anathemas—only the psychiatric lingo is missing. Foreign languages are largely restricted to the newsreel sequence, but in compensation an even larger use is made of cultural *objets d'art*, ranging from the Xanadu architectural acquisitions to the folk-art sled and glass-ball bibelot. Though *Kane* does not include an imitation Hollywood film, it precedes *Zelig* in the use of simulated home movies. While *Zelig* limits its focus to American life in the 1920s and 1930s, *Kane* offers a set of representative images of the nation in the first four decades of this century.

It may be concluded, then, that *Zelig* became a rich field for heteroglossia in part because its immediate model was itself heteroglossic. By multiplying their channels of transcription, both films gain the power to embody, as well as parody, the heteroglossia of the early modern era. Most cultures are, in greater or lesser degree, heteroglossic, but it was in the first postwar period of this century that the resources for transmitting the artifacts and discourses of an international culture came into their own. From this standpoint, *Zelig* may be seen as an exemplary film of the media age—exemplary not only in providing ample selections but in holding them up for critical scrutiny. As one of the intellectual commentators puts it, "All the themes of our culture were there—heroism, will, things like that. But when you look back on it, it was very strange" (p. 4).

We are treated, then, not only to the reorientation toward stories and their tellings that occurs in multiple narrations generally, but to the semiotic and critical activity that occurs in intensively dialogical works. Other films, preeminently those of Godard, exhibit some of these features, and all of them have perhaps made an appearance in one film or another. But it remained for *Zelig* to bring them together, thus becoming a high achievement in dialogical cinema. It is not alone in his subject matter that Woody Allen establishes the image of a human chameleon, but in the absorptive and transformative behavior of his filmmaking as well.

Beyond exhibiting the resources of dialogical and heteroglossic cinema, beyond its wide-ranging parody of cultural processes, a historical period, and a classic film, *Zelig* provides striking indications of the potentialities of multiple narration in film art. Implicit in its strategy of narrating its hero's story from an assemblage of documents, witnesses, and media forms is the esthetic principle that complexity in narrative method is good, simplicity and univocity not as good. Though it is multiplicity that is the hero's problem and the sign of an underlying social malaise, the film does not stint the multiplicity of means devoted to making this point. Multiple narration in cinema can generate considerable complication and even mind-boggling indeterminacy, but these lead the way to ultimate mystery and clarity in films like *Citizen Kane*, *Rashomon*, and *Zelig*.

7

Written Narration:
Letter from an Unknown Woman and *Diary of a Country Priest*

S O MUCH DISCUSSION has centered on Max Ophuls's *Letter from an Unknown Woman* (1948) that it threatens to become a cult classic. This would be a departure from the norms for cult films, as *Letter* is an unhappy-ending romance set in an unfamiliar milieu (turn-of-the-century Vienna) and something of a "woman's film"—though the criteria for this putative genre have never been clearly established.[1] While feminist critics have not been alone in sensing that complicated images of women are projected here, the paths by which these images are communicated have not been traced through all their windings. For its commentators, it seems, *Letter*'s psychological themes and sexual politics have been conveyed without benefit of narration, although the title staunchly names its mode.

What difference does it make that this film is a letter narration? One early indication of its importance is suggested by the opening scene: a man returns home in the wee hours from a night on the town, under challenge of a duel, and sits down to read a lengthy missive about apparently unrelated matters. The letter turns out to deliver an explanation for the duel, to which he has committed himself without being aware of the deeper grounds for quarrel (a husband's dishonor). He plans to make off without fighting, in his insouciant way, but the letter causes him to delay—arrests him, in more than one sense— with anticipated fatal consequences. If a protagonist can be undone by a piece of narrative writing, we should be attentive to the role of narration not only in living but in dying.

By the time the film closes, with the protagonist going out to his duel fully expecting to be killed, we have learned with him to take writing seriously. It has the power to inflict a mortal wound; like homeopathic drugs whose effect is similar to the disease, the letter carries a formidable dosage. Unlike a poison-pen letter, this one is designed to confer a benefit with enlightenment, but the effect is much the same: this is knowledge that brings despair and death. When it becomes explicit that the writer is herself dead by the time the text is read—and that her immediate provocation for writing is the death of the writer's and recipient's son—the full horror of this "letter from an unknown" dawns on us, as it does for him. Unlike the dramatized narration of the ghosts in Ophuls's *Tender Enemy*, who address each other, and the voice-over narration from beyond the grave in *Sunset Boulevard*, directed to the audience, this letter narration delivers to a living character a message from another realm. As we watch it "spook" him, we may well share the same frisson, a polite version of the thrill of horror films.

All this seems a far cry from the Stefan Zweig novella, both in psychological content and in narrational form. The Howard Koch scenario's alterations of its source have been generally recognized; its elaboration of the framing situation to involve a duel to the death is the change most pertinent here. Yet the effect of the letter in the story is equally redolent of morbid overtones: "It seemed to him [the recipient] as if a door had been flung open suddenly by an invisible hand, and a cold current of air from another world flowed into his peaceful room. He became conscious of a death and conscious of undying love. Something struck a chord in his innermost soul, and he strove ardently to reach out in spirit towards the unseen presence, as though he were hearing distant music."[2] By having the protagonist go out to die, the film's finale acts out the story's metaphysical rhetoric of a transaction with the dead. It is therefore no sentimental flourish but a constituent of the story's theme that the deathbed writing and subsequent reading of a letter culminate in another death.

Another alteration of the original text further exploits its resources; whatever the scenarist's immediate goals in adaptation, the outcome was a more incisive work of art.[3] Zweig's text begins with two paragraphs of omniscient narration and ends with two more; the third-person sentences I have quoted are characteristic in form. Between these opening and closing passages stands the letter-text, constituting almost the full thirty-odd pages of the novella. The relation of frame and main text is quite different in the film: there are frequent shifts from the narrational situation to the enacted story and back, each of the four main sequences being framed by scenes of reading (shots 7f., 81, 96, 200f., and 327f.). While the fiction offers a letter that tells the whole story, the film dramatizes the process of reading, interpreting, and suffering the consequences of written narrative.

The letter is first seen as a substantive entity, a packet; then its several pages are quickly scanned by the camera, emulating the recipient's perception of an object in a point-of-view shot. It is also shown, during an enactment, being written; when the letter refers to its own composition, the scene of that activity is visualized (shot 326). Finally, the letter's last page is displayed (shot 327), with a fallen drop of ink and an appended note from another writer (partly typed and partly in script) to explain the interruption. The film, then, far more than the novella—and more than most letter-narration films—takes seriously the material reality and communicative function of an epistolary text. By connecting the drama of communication with the drama of narrated events, it refuses to allow the letter to remain a mere envelope for the story it delivers.

In this larger drama, three distinct temporal phases come to attention. First in story time comes the life of the narrator-protagonist, Lisa, the secret and largely inner events recounted in her letter. Next comes her act of writing, like all autobiographical activity a form of repetition. (It also concludes the first temporal sequence, since writing is among her last living acts.) Cinema's habitual rhetoric of doubling sound and image furthers the sense of recapitulating the first phase, since the scenes from the life described are doubled by the narrator's voice-over. Finally, there is the dramatic activity of Stefan's reading, which constitutes a further repetition in the form of a mental visualization of Lisa's life. (I shall return to this point.) The film acts out, then, not only its main story but that story's replication and transmission, not only Lisa's life but her artful recomposition and Stefan's reexperience of it.

Since these three phases, of living, writing, and reading, are not fully run through but are interwoven and elided in the film's presentation, we may be inclined to neglect not only the distinct events of narrating but also those of reading with imaginative response. Yet, as I shall try to show, we have reason to take the scenes of the past as enacting the letter's statements as they run through Stefan's mind. One indication that the film traffics in such subtleties is a further repetitive sequence near the close. When Stefan, having read the letter, recalls his own involvement in the events it describes, he fleetingly reviews a number of previously seen shots of them in a mindscreen montage sequence (shots 329–36). Like a syllabus these shots recapitulate a narrative that has been thoroughly coded as a set of verbal renditions and their mental equivalents.

Returning to the principal enactment of the past: As with most voice-overs, we hear Lisa's voice and readily assume it to be the narrative source to which the visualization corresponds. But each past sequence is introduced and rounded off by a scene of reading, in which images of receiving a message and reflecting on its contents are vividly presented. The acting out of Lisa's letter is partly ascribable to its reader, who processes her words and mentally reviews the events they recount. When Stefan enjoyed his neighborly proximity, brief affair, and renewed encounter with Lisa, he saw little or nothing of her; he now reviews the scenes as she experienced and describes them. The letter constitutes a repetition not only for its writer but for its reader: he lives over again, more fully than before, what he and Lisa have shared, in the form she has given it.

These apparently technical considerations have a bearing on a crux in recent interpretation of the film. For Robin Wood and George M. Wilson, the visualization of Lisa's story is acknowledged as not completely from her point of view. Despite the warm emotional charge of her narration, we are able to see her story with some degree of detachment, and this detachment must derive from another perspective involved in the story's presentation. While avoiding the tactic of ascribing this added view directly to the director or scenarist, they also omit Stefan's mental reception of Lisa's words as a contributory perspectival dimension. Instead, the enactment is to be understood as, at least in part, an "objective presentation" (Wood) or report of *"actual* occurrences" (Wilson).[4] There is a hint here of the view, perhaps first promulgated by Jean Mitry, that a flashback is inevitably taken as an actual event, even though it is doubtful that a viewer with so visceral a response could follow the action of films as narrationally complex as this one.

One can readily chime in with Wood's suggestion of the submerged presence of a "film *against* Lisa" and Wilson's account of the systematic way in which the film "incorporates both the more and less sympathetic aspects of Lisa's character," without positing that the enactments of her narrative are "objective presentation" or "actual occurrences." But to do so we must reflect on the enormous variety in flashback practice, which overrides any effort to prescribe the way in which a coded activity like enacted narration will logically or phenomenologically be understood. The ambivalence of our response to Lisa, and indeed the ambiguity in almost every reading of the film, may come to be seen as appropriate to the medley of viewpoints that the film orchestrates.

Much depends on the audience's, and the theorist's, flexibility in receiving not only the enacted story as marked by its narrator's personality but flashbacks in general. Wilson's logically drawn alternatives—either a "visual translation" of the narrator's statements or a presentation of "actual occurrences" that the narrator merely accompanies—state two poles in a wide range of flashback practices that have been used in the course of film history. This is not the place to pursue the evolution of codes that has been begun by David Bordwell and his associates,[5] but their evidence suggests that flashbacks have been employed and recognized for a variety of purposes. While the general rule is that considerations of plot coherence and causality have been uppermost, allowing for the "classical cinema's" frequent fast-and-loose shifts in the narrational authority for enacted scenes, there has always been room for character subjectivity. In certain well-known cases, audiences have been assumed to be capable of using narrational frames as consistent markers of the subjectivity of the enacted scenes, that is, to correlate the narrator's verbalized traits and the visual evidence of the enacted scenes. How else, in *Citizen Kane*, could audiences have responded to scenes that seem to come from different films: the American Gothic *mise en scène* of Kane's guardian's memoirs, the comic buoyancy and youthful idealism coloring the scenes in his journalist friends' accounts, and the darkly moribund atmosphere conveyed by his wife's and butler's concluding reports? Indeed, if prevailing practice had established an "actual occurrences" norm for flashbacks, why the need for the "striking effort" that Wilson perceives in *Letter* to "make it clear that the perspective that the film offers upon this history is *not* to be identified with Lisa's" (p. 106)?

While the detailed *mise en scène* of cinema's flashback scenes must always exceed the verbal specifications of a narrator, only documentary and pseudo-documentary narrators call on us to view the visual evidence as objective data. Enactments of internal narration can range from the matter-of-fact renditions of responses to police inquiries—including, of course, false statements objectively shown—to impressionistic and expressionistic visualizations of emotional and even hallucinatory storytellings. Letters and diaries will, however, almost inevitably be enacted with palpable marks of subjectivity, since they intimately express the writer's personal responses to other characters, or to him- or herself.

The language of Lisa's writing supports its function in initiating subjective flashbacks. Her introduction to the first enacted scene sets the pattern: she reports her attitudes now, at the time of writing—"I think everyone has two birthdays, the day of his physical birth and the beginning of his conscious life" (p. 36). But she also distinguishes them from what she thought then, in the past she sets out to describe: "Nothing is vivid or real in my memory before that day in Spring. . . . I wondered about our new neighbor who owned such beautiful things" (p. 36). Lisa's narration is explicit about her subjectivity, both what she feels in commenting on past events and what she felt when participating in them. And in calling on her reader for more empathy than he has ever shown, she also calls upon our own reserves of nuanced imaginative response.

Yet audiences and critics are undeniably responding to

something when they find that Lisa's perspective is not the only one by which the past is seen in this film. There is another operative (not merely an implied authorial) perspective, always latent but only occasionally realized in letter-narration films.[6] Letters are texts and are invariably represented by voice-overs in cinema; but they are also material objects of exchange, and their reception can become a dramatic event. Particularly when the letter recounts a past already partially known to the recipient, the letter plays the role of a stimulus to memory. As such, it generates responses of the kind that are coded in films as memory flashbacks. We witness, then, not only a text and a voice but a reader and his or her consciousness.

Even without narration, cinematic flashbacks can be coded to mark the subjectivity, including the psychic and perceptual distortions, of a character remembering. (The next chapter will have more to say of flashbacks in relation to mindscreen narration.) The remembering character is regularly shown in close-up, sometimes the result of a zoom in, exhibiting well-known acting cues that indicate intense mental activity; the transition to the events recalled is usually made by means of a dissolve; and the enacted memories are often signaled as mental products by the quality of the lighting or by musical intimations of returning to a remembered world. How, then, are the past story scenes of this particular film coded?

Letter from an Unknown Woman has a distinctive manner of effecting its flashback transitions: by that form of dissolve better described as a slow fade-out/fade-in. For example, in shot 10:

> As Stefan reads, the camera slowly tracks in to MCU of his face. The focus blurs and fades out.
>
> [Shot] 11. Fade in to blurred MCU of a man seen from behind. . . . The focus becomes clearer, and the man, who is lifting a large antique lyre, turns to the camera. . . . The camera then pans with him as he turns and passes what appears to be a window to his right. Lisa, an adolescent schoolgirl who is watching with open-mouthed fascination, is framed in the window.

The subjectivity of this enactment would seem to be beyond question, but we may well ask, Whose is it? In part a visualization of Lisa's text, the scene also reflects Stefan's visualizing process, for the fading out and in emphasize a shift from present awareness to the dawning of an idea of the past. Yet Stefan was not present at the precise moment described; he visualizes as Lisa ordains, focusing on Lisa's childhood wonderment at his own cultured furnishings while he is moving in next door. This reported subjectivity is probably the most prominent one, calling upon our empathy with the naive, child's response. There is, moreover, another observer in the scene, for Lisa alludes to the presence of Stefan's butler as a witness to her own responses. When John rather pointedly turns toward the camera, we take him to be observing Lisa, but within the matrix of her reported view of the scene. We have thus not one subjective viewpoint to conjure with but three (and possibly four). They may be summarized as Stefan's imaginative reenactment of Lisa's verbal account of her state of mind when a child—which was perceptible to another character at the time, the mute butler.[7]

When the audience hears Lisa's voice, only its more impressionable members take it to be her ghost speaking to Stefan after her death, although there may be some frisson of narration from beyond the grave. The presence of a letter in Stefan's hands suggests that the voice-over that accompanies the image is of a special kind. Since we are able to follow the code marking the visualizations as partially those of the letter reader, we may also be considered competent to take the voice as manifesting another set of events in a consciousness. Those events are Stefan's mental acts of reception, and the voice-over is to be understood as an articulation not of the written words but of his activity of reading them. While this may seem excessively sophisticated for an audience to be aware of, it engages a readily anticipated intuitive response.[8] This voice dramatizes the flow of Lisa's written words *as Stefan receives them*; it enlarges the code of voice-over functions by inducing a sense of ongoing participation in the mental processing of a text.

It is perhaps easier to account for the psychological resources on which this expanded film code draws than to diagram the process in narratological terms. The voice-over corresponds to that mental equivalent of sonic form in which, some psycholo-

Letter from an Unknown Woman: Scene of reading—Stefan,
Lisa's letter, and John's knowing gaze

gists believe, written language is processed by readers[9]—and
almost certainly when the writing is the imagined speech of a
person whose voice we know. But how are we to describe it
within a system of story communication? The situation cannot
be called "dialogical," for that would involve speech about
speech and we have here only Lisa's utterance. Nor does it lend
itself to analysis under one of the concepts suggested by Genette
and elaborated by other narratologists, the concept of "focalization."[10] This refinement of traditional notions of literary point
of view posits that when a narrator describes events according
to what a character knows or thinks about it, the event is narrated
with that character's focalization. When the narrator is a character, we may discover him or her focalizing another character's
version of events. But the relation that we witness in *Letter* is
not that of a narrator reporting a character's perspective, but
that of a non-narrating character assimilating a narrator's per-

spective. We must therefore consider new terms for narrative situations in which one character's narration is filtered through the skein of another's consciousness.

To the battery of terms for cinematic point of view and literary focalization that have been employed, we may add *dual perspective*.[11] The most common form of this doubling in literature occurs when what one character sees or thinks is presented as another character imagines or intuits it. Novelists like Henry James and Virginia Woolf have labored to devise subtle methods by which to render one character's consciousness of what another thinks or feels. But there is a long-established rhetoric for such renderings in the tradition of epistolary novels, which not only record what one character thinks another is thinking but require that we interpret from their words and deeds what the recipient of each letter thinks as he or she reads.[12]

We may reflect, more generally, on the dual perspective in letter narrations in film and fiction. The imaginative sympathy involved in grasping how one character may receive another's narration is no less necessary in experiencing such films than it is in response to epistolary novels. When the latter fully exploit their resources, they call upon us to grasp not only what the writer meant when writing but what the reader felt when reading. Film adaptations of such novels risk losing that difference if they depart from the letter-narration mode—with the result that the local ironies in the screen adaptations of *Les Liaisons Dangereuses* pale beside the structural irony of Laclos's dual-perspective novel.

The doubling of perspective begins in *Letter*, as in any other internal narration, when one character reports another's state of mind. For example, Lisa gives an account of her husband's wounded feelings, and the enactment delivers not only his words, which she presumably indicates, but also the gestures that she perceives as expressing them, like his not looking at her during their climactic scene. But letter narrations go beyond intimating the writer's and others' feelings to suggest the reception of that intimation. In the present example, we must think of Stefan's perspective on Lisa's account of the scene. He learns from it not only the identity of the man whom he is about to duel and the underlying reasons for the challenge, but also the feelings of that unhappy husband. It may seem a baroque construction, but *Letter from an Unknown Woman* develops a progressive revelation to a relatively self-enclosed protagonist of feelings that he has never known—including Lisa's consciousness of her husband's feelings. And though this structure of consciousness has not been reported in the critical literature,[13] I do not believe that it is alien to most sympathetic viewers of the film, who are fully competent to process it.

These considerations, none of them perhaps tendentious, open the prospect of distinguishing the several participants in an intersubjective constitution of perspective, which the audience is invited to share in films as complex as *Letter*. A full accounting of its perspectives would include not only its often extraordinary visual point-of-view shots, its personalized attention to (or call for identification with) the lives of its twin protagonists, and its presentation of both romantic and, by indirection, antiromantic ideology, but all of these as they are articulated by Lisa and processed by Stefan in the ongoing drama of communication and reception. Whether this film is a typical or a particularly advanced case of letter narration, it fully exhibits the synthetic processes by which writing and reading add their own measure to the finely distributed network of cinema's mimesis of consciousness in action.

If this account of *Letter*'s narration meets the case, what are its implications for the psychological and moral dilemmas that have troubled criticism? Judgments of the film's theme largely devolve from judgments of the protagonists. Everyone, including Lisa, recognizes that her romantic love is excessive, but tastes vary as to the amount of salt with which we are to take her tale, the degrees of irony or sympathy required of us. As fetchingly played by Joan Fontaine, she is hard to dislike, and clearly the "classical narrative system" that fosters audience identification, "suture," and other seductive processes is hard at work to draw our judgmental teeth. Yet when we consider her from Stefan's perspective, as required by an awareness that we are reading along with him, we can only join him in being awed by Lisa's depth of feeling and appalled by the consequences of her monomaniacal design of her life. Stefan guides us in a properly ambivalent view of her, one that responds to her heroic contours and to the enormous costs they exact—of herself most of all.

If we follow Lisa's self-presentation as it is progressively received by Stefan, we may be able to account for the impression that the film is not merely her story, her narration, her perspective. There is no need to invoke an objective or authorial perspective within the film—although its creators have managed affairs to produce the effects we are tracing—to explain our capacity to see Lisa's limitations. She is not the narrator of the film as a whole, but only one input—the most extensive one, to be sure—in an intersubjective construction of a story larger than hers alone. Nor does reading-along-with-Stefan privilege his perspective as an authoritative or even an encompassing one. The goal of such wider distributions of imaginative sympathy is not to relativize judgment by showing the characters' conflicting interests and needs—that is, by sharing the "other side's" point of view. Our observation of Stefan's reading only confirms other impressions of him as a pathetic egoist, as when we see him belatedly infatuated by the photos of his son that Lisa encloses. But awareness of Stefan's response helps us to see the story whole, Lisa's life story extending beyond its telling to reach wider effects.

Stefan apparently finds something in the letter to make him submit passively to his death; that something may not precisely be an accusation calling for self-punishment, but it certainly does not flatter his self-image. While Lisa conveys an explicit image of herself as a misguided but sincere romantic, she also conveys—beyond a plangent reproach for his neglect—a devastating portrait of her loveless lover. He is shown not only as a womanizer but as a wastrel who has squandered his artistic talents. (In failing to have even a déjà-vu sense of Lisa, though it has been ten years, he may also be thought remarkably unobservant, not to say stupid.) The point of her message is not merely to sigh an "If only . . ." but also to deliver a barbed "You fool!" If these implications seem too severe, or not enough so, they must be posited as leading Stefan to the conclusion that he is better off dead.

With all her self-criticism and self-destructiveness, Lisa is yet another incarnation of the femme fatale figure, passive and yielding variety, that has appeared so frequently in modern culture and especially in cinema history. The subject has been studied by art-historical, sociocultural, and feminist specialists, and I shall have little to say in its explanation, certainly nothing in its defense as a portrayal of women's lives and influence. But if we seek the cultural perspective from which this film proceeds— the shared mentality of the Viennese Zweig, Hollywoodian Koch, and cosmopolitan Ophuls—it is one that readily perceives women as inclined to sacrifice all for love, bringing down themselves and their loved ones with considerable self-loathing and an iron will. (There exist, of course, plenty of masculine equivalents in film and fiction, but they are usually seen as passive victims of the active version of the femme fatale.) For all its lavish sympathy, the film's weight is loaded against Lisa as a moral being, and admirers of women can take little comfort from the fact that she is allowed fully to express her lifelong *amour fou*.

Despite its central position in the film, Lisa's letter is a classic instance of unreliable narration. Lisa's unreliability is reflected not in an inaccuracy in reporting story events but in her fatalistic interpretation of them. This is especially marked in her repeated claim that she has no choice.[14] This conviction is so insistently repeated that it matches her own compulsiveness in behavior; it is the "bad faith" rationale of that compulsion. One need only recall the long train of moribund lovers in nineteenth- and early-twentieth-century literature and opera to recognize in her the language of the love-death: "I knew I couldn't live without you" (p. 57); "I told him I wasn't free" (p. 68: rejecting her suitor, she uses a colloquial phrase with wider resonance); "I know now that nothing happens by chance. Every moment is measured, every step is counted" (p. 106); "Somewhere out there were your eyes . . . and I knew I couldn't escape them" (p. 109). This ideology appears not only in her narration but in reported dialogue; "I'd do anything to avoid hurting you, but I can't help it," she tells her husband. When he philosophically challenges her, "You talk as though it were out of your hands. . . . You have a will, you can do what's right, what's best for you, or you can throw away your life," she replies, "I've had no will but his, ever" (p. 113). Believing herself to be a fully determined creature, she effectively reduces herself to being so.

There are other films in which lovers obey the heart rather than the head, but few in which they testify so stridently to their unfreedom, whether in astrological, psychiatric, historical materialist, or other determinist rhetorics. In this respect, *Letter* goes beyond the long train of sexually dominated lovers, both male and female, of which Josef von Sternberg's films of the 1930s are the classics. With the exception of the dramatically narrated *The Devil Is a Woman* (1935), the protagonists of these films are notable for their inarticulateness. (One need only recall the trail of lovers who follow each other off to the desert in *Morocco* [1930].) *Letter from an Unknown Woman*, in contrast, gives fatal fascination a voice, allowing that form of consciousness— whether or not we call it "false consciousness"—to articulate its nature and needs in sustained introspective writing.

Yet narration is rarely innocent, for others may receive from it not only one's story but traces of one's prose style, with the heavy dose of ideology they carry. The last sentence of Lisa's letter reads, "If only you could have recognized what was always yours, could have found what was never lost. If only . . ." (shot 326). Fully mystified, Stefan hears these words again, in the form of a second Lisian voice-over, but this time it is the equivalent not of his reading but of his memory, as he recalls the letter's text. Ascribed to him now, the assimilated words have become part of his own mental structure: "Oh, if only you could have recognized what was always yours, could have found what was never lost" (shot 347). It is the last thing we hear him think, after his "Ready, gentlemen," and it is the last line in the film. This language of paradox, as heard in Lisa's voice-over but derived from Stefan's mental processes, is sufficient indication that he goes to his death under a charm.

Stefan has acquired Lisa's ideology with her rhetoric; in the final scene he is visibly and thoroughly mystified. In overtones of the horror films that *Letter*'s low-key lighting and thematic morbidity recall, he is now possessed and does the will of an invading spirit. Rather than the hopeful "redemption" with which critics have attempted to find nobility in his death, this is no tragic finale but mournful testimony to the power of Lisa's letter, of narration itself, to function like a machine programmed by a now dead hand. In the list of those who have paid for Lisa's compulsive devotion, Stefan is the final victim; that the motive for his quasi-suicide is a recognition of his life's vacuity does not relieve the letter writer of responsibility for thus enlightening him. While we may not generate as much sympathy for him as for Lisa, he is in some degree our surrogate or stand-in. We can learn from his trials of reading to recognize the complexities of intersubjective storytelling and the insidiousness of ideological "bad faith"—but only if we recognize the ways of their uncanny disseminator, the mechanism named in the film's title.

o   o   o   o

Despite its gross differences in subject and manner, Robert Bresson's *Diary of a Country Priest* (1950) is in some respects the tongue-and-groove complement of *Letter from an Unknown Woman*. The letter is presented as already written; the diary (or journal, following the French title) is shown being written. The letter tells what has happened, in the mode of autobiography; the diary tells what is happening, at times in the manner of eighteenth-century epistolary novels in which the writer reports action "to the moment." The fact that letters too have been composed in this way suggests that the contrasts we are considering are not inherent in the nature of letters and diaries. But Bresson exploits one potentiality of diaries to the fullest in this film: a writing activity that often takes place in close relation to ongoing events, keeping a diary also makes a visualizable object, an instrument of personal communion, even a little shrine for those devoted to it.

Beyond their formal differences, these films reveal two very different writers. Both are sharply self-critical, but while Lisa's self-deprecation is countered, even in her report, by others' appreciation of her (her first suitor, her husband, even Stefan), the priest's self-criticism is reinforced by the low opinions of almost all those he encounters (the gentry family, the townsfolk, even the sympathetic doctor and avuncular vicar). We sense, then, that the one protagonist is her own worst enemy, while the other provides a spiritual touchstone by which the people of the ordinary world are found wanting. Both are self-tormentors, but

Lisa's text sows another death while the priest's quite possibly has healing powers—if it is not the relic of a saint. Finally, Lisa resorts to fatalistic notions of her life, while the priest leaves determinist explanations to others, the favored one being the Zolaesque explanation of his physical and mental debility as hereditary alcoholism. Although canonical providentialism is espoused in the film—and is reasserted in the hero's final words after receiving last rites from an unfrocked priest, "Does that matter? All is grace"[15]—his world and his actions lie open to the concept of freedom.

This contrast between a self-constructed, mentally closed world and a socially meager but spiritually free one is cinematically matched in the films' differing ways of conducting their narration. Not only does *Letter* show a text already achieved, while *Diary* shows one in process of composition, but the voice-overs of the two films serve very different functions. As we have seen, Lisa's voice signifies her words running through Stefan's mind, the writing as read. In contrast, Leydu's voice—in the absence of a proper name for the character, I employ the name of an actor totally identified with his role—is the sound of his mental activity while setting down the words. We often hear specific phrases while watching them flow from his pen: This is the voice not of reading but of writing.[16]

The special relations of the sounds and images of writing have consequences for our experience of the film. When it is not accompanying shots that show him writing, the priest's voice-over is heard during story sequences, accompanying the enactment of his narration. Early on, for example, we hear him say, "I went to see the Vicar" (of Torcy) and we see him arrive at the door; no apparent departure here from conventional voice-over in the past tense. But though we do not see the matching words in this and similar cases, the previous visualization of the diary leads us to hear them in a different way: not the ordinary, distant and unlocalizable voice of memory, but a notation much closer to the event. They carry a force roughly equivalent to, "I just went to see the Vicar . . . and what an experience it has been."

But the implied equivalence of sound and text may convert an apparently immediate exclamation into a retrospective musing. Near the opening when we hear Leydu say, "My parish, my first parish," and see him look around at his new surroundings, we may be initially inclined to take the voice-over as emanating from the figure we see and as expressing his immediate responses. Since the exclamatory words are those of a written text, however, we learn to take them not as part of a dramatic action but as a later summary, even when not in the past tense.

Generalizing from this observation, we may observe that even when diary narrations employ the present tense, they stand at a remove from their stories. Though lacking the temporal distance for a rounded perspective on the past, they maintain an irreducible distinctness from the events themselves. They may be written "to the moment" yet stand apart from the story in a time and space of their own. This double status of diary narration—comparable but not equivalent to the presence/absence we have noted in voice-over—gives it its peculiar resonance and distinctive narrative powers.

The space-time of the diary is not, moreover, a merely hypothetical realm. On nineteen occasions, the voice-over accompanies shots of the diary as it is being written. I shall call these shots—roughly equivalent to facial closeups—of the page and a hand with a pen *writing closeups*. More often than not, these shots show some of the words already written down, and they end as the voice catches up with the writing of the last word. In the second writing closeup, for example, the shot begins with the pen in midsentence, the voice begins with the opening of the sentence—"In refusing to admit that my health is bad, am I only considering my duty?"—and both shot and voice end as the hand writes the final word, "*devoir.*" In these scenes, the voice-over not only narrates story events but articulates the writing action, which, as we shall see, becomes story in its turn.

These nineteen shots may be considered a variety of dramatized narration. Instead of seeing and hearing one character tell a story to another, we witness the solitary act of writing, equally a narrative activity. The voice-over does not disturb the quiet drama of the scene; we are asked to contemplate a man performing a significant though isolated action. *Diary of a Country Priest* may be considered the film par excellence of the drama of writing. In this respect, Bresson not only made a film faithful

Diary of a Country Priest: The diary, with ivy motif, among other
sacramental objects (shadows of wine bottle and glass)

to the meditative prose of Georges Bernanos's diary-novel, but
brought to cinema a range of human activities not readily accessible to so public and social a medium.

As a perceptible representation of a partly overt, partly mental process, dramatized writing has affinities with interior monologues, in which a character is shown thinking or remembering
while his or her thoughts are spoken aloud. It is, on the other
hand, important that the voice-overs that accompany these
scenes are not merely mental correlates. They are articulations
of the narrational process for, together with the visual aspects,
they present the coming into existence of a text. In these
scenes—matched by only a few films like Buñuel's *Robinson Crusoe* and Hamer's *Kind Hearts and Coronets*—a solitary and silent
human activity is extensively dramatized, while in the soundtrack writing finds a voice.

Among these nineteen dramatized writings are four in which

Diary of a Country Priest: A writing closeup (poised to
write "duty/*devoir*")

we see not only the diary pages and a hand writing but also the
writer at his table; I shall call them *scenes of writing*. These are
among the most complex sequences in the history of film narration and are worth studying in some detail. The first to occur
is straightforward enough: writing closeup 7 cuts to a full shot
of the priest at his table, recording his first visit to the local
squire, whom he at that time naively takes for a "friend, ally,
companion." The shot continues, tracking back as he closes his
diary, goes to the window, and looks out past the camera, hearing a dog bark and a gun go off. The scene turns out to be
transitional; what he sees, we gather, is the Count hunting, for
in the next sequence the latter delivers a freshly killed hare to
the priest.

The next of these scenes of writing is considerably more
complex, but with correspondingly greater substance. After an
extended voice-over in which Leydu describes his difficulties in

praying, we see him move from the window and kneel at his table. There follows writing closeup 12, which we can judge from its verb tense—"Something seemed to snap in me, in my chest"—to be a flashforward to a later moment of writing. Then comes the scene of writing proper: a medium shot from the level of the tabletop, as he writes and pauses, the voice-over continuing. When we return to the scene of his prostration on the floor, we can recognize it as an enactment (with voice-over) of the events he is narrating. The shot ends with the priest getting up and taking his pen—to write the account of the events we have just seen, including those in the present shot. It is not enough to say that this is to-the-moment narration, or a dazzling *mise en abîme* construction; it is rather that the scene of writing includes both story and narrating, both the subject matter of spiritual crisis and the activity of inscribing it. The contiguity of these events—the crisis at the foot of the table and the writing while sitting at the same spot—turns the writing table into the common space of inner experience and verbal expression. Writing is both the medium in which the crisis is narrated and also a field for the struggles of that crisis.

There is a difference, to be sure, between writing as narration and as story event, but when the two occur together in space and time, the distinction tends to become moot. One might hypothesize, at this early stage, that the story of Leydu's spiritual crisis in *Diary of a Country Priest* is not framed by a narration that describes it, but involves the writing itself, so that narrating becomes a phase of story and the story inseparable from its narration. Such a relationship between story and storytelling is perhaps realizable only in a diary situation, given the potential for inscribing events immediately and the concreteness of the medium in which they are inscribed.

The two later scenes of writing move in the same direction. After the Countess' death and the priest's visits to the manor, we have a long shot of him through the window as he writes at his table, snowflakes falling near the camera. His voice-over declares, "Her ladyship was buried this morning" (presumably the words he is writing); the shot then follows his activities within the room—pouring wine and setting it on the hob to warm, returning to the table and continuing to write. There follows a writing closeup (16), "One must pay for that surely," the pen firmly underlining *"sûrement."* Next a dissolve—the film's most frequent transition to scenes and closeups of writing—to the hand turning over some heavily scored pages and tearing one of them diagonally (16 bis—dramatized *un*writing). Then a medium shot of the priest at his table, a closeup of the page as the hand writes "and the temptation came to me to . . . ," and a return to the medium shot as he looks up from his words. Fade out. The scene of writing, then, can show the self-critical and self-referential activities of writing: reevaluation and emphasis, correction and deletion, ellipsis and reflection. But through these writerly activities there runs a series of moral waverings and choices, a further phase of the spiritual crisis.

The final scene of writing is the Lille café where Leydu takes refuge after hearing the diagnosis of stomach cancer. As the *patronne* chatters on about his meager appearance and his "sermon" writing, the camera zooms in to him at the café table, we hear his voice-over say, "I understood that I had only to remain silent," and only then do we see him begin to write. The writing closeup (18) shows the words "cancer of the stomach"; it is quickly followed by a return to the scene of writing, with a time-lapse dissolve as coffee is served. Another dissolve is accompanied by the voice over, "I must have dozed off"; it is transitional to his waking, with the voice-over, "When I woke up— Oh God, I must write it down." He takes up his notebook and pen but we do not see the words; the voice-over speaks of matins and cockcrow, freshness and purity.

The rhythm of cutting and the self-referential expressions suggest that this is an ongoing activity being described to the moment. Ordinarily, there is some temporal distance between a story event and its narration, but in this scene of writing we are allowed to see events and their recording in close juxtaposition. As the priest determines on silence he writes a vow to maintain it; when he thinks of the diagnosis he sets it down; as soon as he awakes from sweet dreams he inscribes them. The film tends to move beyond mere exhibitions of writing to the moment, toward a dramatization of the activities of consciousness—acted out most overtly in writing behavior.

Diary of a Country Priest appeared at a time of widespread interest in the philosophy known as phenomenology. The earlier writings of the school that came to be known as the New Novel were encouraged in their close recording of sensory, temporal, and other modalities of experience by the French versions of this philosophy. But nowhere in literature is there a more vivid rendering of immediate experience than in this film's scenes of writing. The priest becomes, as it were, his own phenomenologist; with disciplined awareness of the contents of his consciousness, he transcribes them simultaneously so as to lose nothing. At such moments, living becomes conflated with writing, ongoing experience with self-conscious reflection on it.

We may suppose that a substitution of writing for living betrays an exhausted vitality, and indeed the priest is winding rapidly down. Yet it is not that, with so little life left in him, there is only writing to be done. The film's larger drama reveals that, with every social form of action emptied of significance—largely through the misunderstanding and worse foibles of others—the priest's only meaningful behavior lies in writing. By transcribing life events, even those as fragile as his own, into text, he confers immediate symbolic value on mundane existence. The country priest—if we regard his story in a context wider than its origins in Bernanos's and Bresson's religious musings—becomes a hero not strictly of the sacramental but of the more general transmutational power of written language.

We approach here the film's closing scenes and its final line, "All is grace." The circumstances must be specified in some detail. The last writing closeup is an unsteady scrawl: "He [the unfrocked priest, Dufrety] agrees to meet the Vicar of Torcy." It gives way to what may conceivably be counted as another scene of writing (or unwriting): in a medium shot, the priest's hand lets fall the diary and pen, ending in a vain effort to grasp the book's pages. There follows an epilogue, a dramatized *reading*[17] in which a typed envelope is seen in closeup; a hand opens it, exposing the typed page within. We hear a voice-over by another actor, representing Dufrety's letter. As the letter narrates the priest's last actions, there is a fade to black; by the time the voice-over reaches his dying words, a cross (or shadow of a cross) touching the four edges of the screen has faded in.

This finale has, as may be imagined, been much commented

on from both religious and secular positions, and I shall not attempt to adjudicate between them.[18] As a visual complement of the priest's last words and of the life he has lived, it is un-impeachable: he has aspired to Christ's innocence and self-sacrifice, has lived under their sign (a crucifix is prominent in his room), and so his death is appropriately narrated in the visible presence of his chosen symbol. Leydu has also learned to confer significance on mundane life by writing, translating things into signs in a secular equivalent of the priestly power of transubstantiation.[19] If believers need not be distressed by Bresson's humanistic but respectful emulation of religious themes, nonbelievers may find that the cross serves as a dramatic symbol for a universal process: the making of meaning, by words or by the Word.

Certain narratological objections may, however, not be as amenable to ecumenical welcome. Apart from the dramatized writings and readings themselves, all that we see is given as it proceeds from written narration. (The letter epilogue represents a shift, to be sure, from one writer to another, but the representation of the new source is equivalent: a visible text and a voice-over that sounds its words.) The gradual appearance of the cross, however, suggests the emergence of another source of signs, an authorial will that has chosen this symbol as the visual fulfillment of his theme. Bresson's self-effacing strategy, which has raised a character to be not merely the narrator but the consistent perspective on his own story, institutes at the close a new and implicitly higher perspective. One may find this a betrayal of previous narrational commitments, somewhat like the error in the final sequence of *The Cabinet of Dr. Caligari*.

Alternatively, one may object that the emergence of the cross represents a shift in the film's mode of presentation, from written narration to a discourse of graphic symbols. Everything we have seen to this point has been conducted in a realistic *mise en scène*, enacting a relatively prosaic narration. In the epilogue, the mundane world, even one transmuted by writing, gives way before a numinous symbolic apparition. But upon reflection it is seen that other symbols have been exhibited much earlier and have helped to bring us to this outcome.

The opening shot may be taken as an establishing shot for

the space of writing; a closeup serves this purpose, rather than the more familiar extreme long shot that shows the large contours of film action. The cover of the priest's diary is shown, with the word JOURNAL written in block letters above the printed word CAHIER; it is a school notebook, the pages lightly printed in squares. Despite the fact that the hand—which turns the cover, removes a heavily inked blotting sheet, and exposes the opening page of writing—does not write more, we may consider this the first of the writing closeups in the film.

There is a slight zoom in to the page as the voice-over reads, "I do not think I shall be doing any harm if I note down day by day quite frankly the humble and indeed insignificant secrets of a life which in any case contains no mystery." By the film's end we have learned the full literalness and the lovely irony of these self-effacing words: the humble becomes the significant, the life without mystery acquires infinite aura. But while the transparent authenticity of ordinary reality is insisted on—by the priest and by the film's style in presenting it—another element of the visual field suggests a different mode of signification. Along the left side of the notebook cover runs a vine—whether printed like the word CAHIER or drawn like the word JOURNAL remains unclear. This branching line, with its suggestions of living growth and its similarities to the flowing lines of writing, suggests that the priest's own text contains symbols of the same order as the cross. For the vine is ivy, whose tenacity made it the traditional symbol of faithfulness and, because it is evergreen, of eternal life.

If one were to propose the film's proper symbol, however, it would be neither cross nor ivy but instead a concrete element of its fictional world. As the priest packs to leave his parish on his journey to Lille and death, he picks up the now sizable stack of notebooks in which he has written his "secrets of a life." These he packs and takes with him, but we never learn their fate; we can only hypothesize the fictional transmission process by which they became Bernanos's novel and Bresson's film.[20] Yet this image sums up a group of those we take away from the film: the nineteen writing closeups, the four (perhaps five)[21] scenes of writing, and the several notebooks that carry this precious burden of the inner life.

8

Mindscreen Narration:
Brief Encounter
(with a Bow to *Daybreak*)

I N NEVERS she had a German lover when she was young. . . .
I was unfaithful to you tonight with this stranger. . . . We're
going to remain alone, my love." At first in "interior dialogue,"
then in interior monologue, the heroine of *Hiroshima Mon Amour*
tells her story once again, extending it through past, present,
and future, and addressing it to another as much as to herself.
No one hears her in these scenes of narration; at first she is alone
in her hotel room, and later her dubbed voice is heard by the
audience but not by potential auditors as she moves through
the city streets.

Many kinds of descriptive terminology could be applied to
this remarkable narrational activity, depending on the emphasis
desired. Psychologists and philosophers of language have addressed related phenomena under such rubrics as "mental
speech."[1] In literary terms, one might characterize the sequence
as a stream-of-consciousness passage, mixing reveries of the past
with present perceptions and feelings. An additional way of
speaking about such scenes, more closely geared to their function in the films where they are placed and to the cinema codes
by which they operate, is to consider them as *mindscreen narration.*[2]

To summarize what has been said in chapter 1 by way of
relating such storytelling to other kinds of internal narration:
The character is shown in a dramatic setting and is heard—or,
since the audience is not addressed, overheard—narrating.
Other characters may be present but do not hear the words,

although the nonvocalized sentences may be couched in second-person form. The variety of phrasing, from self-address to pretended address to another, is comparable to that of diaries and letters, leading one to place mindscreen narration between dramatized and written in a schema of storytelling situations.

Why not call it "interior monologue narration," then? In chapter 4, it will be recalled, interior monologue was related to other uses of dubbing technique by its seen/unheard dimensions: the character is seen by other characters but his or her voiced thoughts are not heard by them. In *Hiroshima*, the heroine is sometimes meditating while alone, and this may seem to break the pattern of interior monologue. Yet there is no qualitative difference between the dubbed voices of the two scenes, and it would be appropriate to modify the "seen" stipulation of interior monologue to "potentially seen"—that is, the character is shown thinking in a story-world setting, although not necessarily seen by others at every moment.[3] In a more elaborate interior monologue film, Masaki Kobayashi's *The Human Condition* (part 3: 1961), the hero's dubbed voice is used in scenes in which he is walking among other retreating soldiers, while being interrogated by his Russian captors, and when utterly alone in his final withdrawal from mankind.[4] Through all these degrees of isolation, the voice is felt to be continuing an extended interior monologue.

Yet Duras's term "interior dialogue" responds to another feature of the *Hiroshima* hotel-room scene: while looking into the bathroom mirror, the heroine intermittently speaks aloud. I have described this in passing as normal talking-to-oneself, but it is less tendentious, perhaps, to relate it to the dramatic traditions of *soliloquy*. Theorists of theater, cinema, and modernist fiction have described the convention in ways that respond to the differing conditions of their media, and no consensus exists in applying the term to films.[5] As a general human activity, however, it is the feature of speaking aloud, either alone or in the presence of others—and, in the latter case, remaining unheard by them—that characterizes soliloquy. (A dictionary definition: "Act of talking when alone or as if alone; an utterance or discourse by one who is talking to himself or is regardless of any hearers present.'') In films, this characteristic is sufficient to distinguish soliloquies from interior monologues, where the voice is dubbed.

The distinction brings about the need for a term more inclusive than "interior monologue narration," for there are films that use soliloquies occasionally or extensively to narrate. *The Seven Year Itch* was discussed in chapter 2 as a problematic direct, on-screen narration, where the account served to represent the innovative storytelling of the 1950s. Yet since the protagonist does not directly address the audience but utters his fantasy scenarios at random and is overheard by the audience, we may also describe this as soliloquy. (A direct address to the audience from a story-world situation would be distinguished as an "aside," as in the Woody Allen films discussed earlier.)

The reason for this protracted exercise in definition may now be clear: soliloquy and interior monologue are cinematic codes for exteriorizing thought. Their conventions work to the same end in making unspoken thoughts available to the audience, whether the character is alone or in the presence of others. In the one case, viva-voce speech, in the other, a dubbed voice— both are taken to be equivalents of mental language. When this language undertakes to tell a story, we have a narrational activity that calls for a covering term to represent a common mental origin. Thus, *mindscreen narration*.

The mindscreen narrational code may be summarized as follows: A character is heard storytelling, not just seen thinking. (In the latter case, we can speak only of *mindscreen* codes for rendering a character's memories, dreams, or other mental processes.)[6] The teller does so in a story-world situation, but is not heard by other characters. (This visibility minimally distinguishes a mindscreen from a voice-over narrator; the latter may also be engaging in mental rather than communicative activity, but the invisibility of the narrator makes it difficult to determine this.) The conventions that enable the audience to overhear this mental speech are dubbing, over shots of a nonspeaking character (interior monologue), and speaking aloud, while alone or "regardless of any hearers present." And the discourse is noncommunicative, irrespective of second-person forms that may be used in a pretended way; its grammatical freedom also makes it difficult to be sure whether the character is talking to him- or herself, with another in mind, or at random.

Since enactments of mindscreen narration usually follow from such utterances, it may be useful to review the methods by which scenes linked to a character's mental processes are signaled in cinema. Filmmakers have in the course of time developed (and modified) the codes that induce audiences to follow their characters' mental activities.[7] These include fairly well-established flashback signals to indicate that a character is remembering; visual and aural distortions to represent disturbed states of mind; point-of-view positionings within and between shots to suggest visual and other kinds of attention. Drawing on each of these, mindscreen narrations employ the acting gestures expressing concentration or rumination, the dissolves and other marks of transition to and back from enactments, the swells of music, changes of lighting, and other indicators of emotionally heightened engagement with past events. But the conventions of mindscreen narration also include the verbal features that mark the mental activity as storytelling.

Many of the features of mindscreen narration may be illustrated in an exemplary case. Billy Wilder's *The Spirit of St. Louis* (1957), with a scenario by Wilder and Charles Lederer, is as inventive as *Sunset Boulevard* and *The Seven Year Itch* in its narrational procedures. As Lindbergh lies awake before his flight, the dubbed voice accompanying his screen image narrates scenes from his earlier life. While flying the Atlantic, he continues to reminisce in interior monologue but also soliloquizes about his current predicaments (e.g., icing wings, navigating by the stars) and visibly mumbles in a stream-of-consciousness style while trying to keep awake. While some of these instances of talking-to-oneself are psychologically grounded, at least one is an absurdity accepted as a convention: the hero tells a fly that shares his cockpit the outlines of his flight plan, a homey touch that only a Jimmy Stewart could have carried off. Here Lindbergh, isolated in his solo enterprise, not only mentally articulates the immediate events of ongoing action but finds ways to summarize the project as a whole. Mindscreen narration amply fulfills its potentialities, shaping the large contours of the heroic tale while foregrounding the narrator's present reflections and his poignant inability to express them to anyone. At the close, there is a marked shift to the storytelling mode of retrospective voice-over: accompanying shots of the hero taking his well-earned rest, his past-tense sentences sum up the scene from a historical distance.[8]

While the number of films employing mindscreen narration systematically to tell their main stories is limited, it is often used transiently to recall incidents in the lives of temporarily isolated figures. In addition to adventure dramas in which the hero undertakes a solo mission—*The Spirit of St. Louis* is exemplary—there are numerous crime or spy dramas in which a hunted or hunting protagonist, temporarily secluded, reviews phases of his career leading to his present plight.[9] Before turning to an example of the latter, we may also recall films with more literal forms of physical or psychic separation than those of the lone-adventurer or hideout type. Dalton Trumbo's *Johnny Got His Gun* (1971), the story of a massively injured veteran unable to communicate with those who surround his hospital bed but whose voice we hear throughout, is a ghastly instance. Psychiatric films may also be placed under this head: the analysis in Compton Bennett's *The Seventh Veil* (1945) begins with a memory flashback to a childhood trauma, precipitates the main story by mindscreen narration, and ends with dramatized storytelling by patient to doctor.

Such variable usage suggests that the evolving cinema codes were less concerned to emulate the psychological explorations of stream-of-consciousness fiction than they were to exploit the narrative potentialities of restricted or pressure-laden personal situations. Yet mindscreen narrations were not limited to being tools for conveying the main story but were seized on for dramatic scenes of self-confrontation. They thereby extended cinema's powers to a point where it could foreground the tendency of men and women to recite their stories to themselves, even when there is no one else who can or will listen.

The archetype of the isolated individual reviewing the past is the hero of Marcel Carné's *Daybreak* (1939; scenario by Jacques Prévert, with credit to Jacques Viot). The film has achieved its place in cinema history by presenting its working-class milieu in the style designated by André Bazin as "poetic realism."[10] The ideological implications of a working-class tragedy have occupied much of the debate on this film and its style, as they do in discussions of other kinds of realism. The Carné-Prévert version of the proletarian hero, not as an allegory of exploitation and class-consciousness but as modern tragic figure, has failed to please partisans on the left and on the right, ever since the French censor banned it for depressing prewar morale. By moving beyond issues like the authenticity of its *mise-en-scène* and the political implications of its closing suicide, an account of the film's narrational program may hope to touch on some of its unique qualities and bolster its special place in cinema history.

The story of a factory worker who loves a florist's clerk, discovers her longstanding affair with a slimy vaudeville charlatan, and eventually kills the latter before committing suicide is by now marked as a period piece. *Daybreak's* importance derives from its treatment of this somewhat trite material, not only in the high quality of its execution—the acting of Jean Gabin, the sets of Alexandre Trauner, and more—but in its narrational strategy. Beginning with the murder during an evening encounter and ending with the suicide at dawn, the film enacts the main story as the protagonist mentally reviews it in his small room during "the long night," to use the title of the ineffective remake by Anatole Litvak of 1947.

So extensive a flashback, or series of flashbacks, was not unprecedented in cinema history—*The Story of a Cheat* and *Tender Enemy* had recently appeared—but the film's rigorous program of mindscreen transitions to the past must have been a challenge to the audience. Or so the producers believed when they required the addition of a title card even before the credits: "A murder has been committed . . . As he sits alone, shut inside a small room, a man tries to reconstruct [*évoque*] the events that led to his becoming a murderer."[11] The verb "*évoque*" nicely designates the situation in which story events are not told but are called to mind; it implies an active process of mental rehearsal—also emphasized in the translation as "tries to reconstruct." Thus the film challenges the audience not simply by its large-scale anachronic narrative order but by requiring it to contemplate a man contemplating himself.

Daybreak may therefore be considered to stand on a watershed line in cinema history, despite the possibility of tracing all its particular features to prior practices. While systematizing the subjective flashback, previously used for story segments, to present the main story, the film elaborates the scene of evocation with the same intensity and interest that it gives to the enacted scenes of the hero's life. By the end, we know that scene, the tawdry room and its prosaic contents, intimately, and the closing shot of dawn's rays and police tear-gas transfiguring the suicide's corpse suffuse the well-explored interior space with an aura of tragic significance. If, as Bazin's account of "poetic realism" would have it, the ordinary is made extraordinary, there is a heightened significance in the fact that almost every object in the room has become an instrument in the hero's project of recalling and questioning his past.

Daybreak is insistent on its presentation of a mental reenactment. Its code of subjectivity includes signals that, as they become familiar, encourage the audience's tacit awareness of the immediate transitions and the larger rhythm of presentation. This code includes shots of the protagonist framed in his mirror or in his room's one window; camera movement toward him or toward his reflected image; a somewhat ponderous musical leitmotif; and a slow dissolve to the remembered scene. Two of these shifts involve a cut from the reflecting hero to a point-of-view shot of his bulky wardrobe, a zoom in toward it, and a dissolve to the past, the wardrobe becoming a screen for memory images.

There are three long flashbacks, the first recounting the love story through its stages of meeting, blossoming, and initial crisis, when a rival is perceived; the second showing the rise and fall of a consolatory affair with the rival's castoff mistress; and the third, the murder scene, in which corroborating evidence of the loved one's infidelity—and the charlatan's death-wishful goading (he even provides the murder weapon)—lead to the debacle. The opening and closing scenes in the virtual present, together with the two interludes between the flashbacks—in which additional ongoing events involving the police take place—makes this a seven-part structure of a complexity that may well have daunted its early audiences but that we can now appreciate for its rigorous control in juxtaposing past and present actions. For it is the drama of bitter recollection that stands as the emotional center throughout, ultimately becoming the "main" action as it leads to a violent halt to remembering.

For all its skill and amplitude in subjective presentation, *Daybreak* does not fulfill its potentialities as mindscreen narration. We may trace the precise limits of its employment of the latter mode, for it does avail itself of verbal storytelling for a time. During the first transitional sequence, the hero is shown framed in the window, the camera tracks into an extreme closeup of his eyes, and we hear him whisper, "And yet it seems like only yesterday . . . do you remember . . ." (p. 34). Characteristic of the interior monologues of mindscreen narration, these lines are couched in the present tense, referring to the hero's immediate situation and his current encounter with his memories. At this stage of tantalizing suggestion that further verbalizing of the story and its significance is to come, mindscreen narration stops. The opportunity to follow the hero's mental process of phrasing and covertly expressing the narrative sentences that correspond to his memories is not taken up.

One cannot pretend that *Daybreak* is a lesser achievement for its failure to pursue these potentialities; its employment of other mindscreen codes, especially its use of mirror shots, is sufficiently inventive and rewarding to secure its place in the rise of subjectivity in cinema. But in approaching the narrower sphere of film narration, it has only one toe over the sill, as it were. There is a possibility that its creators were somewhat uncertain, if not of their own ability to formulate a proletarian's narrative of his past, of the ordinary man's capacity to do so in an articulate and interesting way. Yet a fuller use of the voice of remembering might have conveyed the protagonist's dawning grasp of the shape and significance of his fate—giving him stronger claims on the status of tragic hero. By implying but not exploring the psychology of narration, *Daybreak*'s "poetic realism" takes a step beyond, but does not completely transcend, the limited model of the proletarian type figure favored in the decade of its appearance.

o   o   o   o

A film of almost equal popularity appearing just after the war, David Lean's *Brief Encounter* (1945) undertakes to realize fully the potentialities of mindscreen narration. Its heroine narrates the story of her just-concluded love affair while sitting with her husband in a cozy after-dinner ambience. She addresses him throughout, using the second-person pronoun and his proper name, and the form of her discourse is that of a confession, yet she lacks the courage to utter it. We see her in extended closeups but her lips do not move, so we take the accompanying dubbed voice as her interior monologue.

The situation is interpersonal, but communication is not effected; it is thus not dramatized narration as ordinarily conceived. Yet some sort of influence is apparently transmitted, for the film's closing dialogue shows that the sight of her long meditation has moved the husband to more than usual tenderness, even to a kind of intuitive sympathy: "You've been a long way

Brief Encounter: Fred intuits Laura's mindscreen narration
("You've been a long way away.")

away. . . . Thank you for coming back to me."[12] Mindscreen narration is here shown to have a variety of potential effects. Not only does it, by a marshaling of cinematic conventions, convey a story to the audience; it also hints at the pervasive influence of even unspoken narration in personal relationships. An intensely ruminating mental narrator can subliminally affect other characters and induce responses they do not fathom; while such narrating alone cannot overcome his or her isolation, it can have dramatic consequences.

Unlike the contemporaneous Hollywood genre loosely described as the "woman's film," *Brief Encounter* makes consciousness and not sentiment its stamping ground. It is one of the relatively few films that systematically present point-of-view shots with the female protagonist as the viewer, not the viewed.[13] The scenes of narration provide not only shots of the heroine looking at her husband with intense concentration, but also shots of him in which the back of her head and shoulders occupy frame right. While his eventual intuition of her mental state may be regarded as an isolated instance of a male figure's dual perspective—not so developed as Stefan's in *Letter from an Unknown Woman*—it is in her awareness of him as she narrates that this condition is explored at length.

In place of the standard romance of unfulfilled or thwarted desire, we find a drama of consciousness in which desire and unfulfillment themselves become subjects for speculation by the introspective narrator. *Brief Encounter* dramatizes the active role of consciousness to a degree rarely seen, before or since, in cinema history.[14] Noël Coward, in adapting his own play, was no Conrad or Joyce in his concern for the perspectival intricacies of storytelling, yet the scenario's elaborate structure of narration does trench on their domain.

This is especially the case in the film's foregrounding of time. Throughout the film, the two orders of story time and narrating time are presented in standard alternating form. We see the heroine in a mundane domestic setting at the beginning, middle, and end of her narration, as she tells her story in her habitually well-ordered way. Between these scenes of narration, we see the enacted story scenes, each introduced or closed by her temporal markers: "The next Thursday . . . ," "All that was a week ago. . . ." As the title's temporal reference suggests, the film develops a contrast between the regularity of the heroine's unromantic marital life, lived out in the humdrum rhythms of diurnal time, and her construction of an idyllic counterrhythm of romance, marked at a number of moments by an aura of temporal suspension.

Yet the alternative realm of romance is not an escape from time but a submission to it. The story recounted is as elaborately, almost painfully, structured by time as the prosaic scene of narration. In the *mise en scène*, plotting and dialogue of the main story, time is made an issue. Clocks appear regularly in the railroad station scenes, the lovers' meetings are shaped by a number of temporal orders like the heroine's weekly shopping trips to town, and the dialogue is filled with anxieties about train times. We see a clock in the very first shot, high above the railway platform, and it becomes a presiding authority over the lovers who scurry below. We learn that their "brief" affair, from meeting to parting, lasts exactly six weeks, and we become as attentive as they are to the comings and goings of their trains—so that one can, with practice, recite the timetable for certain stretches of Midlands rail traffic almost as competently as they. Minutes, hours, and weeks are strictly rationed in the love story, but they are also carefully accounted for in the narration, so that the realm of consciousness becomes, as in major modern works in other media, time-consciousness.

The opening sequence is not a narrated one but a dramatic event on the day the narration takes place; it may be seen, in retrospect, as setting up the occasion for narrative activity. A trainman moves across a platform at "Milford Junction," passing in front of a clock showing 5:35, and enters a waiting room buffet. During the next eight minutes of story time—presented with few cuts, in an approximation of "real" time—the trainman and a barmaid carry on a flirtation while the protagonists at a nearby table are shown in deep dejection, before being interrupted by a gossipy acquaintance. The man at the table goes off to his train, the 5:40 for "Churley"; at that time, as a wall clock indicates, an express barrels through. The woman dazedly reenters the buffet; we have not seen her leave, the camera having followed the gossip to the bar for further chitchat. Her own train, the 5:43 for "Ketchworth," is announced and she goes off to board it. We learn much later the subjective aspect of these events. Their successive departures repeat the pattern of the lovers' previous meetings; they are now definitively parting, he having taken a position abroad; the heroine rushes out in a confused impulse to end her pain under the speeding express.

This sequence takes part, as the film develops, in a number of structural relationships. It is soon followed by the scene of narration, after the heroine returns home, and it thus proves to be the final event in her story, with the narration and its subliminal influence subsequent to it. Much of the sequence is later repeated, with the subjective details filled in, as an enactment of her narration. Since this repetition is also the penultimate unit in the film's discourse, the opening action works together with the near-closing one to create an enveloping form for the film as a whole. Starting out as the film does at the end of the affair, the ensuing narration generates a vast anachrony, taking us back to the affair's beginning and completing the loop at the close.

Along the way, *Brief Encounter* reveals its motives for so highly patterned a structure. Mundane events like buffet chatter and commuting rituals are run through in their full banality but gain weight when revealed by the narration to be laden with personal concerns. The narration, itself a mental performance, becomes the agency by which more overt behavior is portrayed as laden with psychological depths. The subjectivity of mindscreen narration is perceptible, then, not only in the storytelling scenes but in the story's enactment. What might have been considered a middle-class affair not much more interesting than the lower-class flirtation in the buffet turns out to be charged with thought and feeling.[15] If modernism may be thought of as characteristically disposed to render significant the humdrum life of ordinary men and women—usually by exploring their internal responses to even the most banal events—then *Brief Encounter* stands squarely within that tradition.[16]

As in *Daybreak*, the mentalization of the ordinary takes place within a *mise en scène* of exquisitely precise physical circumstances. The heroine's life being one of well-schooled middle-class regularity, her narration is riddled not only with temporal indicators but with exact specifications of trivial details. Some of this is traceable to the standard Noël Coward milieu, elsewhere taken up as material for his famous satirical touch. But well-made-play comedy is transcended here as a suburban housewife is taken, for once, seriously, both as narrator and as lover.

From her fact-laden account, we are in a position to order the story fairly precisely:

1. First encounter at the buffet, at about 5:33 P.M. of a Thursday (the scenario specifies "the winter of 1938–39": p. 11); Laura Jesson has a speck removed from her eye by Dr. Alec Harvey.

2. A week later, she goes to Milford on Thursday "again as usual" (we get a full list of her habitual activities), bumps into him on the street, and thinks of him as his train is pulling out.

3. In their third encounter, they meet accidentally at a restaurant, spend the afternoon at the movies, and wind up at the same buffet at the same hour for their return trips.

4. On the fourth Thursday, he fails to keep their rendezvous but catches her for a hurried explanation at the usual time and place as they rush off for their trains.

5. On the fifth occasion, they enjoy a full afternoon of moviegoing (the previously advertised "Flames of Passion" proves to be a bore, though its title makes its own ironic comment on their affair), rowing and drying out in a boatman's shed, a mutual declaration of love, and a furtive kiss in a railroad underpass—followed by her first lie, when the sequence concludes at home.

6. A day of crisis that begins with a distressing recognition by a catty acquaintance at lunch, relaxes with an auto ride in the country, climaxes with a furtive assignation at a friend's apartment and the friend's unexpected return, and extends into a long night walk during which Laura comes to grips with the affair's impossibility. This is the only deviation from a pattern of late-afternoon parting, for they meet again at the station at

9:54 (as we see by the clock), and as they walk toward her train he tells her of an overseas job opportunity and receives her tacit encouragement to take it.

7. Their last day together, from 12:30, when they take another ride in the country, to the parting scene described above, at the usual hour; Laura's day closes with an evening of mentally reviewing the affair after returning home.

Narration by the well-disciplined heroine predictably follows the story order from 1 to 7, without anachrony. Yet a number of elements in the scene of narration mark Laura's account as a complex and creative one. Designating her husband as her desired addressee indicates the peculiar poignancy of her narrative activity, for instead of serving as communication it only reinforces her isolation: "There's so much that I want to say to you. . . . As it is you are the only one in the world that I can never tell" (p. 23). Previously, in a non-narrational interior monologue during her ride home with the gossip, she has expressed her need for and lack of a worthy confidante. Yet her isolation is mitigated by her continued psychic intimacy with her beloved, so that although her narration is in one sense a frustrated communion with her husband, in another sense it is a form of mental congress with her lover. For all the guilty feelings expressed in her confession to (or toward) Fred, there is no gainsaying the visible evidence that recalling her pleasures is itself a pleasure, even now shared with Alec.

We also observe in the storytelling scenes that the film's (in)famous use of Rachmaninoff's second piano concerto is a complicated one. As she begins her narration, Laura tunes the radio to the music, so that the passages from the opening, slow, and final movements that we hear are to be taken as part of the mimetic world—her deliberate choice of an appropriate accompaniment to her reverie. But during an intermediate return to the scene of narration, the normally forbearing Fred rebels against the finale's loudness—perhaps speaking for our own irritation with it—and turns the volume down. Thereafter, it is the slow movement that we hear, and since this section has already passed in the concerto we cannot take the music at this stage to be ordinary "diegetic sound." We are invited to interpret it as the equivalent of Laura's mental repetition of what she has been hearing on the radio: one might call it mind music.

Another segment of the narration raises more difficult questions about the status of Laura's mental language and its corresponding images. The close of the fifth encounter, with its climactic kiss in the station underpass, returns to the scene of narration by what at first appears to be a slow dissolve but turns out on closer inspection to be a briefly suspended superimposition. At the lower right of the station scene, we see for a time Laura in her library armchair, the thinker and her thought shown together; then the light comes up in the superimposed shot to reveal the full domestic setting. Lean and Coward were concerned to articulate not only the lingering of memory in the remembering mind but also the mental narrator's dual space—in the story as well as in the storytelling scene.[17]

The return to the scene of narration issues in the dramatic action involving the radio, described above. But after Fred turns down the Rachmaninoff, a new phase of mindscreen narration is reached. A series of dissolves returns us to Laura in the train coming away from the climactic kiss. This carefully composed sequence begins with a two-shot of the character and her reflection in the train window. The visual doubling is further complicated by our awareness that the scene with its doubled image forms part of the story she tells. Although Laura does not specify that she saw herself reflected in the window, we may take the shot as an equivalent of her words, "I had to think" (p. 58), that is, as the enactment of her report of past self-consciousness.

As if this were not sufficiently self-reflexive, the window acquires further reflective functions. The scenario makes explicit the relation between mental and visual spaces by activating a nice ambiguity in the word "screen": "As LAURA turns to look out of the window, the camera tracks and pans slowly forward until the darkened countryside fills the screen" (p. 58). The screen of film images at first shows Laura in the train looking at or out the window; we see not what she saw but an equivalent of her narrative of past events. A portion of the film screen then becomes the space or screen of her visual and mental field as she remembers what she saw and imagined in the window: we see her reflection, the trees and other pieces of the world outside, and the fantasies she entertains. Laura herself is quite explicit about her use of the window as a space for imaginative visualization: "I stared out of the railway carriage window into the dark and watched the dim trees and the telegraph posts slipping by, and through them I saw Alec and me" (p. 58). There follows a mindscreen montage—intermittently superimposed over a shot of the window and passing objects—of her fantasies of living the high life with her lover at various pleasure spots. We must take these film images, then, as equivalent to reported memories of fantasy images. They are typical of a narrator who scrupulously includes not only what happened in her story but what she thought, felt, and even imagined.

The lavish fantasies are reported self-critically by the narrator—"I imagined being with him in all sorts of glamorous circumstances. It was one of those absurd fantasies" (p. 58)—so that an almost ludicrous lushness is employed in the acting and *mise en scène* of their enactment. Their illusoriness is also conveyed by the rapid cutting of the montage, suggesting a will-o'-the-wispish insubstantiality—the celerity of thought, especially of self-deluding thought. The sequence as a whole contains, then, indicators of mental activity in the present narration, in the story episode (thinking and fantasizing in the train), and in the imaginary realm conjured up during that episode. Laura's mental narration of psychological experience includes reflections on the quality of past imaginings and their intersection with other realities: "Then the palm trees changed into those pollarded willows by the canal just before the level crossing . . . and all the silly dreams disappeared, and I got out at Ketchworth and gave up my ticket" (p. 59). We come to recognize certain phases of *Brief Encounter* as concerned with subjectivity at every level of the narrating and of the story.

Laura's narrative of past events, both those at Milford and Ketchworth and those that can be said to have occurred in her mind, is established as the main story of this film. Its cumulative effect is to suggest that mindscreen narration assembles cinematic codes to convey an intrapersonal as well as an interpersonal drama. The episode in the train is seen to be made up of a tissue of psychological processes; nothing happened to Laura on the train, but she led a busy life there. As we follow her narration, we see her engaged in various kinds of thought: self-examining, remembering, fantasizing. We also learn her present attitudes toward those mental activities, so that mindscreen narration may be said to report thinking about thinking. Cinema is, it seems, capable of rendering not only immediate responses but longer phases of psychological development, tracing the course of attitudes over time, recounting a history of the emotions.

Let us consider *Brief Encounter* as a story of the emotional life. By comparison with most current romantic dramas—or even with contemporaneous films in other national cinemas, like the French—nothing much happens in this love affair. To put it crudely, it is a story of lovers who do *not* go to bed or, more sympathetically, of lovers who find that their cultural constraints and personal moralities render them incapable of adultery. This negative tale of what does *not* happen has its positive equivalent, the eventful record preserved in Laura's mind of all the feelings she did experience—including love and loss and past reflections upon both. Laura's mindscreen narration is, then, largely about psychological events: what she thought and felt as she had her love affair. In line with the broad tendency of modern fiction to turn the micro-movements of inner experience into the stuff of storytelling—both of the story and of the telling—films like *Brief Encounter* move toward the full subjectivizing of narrative.

In joining with this tendency, although perhaps not committed to its avant-gardist accouterments, Lean and Coward gave their heroine a narrational capacity rarely found in films but closely resembling that in the great tradition of introspective fictional narrators. Laura is well equipped to recount not only past events, with keen awareness of both her past and present feelings, but also her intuitions of the responses of others, her consciousness of their consciousness. Laura's imaginative sympathy with Alec allows her to picture not only his feelings but his unseen actions, such as his coming away from one of their dates, returning home, and rejoining his wife. She is even capable of narrating events that do *not* occur, or in which something does *not* happen, as when she portrays him as failing to tell Madeleine about herself.

Laura goes on to explore the difficult mode of prophetic narration, anticipating the heroine of *Hiroshima Mon Amour*: "There will come a time in the future when I shan't mind about this any more—when I can look back and say quite peacefully and cheerfully, 'How silly I was.' No, no—I don't want that time to come ever—I want to remember every minute—always—always—to the end of my days" (p. 19). Her floating of these images of the future involves a further refinement of narrational skills. Like the interior monologuist of *Hiroshima*, Laura tells of a time of distancing from the emotions, by indifference if not by death. But she raises this anticipation to a critical sharpness by negating it, projecting an alternative outcome in which she remains fully aware of her experience. In devising alternate endings for her story, Laura gains stature as an autobiographical narrator, giving shape and significance to her otherwise humdrum life.

Lacking a sequel, we can only speculate on how these prophecies turn out. But it is in keeping with the film's subjectivizing of story and narration that the imagined future should emerge as its ultimate denouement. *Brief Encounter* may project a story of what does not happen, but it is even more winningly a drama of what does—and what happens is the rich funding of its heroine's emotional life. If cinema, a non-narrated medium in which most stories are expressively dramatized, can also present narrations in which the full flow of inner experience is made available in words and images, there may be no loss in limiting "film narration" to narrated films, as it has been here.

◻

Continuation:
Questions for Research

IT WILL BE EVIDENT to any fair-minded reader that the preceding pages have not exhausted their subject. I too am conscious that there is more to be observed in cinema, in narration, and in the specific films discussed than has been pursued here. My effort to delimit a subject in which answerable questions are asked only raises further questions—about the verbal rhetoric of the storytelling situations, about their interaction with each film's visual and sonic texture, about their relation to the code of subjectivity, about. . . . Yet there may be methodological advantages in choosing a scope somewhere between cinematic narrativity in general and a focus on a specific mode like voice-over. These advantages may show themselves not only in the doability of the present enterprise but also by generating further questions that seem worth attempting to answer. Since the instrumental, rather than definitive, concepts and terms introduced here are designed to open rather than close discussion, I conclude with a view of future prospects.

The general question might be phrased, What else in cinema might be studied, where narration makes a difference? If my amateur statistics reflect a reality, that roughly one of six sound films is narrated, the approaches practiced here may be applied with some regularity to films as they are currently released. There are, as well, many non-narrated films in which storytelling makes an important contribution, sometimes a crucial intervention in the theme or plot. One has only to think of the powerful though dry narrative in *Jaws* of shark-infested waters after a naval battle, or the dry and enacted explanations of the future story in *The Terminator*. With heightened attention to storytelling scenes, we may find more movie reviews that note not only plot and characters, actors, and other production values but also the fact that the story is told by one or another kind of narrator. Most reviewers, far from fretting at such distinctions, ignore narration altogether, apparently on the assumption that audiences are not much interested in how the story reaches them. But avoiding the storytelling source can reduce a commentary to incoherence when a film carries its narrational perspective into the characterization, *mise en scène*, and theme.

The virtue of consciousness-raising in the sphere of narration may be gauged from the controversy over Milos Forman's *Amadeus* (1983). Many who were outraged by the demeaning presentation of Mozart—acting like a modern teenager at times, with a raucous laugh, modish hair styling, and other hip trappings—seem to have ascribed his portrayal to the anachronistic filmmakers rather than to the contemporaneous narrator, Salieri. With all the inputs of the director, the actor (Tom Hulce), and the scenarist (Peter Shaffer, from his play), narrative authority flows from the intensely realized scenes of dramatized narration in which the half-cracked, institutionalized composer unpacks to a would-be confessor his ambivalent views of his genial rival and bête noire. We have learned to take the Expressionist *mise en scène* of *The Cabinet of Dr. Caligari* to be the visual equivalent, not the explicit specifications, of its distorted framing narration. Are we not to take the pop elements of *Amadeus* as expressive, not literal, equivalents of another tale told in a madhouse?

As in *Caligari*, certain elements of narrated films may derive from non-narrational sources: in *Amadeus*, for example, the unnarrated closing presentation of Mozart's legendary pauper's burial. The larger questions persist: What codes enable audiences to discriminate the perspectives of the filmmaker(s), the narrator, and the central character? The elaboration of subjectivity codes in Edward Branigan's *Point of View in the Cinema* and the enlarged varieties of perspective in Seymour Chatman's *Coming to Terms* need to be supplemented by attention to the role of verbal storytelling in the shifting manifold that controls many films' attitudinal burdens.

To nag at *Amadeus* a bit more: An awareness of narration may lead us to savor the full value of F. Murray Abraham's Oscar-winning performance as Salieri. The actor's interpretation of the aged and decayed minor composer covered the full emotional range from comic reduction to Lear-like tragic loss. One of its rarer achievements may, however, have been lost in the general admiration: the character's stature as a historian, his ample and precise verbal imaging of Mozart and his times— beautifully articulated by the actor's fine voice and rhetorical skills. Salieri's capacity to describe artistic inspiration and personal idiosyncrasy rose and shifted with the subject matter; even when not doubled by enacted scenes, the narration evoked creative power by exhibiting the same force in its own language and delivery.

One of the subjects to have been neglected in the push to determine cinematic narration, enunciation, and "film language," on the dubious model of the diegetic arts, has been the actual, verbal language used in films. A good place to begin would be the rhetoric of narrative discourse (using those words in their nonmetaphoric, disciplinary senses), to include such pragmatic activities as those Salieri engages in—description, argument, and evaluation (epideictic praise and blame, not only of Mozart but of God). Rhetorical analysis appropriate to cinema would of course be guided by the relations among words, images, and sounds; that is, it would be up-to-date on kinesics, proxemics, and other paralinguistic studies. Such attention to language would enable a full account of the climactic scene of composing the Requiem, with its multiple channels of articulation, including the composers' technical register of terms for symbolic notation, the musical equivalents (instrumental line by line), and the narrator's *ekphrasis* or description of a nonverbal work of art, in this case invoking the rhetoric of the sublime.

The most palpable effects of narration in this film, as in many another, lie in characterizing the titular hero. Salieri's unreliable narration manages to generate a more humane portrait of a legendary composer than most others in the long string of movie biographies. The payload of storytelling is, moreover, delivered in the characterization of the narrator himself. Salieri comes through not merely as a distorting filter but as a complex and impressive figure, in consequence of his ability not only to appreciate Mozart's creative heights but to describe them with brio and conviction. Insofar as films invite audiences to identify with ordinary mortals, friends, or other witnesses through whom we gain access to divinely or demonically inspired figures, *Amadeus* follows a well-known strategy whose fictional equivalent would be Thomas Mann's *Doctor Faustus*. The incisive self-definitions of Salieri's discourse also enable him to stand out as what he calls the "champion" of mediocrity—not, perhaps, the most elevated character type, but one fully due our attention. The dual activity of self-characterization by narrators amid their characterizing of others is not a specialized haunt of narratologists but a concern of everyday behavior, elaborated in literature and cinema and well worth studying in both.

To digress on character for a page: Almost any year-end survey brings the issue up—today's films need characters, lack characters, occasionally create characters. No one can legislate memorable character studies into existence, since they derive from the world-views of each cultural period and the insights of individual creative artists, and the present may be unfavorable for portraiture in depth. Motion pictures, in particular, whose very name invokes the visual and the kinetic, may be at an inherent disadvantage in building up a structure of inner and outer traits—of passive, contemplative dispositions along with active ones—though they are highly equipped to render immediate psychological experiences. That depth of character is nonetheless accessible to the medium is evidenced by the so-called transcendental cinema of Dreyer, Bresson, Ozu, Tarkovsky, and others, which actually renders fewer otherworldly than immanently human qualities. Its characters are temporally layered, that is, exhibit a history that conditions their varied, sometimes conflicting, spheres of reflection, commitment, and activity. Since narrators are in a favorable position to provide this temporal dimension, they constitute a valuable resource for enhancing characterization. No requirement, of course; while the others mentioned often invoke narration, Ozu, to my knowledge, does not. (See note 11.)

Most of the films closely studied above provide striking examples of this potentiality realized. Where the protagonist is schematic, as he is by design in *Orpheus*, the admixture of an external narrator expands his stature, even fusing with him to project a conjoint archetype of the poetic temperament. When the protagonist's inner life might otherwise be inaccessible because of his psychic derangement, he may like Francis externalize his mind's workings in the course of narrating his fantasies. Even when character structure is most problematic, as in the case of a Zelig, the combination of varied means and sources of narration can fill out a rounded perspective on a perhaps nonexistent central identity. As for the mixed perspicuity and mystery of the protagonists of *Hiroshima Mon Amour*, *Diary of a Country Priest*, and *Brief Encounter*, there is little need to underscore the contribution of their self-portraiture in narrative form. And in films like *Sunset Boulevard* and *Letter from an Unknown Woman*, the narrators succeed in casting a penetrating light not only on themselves but on the significant others in their lives.

Yet psychological depth has become a problematic category and perhaps no longer an incontestable desideratum, given the new schools of psychoanalysis and new ideas of personhood that have entered film studies. Current talk of cinema psychology follows the direction, if not the terminology, of the earliest film theoreticians in focusing on the audience's rather than the filmmaker's or the character's mind.[1] There are few recent discussions of character as such, although some of the best criticism of individual films contains unblushing character interpretation.[2]

The disuse of character runs in tandem, it seems, with a more sweeping distrust of subjectivity, given our increased awareness of the insidious power of the cinema apparatus and the manipulative instincts of the film industry to induce not only ideological "false consciousness" but spurious identification in its wake.[3] With the theorist's eye cocked for illusory promotions of subjective consciousness, as well as personal seductions by the stars' charisma, the filmmaker is encouraged to elaborate other ideas of personhood. The current trend in characterization—toward not mere flatness or typicality but comic-book unbelievability—results not from a dearth but a choice: it is the cinematic equivalent of the minimalism, alienation-effects, and self-conscious "historicism" that mark postmodernism in the arts generally.

No one would dream of demanding that film criticism take up a line of inquiry that has become outmoded elsewhere; in literary studies, for example, character-oriented criticism has come to seem a relic of another age. If we reflect on when that age ended, however, we recall that character as focus and as problem not only was a Romantic and Victorian preoccupation but was vigorously explored by modernist writers, both creative and critical. Since most of cinema history falls within the span of the modern period in the arts, it behooves us—even from a postmodern perspective—to understand film characterization and subjectivity within that context. In such a rethinking, the role of narration will come to higher prominence, for just as modern writers were delving into newly opened psychological strata by innovations in narrational technique, filmmakers were experimenting with narration in pursuit of similar ends. Considering cinema in the light of modernist esthetics raises new questions about the psychological and formal functions of film narration, questions that will be framed rather than answered here.

As noted at various points along our way, narrated films often bear the impress of cinema's relations with modern fiction during the latter's heyday. Since the relationship has been canvassed in a number of studies that center on fiction and use cinema as a means of distinguishing its modernist features, it may be useful to reassess their findings and decide where a film-oriented approach might best begin. Early formulations of the idea that modern novels are "cinematic" tended to be swayed by palpable similarities—seemingly objective presentation, abrupt transitions or intercutting, and other stylistic traits—into crediting cinema with the initiating role. Claude-Edmonde Magny's seminal view of the influence was a unidirectional one: "Almost all the innovations introduced by the American novelists into novelistic technique—except for interior monologue . . . —seem to be borrowings by the novel from film."[4] A partially reversed and perhaps wiser, because weaker, relationship was later drawn by Alan Spiegel: certain passages in nineteenth-century novels (especially Flaubert's) anticipate, and others in twentieth-century novels resemble, film techniques like parallel and alternating montage, "panoramic" shots (high-angle long shots, not what are called "pans" in cinema), and closeup inserts that isolate objects or details of a scene.[5]

A more sweeping version of Magny's influence claim has recently been made: that the emergence of cinema as a cultural way of seeing shaped the revolution in modern literature at large, particularly in narrative technique. For Keith Cohen, the "classic modern" literature of the 1920s was marked by a number of traits derived from basic cinematic properties: a shift of priority from subjects to objects (*chosisme*, "behaviorism," or "external focalization," as it has also been called); temporal distortion, including not only achronological discourse but also foregroundings of the present moment and of simultaneous events; a multiperspectivism born of the mobile camera and from cutting between several angles on a scene; and discontinuities in narrative—elliptical, fragmentary, and psychologically motivated (stream of consciousness or, as Cohen calls it, "montage of consciousness").[6]

While these trends certainly emerge in film and fiction, steps in similar directions are also apparent in the other modern arts— multiperspectivism in abstract painting and sculpture, new temporalities in the tonal systems of music, discontinuities of varied kinds in drama. Just as it would be limiting to single out literature as the only recipient of cinema's influence, it would be reductionist to proclaim one medium as progenitor of these pervasive tendencies. We must keep open the possibility that, within the broad stylistic "dominant" of the age, film and fiction not only have common sources but engage in a continual interaction. A nonprivileging view would take account of literary endowments to cinema with at least the enthusiasm shown in celebrating cinematic fiction. In this accounting, not only would adaptations of modern novels and modernist writers who have worked as scenarists be called into evidence, but the more subtle influence of fictional technique in film narration and other cinematic codes might also emerge.

As well as asking what cinema has done for fiction, then, we may also be interested in learning what modern writing has done for, to, or in films. Their mutual roles may be derived from a theoretical distinction explored in the Introduction and given another turn in discussions of the interrelation of the arts: the

difference between cinema's inherent indications of visual perspective and fiction's need to articulate the visual. "Each filmic
image 'bears the mark of the point of view from which it was
taken,' " as Cohen puts it, citing Magny. "Distance and angle
are built into the image, whereas in any discursive, literary art,
such as the novel, they are subtle and constantly varying factors
that are determined at another level, so to speak, of production."
What this "so to speak" avoids saying we might as well name:
the "production level" of fictional perspective is narration, as
intrinsic to it as are distance and angle to photographic images.
And in fiction's rhetoric of perspectival determinations, which
includes but goes well beyond distance and angle, a resource
lies open to cinema that its more receptive exponents have not
failed to tap.

Though signs of the narrator may be severely reduced in
fiction, its narrative sentences posit not only that certain events
took place but that a speaker, knower, or consciousness stands
at the position from which events are rendered. Although this
narrative voice may be "omniscient" or "nonfocalized," as Genette terms it[7]—that is, not tied to what the characters know or
perceive—more often the narration is focalized by or through
one or more characters ("internal focalization" with its several
varieties). Fiction thus has long experience in rendering the non-
essential but worthy project that filmmakers may take on themselves, of moving from nonfocalized to internal presentation,
conveying limited or subjective views of events within a more
encompassing, quasi-authorial perspective.[8]

We may reflect on the role of modern fiction in encouraging
filmmakers to extend themselves in this demanding exercise.
Film-and-fiction comparatists have heralded the example of
Alain Robbe-Grillet's efforts to make his novels "cinematic" by
effacing the narrator, severely limiting the focal character's perspective, and other stylistic tactics, an enterprise continued by
other means in his own films. Yet equally striking as a paradigmatic case, a film molded by fiction, is the same writer's scenario
for *Last Year at Marienbad*, in which a character's almost continual
narration, while intending to convey a story (and perhaps
worse), takes the form of a literary mode, repetitive and asso-
ciative stream-of-consciousness monologue (in which the author

is also an adept). Not to make Robbe-Grillet's practice an isolated case, we recall the strikingly literary narrational techniques employed in other avant-garde films, like the internal monologue and internal dialogue of *Hiroshima Mon Amour*—not surprisingly, the scenario of another lifelong experimenter in narrating consciousness.

Yet the importation of novelistic techniques into cinema—and not only in passages of narration but in visual discourse as well—hardly begins with the New Novelists' scenarios. As early as the 1920s, French "impressionist" filmmakers like Germaine Dulac and Jean Epstein were discovering cinematic means of rendering subjective experience to equal those of fiction's narrators. Dulac's *The Smiling Madame Beudet* (1922) achieved by montage, distorted images, and other devices the moment-to-moment tracing of a woman's consciousness that her opposite numbers, Virginia Woolf and Dorothy Richardson, were evoking in fiction at the time. Similarly, Epstein's *Fall of the House of Usher* (1926) employed new compositional and technical methods to render less the narrative than the hallucinatory narration of Poe's short story—not the plot but the narrator.

Nor has the literary impulse in filmmaking been confined to the experimental schools. The effort to find cinematic means of conveying the subjective experience in modern fiction came into play in a number of adaptations of the 1930s. In Frank Borzage's *A Farewell to Arms* (1932), for example, an extended montage sequence is deployed to express little of the plot and more the subjective states of the hero during the disastrous retreat from Caporetto. And *Sabotage* (1936), Hitchcock's version of Conrad's *The Secret Agent*, showed the master of audience psychology devising visual and sound sequences to render the heroine's mental tumult and murderous impulses after her husband sends her brother to destruction.

Adaptations of modern novels were not the only sphere in which cinema tried to find its own discursive means to convey the perspectives of literary narration. All too often, their verbal texts betrayed a suspect desire to tap a literary tone and high-art afflatus for an institution that has always had a love-hate relationship with "culture." When adaptations of the classics became a staple of the later 1930s, they settled for historical verisimilitude (or the illusion of it) and transcriptions of the original dialogue (or snatches of it), rarely aiming to recreate the perspective either of narrators or of characters. While the sporadic visual and voice-over resonances of fictional narrators were designed mainly as nostalgic echoes of familiar texts, they prepared the ground for fuller dealings with the advanced narrational techniques of modern fiction. My sketch of this period in chapter 2 must remain only that, absent a close study of screenwriting, particularly of adaptations, amid the recent revival of interest in Hollywood scenarists.[9]

Beyond the industry's aspirations and hesitations to incorporate literary qualities, beyond the efforts of innovative filmmakers to devise cinematic equivalents of fictional perspective, another relationship between film and fiction might fruitfully be explored. It became evident that the rising prestige of modern literature constituted a potential property value to be tapped by movie moguls—witness the early adaptation of works by Nobel Prize–winners like Sinclair Lewis, Eugene O'Neill, and Pearl Buck, and by eventual laureates like Hemingway, Faulkner, and Steinbeck. In the stream of East Coast novelists and playwrights to Hollywood, modernist authors like Faulkner, Fitzgerald, and Dos Passos were also recruited, although with results rewarding neither to the individuals nor to the medium—certainly not to the diffusion of modernism.[10] Although their experimentalism—and that of younger novelists like Nathanial West, Daniel Fuchs, and James Agee—could rarely reach expression in their scenarios, yet the institution must have been subtly modified by the presence of writers with their orientation. It would be worth entertaining the hypothesis that these passing engagements with modern fiction were steps toward Hollywood's increasing interest in narration and subjectivity in the 1940s and thereafter.

The assimilation of modernist fictional methods by the studio system—both what was lost and what was gained—is illustrated by the early stages of Orson Welles's career. The industry's importation of a scandal-raising theatrical whiz-kid was also a fumbling step into the realm of avant-garde esthetics, whether it knew that or not at the time. With Welles's advent, modern fiction became not merely a source of prestige or fine writing but a stimulus to discover cinematic means of conveying narrational perspective and subjective experience. It was this challenge, as much as Welles's budgetary and scheduling deficiencies, that made him anathema to the institution but formative for filmmakers already practicing there (and elsewhere, like Ozu),[11] in *film noir* and other genres of the 1940s and 1950s.

For his initial, unfilmed but highly elaborated project, an adaptation of Conrad's *Heart of Darkness,* Welles specified no less than a framing situation, an extensive voice-over, a set of camera and montage arrangements that would later be called "subjective camera," and a prologue by Welles as on-screen personal narrator, explaining the "first-person" camera technique by means of such visual puns as "eye = I."[12] That some of these elements were, a few years later, picked up by another actor-director for a more flimsy story, *The Lady in the Lake,* indicates only the more overt part of the project's influence. Though Conradian subjective perspective and introspective narrational language did not reach the screen on this occasion, Welles's achievements in a considerable corpus of narrated films would follow from the unfulfilled enterprise. And the narrated films of Joseph Mankiewicz, Billy Wilder, and others could make their way more readily in his wake.

Welles's early career is, on this hypothesis, indicative of the rarely explicit but ramified migration of literary modernism that stands behind cinema's increasing interest in subjectivity and narration in the immediate postwar period. While my choice of films to exemplify the storytelling situations was not dictated by historical considerations, it is notable that two-thirds of them appeared in this period. Together they make up a body of evidence that suggests an influence of modern fiction on film more pervasive than on narration alone. Mindscreen narration, which was approached gingerly in *Daybreak* by an avant-garde poet, was developed in *Brief Encounter* by an otherwise conventional playwright, operating with unwonted attention to modern fictional modes like interior monologue. Cocteau's personal voice-overs and battery of signs of the author brought into filmmaking the boldly authorial voice and the spirit of self-manifestation that had become a hallmark of modern fiction from Proust and Lawrence on. While Kurosawa seems to have drawn directly neither from Welles nor from Conrad for the multiple narration of *Rashomon*, his adaptation of a story by an experimental Japanese novelist of the 1920s makes use of a modernist literary tendency on local soil. Although *Diary of a Country Priest* employs a novelist who can be placed only at the fringes of the modern movement, Bresson's version of Bernanos avails itself of the narrative methods of this carefully controlled diary-novel. Indeed, a film's narrational complexity might go well beyond the fairly elementary technique of its modern literary source, as in *Letter from an Unknown Woman*.

The existence of a variety of storytelling situations that have, as in these films, conveyed perspectival complexities and experiential inwardness suggests that the frequent discussion of film and fiction as inherently different and therefore ultimately untranslatable media may be misconceived.[13] Cases in point may be drawn from a recent symposium of contemporary writers who have had their novels adapted and resignedly join in their fraternity's complaints against Hollywood. One exchange indicates that the desired narrational modes may not always be available to filmmakers, because of passing trends. Responding to a question about the loss of a "sense of the character's interior knowledge" in the adaptation of his novel, John Knowles explained, "That's why in *A Separate Peace* they should have used a voice-over. . . . But in 1972, when this was made, voice-overs were considered very old-fashioned and not done."[14]

Other exchanges indict not the transitory impediments but the limitations of the medium, yet suggest more personal sources of failure. In questioning William Styron, the point is made about *Sophie's Choice*, "How differently one experiences the meeting of Sophie and Nathan and their relationship in the film because we're not getting it through Stingo [the novel's narrator]. We're getting it through our own eyes immediately." Styron's reply falls back on the untranslatable-media canard: "There's nothing to say except the two mediums are different, and that there's no possible way to render certain things that were there originally." This is remarkable for forgetting that the film opens with a voice-over narration by Stingo; the fact that it was not developed to lend a witnessing perspective on the protagonists' tragic affair is the fault less of the medium than of the filmmakers, who failed to take seriously the means at hand. One has only to compare Andrzej Wajda's *A Love in Germany* (1984) to see what can be done with witness narration of similar materials. Modernist techniques are as available to cinema as they still are to literature; it may be the insufficient modernity of the film-makers, as of the novelists in this panel, that impedes their creative usage.

When the question of film-and-fiction influence is raised in this light, it may help to address another historical issue where narration makes a difference. The periodization of cinema history has been subjected to renewed attention, especially as the boundaries of modernism and postmodernism have come in for intensive debate. Since the "First Avant-Garde" of the 1920s was rediscovered by Noël Burch and others, and since Eisenstein's experimentalist milieu has been adduced as a context for Russian montage, a stronger grasp of Continental cinema's modernist esthetics has developed. The "classic modern" in both film and fiction may be safely placed in the interwar decades, when film-makers in France, the Soviet Union, and elsewhere responded to the modernist imperatives of deformation, abstraction, and constructivism. In the years immediately before and after World War II, as we have seen, extensive literarily inspired narrational innovation took place, at least as remarkable as the break-throughs in *mise en scène*, acting, and cinematography associated with Neorealism. Further interactions between the two arts took place from 1959 on, as the New Novel and New Wave made common cause and frequent joint enterprises.

Whether the perceptible similarities between postmodernist minimalism[15] in the literature and cinema of the past and present decades represents a further stage of mutual influence and con-joint reworking of modernism, it is perhaps too early to judge. We can safely say that the modernist literary influence on cin-ema—as well as the cinematic impact on fiction described in revolutionary metaphors by avant-garde theorists—has been and looks to be a permanent revolution or continually recurring one. In the "classic," pre- and postwar, 1960s, and, potentially, postmodernist decades, each modernist phase shows filmmak-ers, like writers, challenging established modes of representation by introducing new ones that in part become conventional in their turn. In the elaboration of cinematic codes for rendering subjectivity (and heightened objectivity), ambiguous narrative structures, and other modernist pursuits, innovative uses of narration have played a consistent role.

Such a history of cinema's relation to modernism would allow for more generous acknowledgment of a watershed period in cinema history, during which literature made its contributions to film's modernity. Between the two main phases of cinematic experimentalism ("classic" and New Wave) would stand not the mythic Fall of avant-garde histories but a period of fulfillment in visual, sound, and other narrative codes. So dominant was the industry's impulse toward story that it could sustain, not always with sympathy or largesse, films of complex storytelling that rank among the finest of any period. This middle phase of high achievement in film narration would represent a modernist advance worthy to stand with the more easily recognized ones of the "classic" and "New Wave" stages. The narrated films of the 1940s and 1950s too added their storytelling voices to the living art of cinema.

◻

Notes

Introduction:
What Is Film Narration, after All?

1. Neil Sinyard, *The Films of Alfred Hitchcock* (New York, 1986), p. 125. For an extended display of camera-as-narrator rhetoric in psychological or existential terms, see William Rothman, *Hitchcock—The Murderous Gaze* (Cambridge, Mass., 1982). The notion is not confined to film criticism and makes its appearance in philosophical esthetics and literary theory, for example, "The structure of a motion picture is not that of drama, and indeed lies closer to narrative than to drama. . . . The percipient of a moving picture sees with the camera" (Susanne K. Langer, *Feeling and Form* [New York, 1953], pp. 411, 413); or, "The animated image, or motion picture, has a narrative function. . . . When we see a film we are viewing narrated material, a novel" (Käte Hamburger, *The Logic of Literature*, trans. M. J. Rose [Bloomington, Ind., 1973], p. 222).

2. For a survey of this distinction, see Gérard Genette, "Frontiers of Narrative," in *Figures of Literary Discourse*, trans. Alan Sheridan (New York, 1982), pp. 127–44. Genette considers all of the fictional text as narrative, including the apparently mimetic direct-discourse quotations; even description and lyrical or authorial expressions become assimilated to the narrative function. Where this leaves cinema and other mimetic arts is less clear, but in *Nouveau discours du récit* (Paris, 1983), Genette expresses his doubts that films are, in general, narrated—a doubt I share, except under the special conditions to be described below.

3. The classical opposition has been undermined, with learning and ingenuity, in André Gaudreault, "Récit scriptural, récit théâtral, récit filmique: Prolégomènes à une théorie narrative du cinéma" (diss., Paris-III, 1983). See Gaudreault's "Narration et monstration au cinéma, *Hors cadre* no. 2 (1984), pp. 87–98, for a brief account of his proposed terms for ascribing narrational force to cinema's montage and photo-

graphic shots, respectively. Another challenge to the standard distinction between mimetic and narrative arts is raised in Seymour Chatman, *Coming to Terms: The Rhetoric of Narrative in Fiction and Film* (Ithaca, N.Y., 1990), pp. 109ff. For Chatman, enacted works like plays and films constitute one kind of narrative, "in the broad sense," because they convey stories; the other kind is recounted stories (" 'narrative' in the narrow sense"). But the criterion that groups enacted and narrated works, their story content, is soon replaced by another: epics and dramas "both present a chronology of events different from the chronology of the discourse. This double chronology is the fundamental property that distinguishes" narrative (p. 110). The very notion of dramatic enactment involves, however, a conflation of story time and discourse time: the story is not told at a remove in time and place but directly performed. Departures from story chronology in dramatic presentation are, of course, possible but require an admixture of narration for clarity (Shakespeare's "Chorus," Brecht's "Story Teller," etc.). Cinema has, to be sure, developed a code for signaling flashbacks without verbal narration, frequently associating them with images of a character remembering, but the resulting double chronology remains an option rather than a defining condition of cinema. Many if not most films with complex chronology are narrated films, as we shall see, and cinema's recourse to narration for such purposes indicates that, like drama, its ordinary discourse matches story time.

4. Baudry, *L'effet cinéma* (Paris, 1978), and Metz, *Le signifiant imaginaire* (Paris, 1976); both partially translated in *Narrative, Apparatus, Ideology: A Film Theory Reader*, ed. Philip Rosen (New York, 1986), pp. 286–318 and 244–78.

5. Two recent critiques of related trends are Noël Carroll, *Mystifying Movies: Fads and Fallacies in Contemporary Film Theory* (New York, 1988), and David Bordwell, *Making Meaning: Inference and Rhetoric in the Interpretation of Cinema* (Cambridge, Mass., 1989)—both confirming the impulse for the present study.

6. Seymour Chatman, *Story and Discourse: Narrative Structure in Fiction and Film* (Ithaca, N.Y., 1978), p. 151; to explain his notation, Chatman adds, "The box indicates that only the implied author and implied reader are immanent to a narrative, [while] the narrator and narratee are optional (parentheses)." These indications have been significantly modified in Chatman's *Coming to Terms*, p. 151, and will be discussed below. Other terms in the model will not be fully discussed. For the "narratee," see Gerald Prince, *Narratology: The Form and Function of Narrative* (Berlin, 1982), chap. 1; despite efforts to generalize it beyond literature, the concept is more applicable to the audience of the character narrators than to that of the "main" narrator of films. The "implied

reader," a construct designed to match the hypothetical construction of an "implied author" from all the resources of the text, is treated phenomenologically in Wolfgang Iser, *The Implied Reader: Patterns of Communication in Prose Fiction from Bunyan to Beckett* (Baltimore, 1974).

7. For the filmmaker's visible presence as a sign of his enunciating the film, see Raymond Bellour, "Enoncer," in *L'analyse du film* (Paris, 1979), pp. 271–91 (published in translation as "Hitchcock the Enunciator"). For the character-surrogates of the filmmaker, see George M. Wilson, *Narration in Light: Studies in Cinematic Point of View* (Baltimore, 1986), pp. 152ff.; but Wilson acknowledges that "it would be harmless but misleading . . . to call the focalizing character the visual narrator of the film or film segment" (p. 133).

8. Sarah Kozloff, *Invisible Storytellers: Voice-over Narration in American Fiction Film* (Berkeley, 1988), pp. 43ff., usefully lists a number of the terms that have been used to answer her question, Who really narrates?; they include, besides "grand image-maker" and "camera," "implied author," "implied director," and "implied narrator." Although Kozloff rejects these terms, settling for the diminished "image-maker," the frequency of answers couched in a source *implied* by the film discourse indicates that her question should read, Who implicitly narrates?

9. *The Rhetoric of Fiction* (Chicago, 1961), pp. 70ff. Wilson, *Narration in Light*, pp. 126ff., refreshingly clears the air of a number of "filmic narrator" theories, concluding that while the "implied filmmaker" may be employed on the model of the implied author, "to place either of these constructs in a narrator's position is to sow misunderstanding all along the line. . . . There are no grounds for recognizing in narrative film a being, personlike or not, who fictionally offers our view of narrative events to us" (p. 135).

10. Nick Browne, *The Rhetoric of Filmic Narration* (Ann Arbor, Mich., n.d.), p. 1; further quotations are from pp. 11 and 15. For an elaborate coding of point-of-view shots that attempts to avoid tying their subjectivity to the figure of a narrator, see Edward R. Branigan, *Point of View in the Cinema: A Theory of Narration and Subjectivity in Classical Film* (Berlin, 1984)̂. Despite Branigan's awareness that in such contexts "the term 'narrator' is a metaphor, an anthropomorphism" (p. 40), he relents: "What is needed is a term to replace 'narrator' which has no realist overtones (an activity without an actor). . . . In the absence of such a new term, we shall employ the old terms to speak of narration" (p. 48).

11. The ground-breaking work in this area is Noël Burch, *Theory of Film Practice*, trans. H. R. Lane (Princeton, 1981 [1969]). David Bordwell, Janet Staiger, and Kristin Thompson have studied the historical

emergence of film codes in *The Classical Hollywood Cinema: Film Style and Mode of Production to 1960* (New York, 1985). The most useful set of categories for assessing film images is the "micro-circuits" in Jacques Aumont et al., *L'esthétique du film* (Paris, 1983), pp. 193ff. Here Alain Bergala (who has served as editor of *Cahiers du cinéma*), lists eight elements of shot-change, seven elements of shots themselves, and a number of additional qualities related to point of view—all of them operating to communicate story information as well as to affect spectatorial identification. See also Bergala's *Initiation à la sémiologie du récit en images* (Paris, n.d.).

12. See, for example, Jean-Paul Simon, "Enonciation et narration," *Communications*, no. 38 (1983), pp. 155–91. The most ingenious system is François Jost, *L'oeil-caméra: Entre film et roman* (Lyon, 1989 [1987]), where Genette's *"focalisation"* is supplemented by *"ocularisation"* and even *"auricularisation"* in order to treat the modalities of the cinematic text as stemming from a hypothetical speaker. Nor is this account content to refer to the speaker as enunciator; it is impelled to treat it as a narrator, identifying the *grand imagier* in his storytelling role as the *"narrateur implicite"* (p. 39). Perhaps the sagest comment in recent French discussion is Jacques Aumont's: "La difficulté est évidemment qu'il est impossible d'assigner aucun *lieu*, dans le discours filmique, aux processus narratifs. . . . Les meilleurs travaux sur le récit filmique ne peuvent—voir le livre de Vanoye [cited below, n. 18]—que viser le récit *dans* le film, et jamais vraiment le film (tout le film) comme récit" ("Le point de vue," *Communications*, no. 38 [1983], p. 20).

13. David Bordwell, *Narration in the Fiction Film* (Madison, Wis., 1985), pp. 21–26, discusses the enunciation approach and concludes, "Because a film lacks equivalents for the most basic aspects of verbal activity, I suggest that we abandon the enunciation account. We need a theory of narration that is not bound to vague or atomistic analogies among representational systems." Bordwell's own theory of narration avoids such analogies by eliminating the excess baggage of a general narrator: "Narration is better understood as the organization of a set of cues for the construction of a story. This presupposes a perceiver, but not any sender, of a message" (p. 62). As formal analysis of discourse cues for story construction, Bordwell's restricted theory of narration succeeds admirably and will be cited frequently below. Yet "narration" without a narrator must be recognized as still another vague analogy, for there is no "producing narrative action" (to employ Genette's definition of narration) that delivers the discourse. Bordwell acknowledges that for him "it would of course be possible to treat narration solely as a matter of syuzhet/fabula relations" (p. 53), although he reserves a role for "style" or non-story-cueing features of discourse.

Notes to Page 10

Reducing "narration" to relations between story and discourse, even with the admixture of a perceiver and of style, empties the term of the idea of productive activity (whose?), not to mention motivated communication between a sender and receiver.

If Bordwell's account is of narration without a narrator, Seymour Chatman's is that of a narrator without discernible acts of narrating. He has developed the concept of a "cinematic narrator" to fill out the requirement that narratives (as he takes films to be) must have a narrator. The concept is thus a scrupulously impersonal one: the agent of showing the film (not necessarily a person) is the *"presenter* of the story, . . . who is a component of the discourse" (*Coming to Terms*, p. 133). But this presenter is contained within the discourse rather than in a situation of producing that discourse, that is, within the film rather than at a distinct diegetic level (to use Genette's terms again). This collapse of the narrator into its means of narrating is, indeed, acknowledged: "The cinematic narrator is the *composite* [italics added] of a large and complex variety of communicating devices" (p. 134). The suspicion is raised that this is no functional agent who or which narrates but only a formal fiction, a name without content. The motive for thus multiplying entities is frankly stated: "In the narrower, traditional sense, Narrative . . . must be *told* by a human narrator. This more restricted definition obviously provides a narrower base for narratology" (p. 114–15). I believe that the narrators who perceptibly function within plays and films provide ample and worthy subjects for narratology's attention, without an appropriation of adjacent territories that requires staffing by ghostly abstractions.

14. Exceptions to this general neglect are found in Pascal Bonitzer, *Le regard et la voix* (Paris, 1976); the section in which the distinction is made appears in the Rosen collection *Narrative, Apparatus, Ideology*, pp. 322–23; also cf. Jacques Aumont, "Off-cadre, en lecteur étranger," *Hors cadre*, no. 3 (1985), p. 183n. A similar muddle and exceptions to it exist in America, for example, *Yale French Studies*, no. 60 (1980), where Mary Ann Doane's essay observes the distinction, while Daniel Percheron's seriously confuses it. The issue is pursued in chapter 4.

15. The significant exception to the situation described above is Kozloff's *Invisible Storytellers*, pp. 42ff., which introduces an ample terminology to deal with the variety of voice-overs. Based on Genette's system, to which I shall myself apply below, Kozloff's arrangement permits clear distinctions between character and noncharacter narrators ("homodiegetic" and "heterodiegetic," respectively) and refines Genette's distinction between framing and embedded narrators in useful ways (adding localized "micro-narrators" on p. 49). But when the issues entailed exceed the borders of voice-over, the discussion lapses into

speculations on implied image-makers (see n. 8). This would have been the place to follow up the distinction between framing and embedded situations so as to distinguish voice-overs from, and relate them to, on-screen storytelling (as I shall attempt to do when describing what may be called "dramatized narration").

16. Another caution: An intense debate on the necessity or even desirability of narrative in films has been conducted, mainly by experimental filmmakers and their proponents. It will be seen that my historical and descriptive accounts of narrated films are nothing to the purpose on either side of the debate.

17. Although urging a return to seeing nondiegetic media, including cinema, as non-narrated, I am in accord with Genette and others that all literary fiction (epic, novel, even epistolary novel) *is* narrated. So-called non-narrated tales (certain short stories by Hemingway are invariably cited) are merely effects of reduced signs of the narrator, extensive use of direct-discourse quotations, and other stylistic manipulations.

18. *Narrative Discourse*, trans. Jane E. Lewin (Oxford, 1980), pp. 227ff. Genette's concept of focalization ("Qui voit?") has been applied to film study in Francis Vanoye, *Récit écrit/récit filmique* (Paris, 1979), pp. 147ff., while distinguishing it from narration ("Qui parle?"). See also Brian Henderson, "Tense, Mood, and Voice in Film (Notes after Genette)," *Film Quarterly* 36, no. 4 (1983), pp. 4–17. The dangers of excessive devotion to the model are illustrated in the Simon article cited in note 12.

19. *Story and Situation: Narrative Seduction and the Power of Fiction* (Minneapolis, 1984), pp. 4–5.

20. Jerzy Pelc, "On the Concept of Narration," *Semiotica* 3 (1971): 12; the entire article is salutary in draining this theoretical bog. The importance of metaphors to discussion in this field has been sketched in Dudley Andrew, *Concepts in Film Theory* (Oxford, 1984), pp. 8, 12–13; although receptive to the discovery of the root metaphors (framed image, window, and mirror) that animate various theoreticians, I am less sanguine than Andrew about the progressive tendencies of the process of metaphor modeling and its subsequent critique.

21. Genette, *Narrative Discourse*, p. 27.

22. "What Novels Can Do That Films Can't (and Vice Versa)," in *On Narrative*, ed. W. J. T. Mitchell (Chicago, 1981), p. 124. "Depiction" has been modified in Chatman's *Coming to Terms* to "*tacit* Description" (pp. 38f.).

23. I use the word "perspective" in preference to the term more familiar in film studies, "point of view," and likewise to the narratological term "focalization" that has increasingly come under requisition.

The fate of literary notions of "point of view" in a predominantly visual medium like cinema has not been a happy one, and even Chatman's expanded concept of its possibilities—"filter," "center," and "slant" to cover the perceptual, character-interested, and ideological senses of "point of view"—cannot dispel the overriding sense of visual positioning as determinant, as in the widely used phrase "point-of-view shot."

24. With all the enthusiasm accorded Brecht's dramatic theory as inspirational for revolutionary cinema—see, for example, Colin Mc-Cabe, *Tracking the Signifier: Theoretical Essays* (Minneapolis, 1985), esp. "Realism and the Cinema: Notes on Some Brechtian Theses"—there has been a curious inattention to the frequent narrational declamations of "epic theater," perhaps Brecht's most decisive theatrical development. The importance of on-stage storytelling in modern drama has come under recent scrutiny, as in Kristin Morrison, *Canters and Chronicles: The Use of Narrative in the Plays of Samuel Beckett and Harold Pinter* (Chicago, 1983).

Chapter 1
Storytelling Situations: Working Definitions

1. The function of narration in signaling time shifts is touched on in Maureen Turim, *Flashbacks in Film: Memory and History* (New York, 1989); unfortunately, its excellent account of visual techniques for rendering subjective transitions is not matched by analysis of verbal techniques.

2. "Fiction" connotes, of course, feigning as well as making, and vigorous debate has been waged over the place of truth and imagination in various narrative forms, including historiography and autobiography. I have participated in this debate in *Figures of Autobiography: The Language of Self-Writing in Victorian and Modern England* (Berkeley, 1983); I avoid it here because fictiveness is not decisive to the narrational modes under review.

3. The opposite proportion probably holds true in the silent era, since most silents were narrated in some degree by means of intertitles (see the homely statistics in chap. 2, n. 3, and discussion of some exceptions in chap. 2, nn. 11–12). Given this near uniformity, I have omitted silent films in offering numerical generalizations about narrated films.

4. As with every abstraction, particularly visual displays, the accompanying diagram can reveal only a selection from the potential theoretical options. Under "written" narration, for example, one might place a number of other genres: the existence of a fiction-writing pro-

gram in *Waxworks* (to be discussed in chap. 2) suggests that this is another potential mode. At a lower level of differentiation, there are opportunities to subdivide internal voice-over into autobiography, "reflector" or observer report, and the cinematic equivalent of *skaz* or vernacular sketch—as in Terrence Malick's *Badlands* or *Days of Heaven*.

5. Since a distinction between external and internal narratees would be often found asymmetrical with respect to their narrators, the terms "audience" and "auditor" better highlight their position and function in cinematic situations.

6. The distinctions among author, narrator, and "author"-narrator have been effectively developed by narratologists for literature: "As Monroe Beardsley argues, 'the speaker of a literary work cannot be identified with the author . . . unless the author has provided a pragmatic context, or a claim of one, that connects the speaker with himself.' But even in such a context, the speaker is not the author, but the 'author' (quotation marks of 'as if'), or better the 'author'-narrator, one of several possible kinds" (Seymour Chatman, *Story and Discourse: Narrative Structure in Fiction and Film* [Ithaca, N.Y., 1978], pp. 147–48). In films, the filmmaker's appearance on-screen or the more ambiguous evidence of the soundtrack provides the "pragmatic context" identifying him with (as) the narrator; I am calling this, the cinematic equivalent of the " 'author'-narrator," personal narration.

7. Some of the announcers or other professionals recruited for the task may be recognizable in documentaries and pseudo-documentaries—even declaring, for example, "This is Walter Cronkite. . . ." There is an elaborate professional code for voice-over narrators, including their control of personal traits, purveyed in handbooks like *Word of Mouth: A Guide to Commercial Voice-over Excellence*.

8. With both these films appearing in 1959, the influence of the rising television medium may be suspected (although Cocteau had previously used many other forms of authorial presence; see chap. 4). Renoir made this film (and the later *Little Theater of Jean Renoir*, where he also appears) for television and is shown here before the cameras in a broadcasting studio. Television's codes for producing the impression of intimate contact have undoubtedly encouraged filmmakers to make on-screen appearances: Fellini began operations in this vein with *A Director's Notebook* (1969), produced for television. Hitchcock too, in *The Wrong Man* (1957), was encouraged by his host performances in the medium to go beyond his fleeting movie appearances.

9. Its prevalence in Allen's films far outstrips its basis in his double duties as filmmaker and actor, and goes beyond his debts to the traditions of comic theater. Its cultural context is the frequent crossing of

narrative levels in postmodernist fiction; Allen's short stories employ similar techniques.

10. The mode's ambiguities call for further inquiry; a start has been made in Marc Vernet, "Le regard à la caméra: Figures de l'absence," *Iris* 1, no. 2 (1983), pp. 31–45; translation in *Cinema Journal* 28, no. 2 (1989), pp. 48–63. My own terms, "on-screen" for external narrators and "direct/on-screen" for internal, attempt to avoid the excessively literal "look at the camera." What is decisive is the narratee; even when a narrator is filmed frontally, he or she may be addressing another character, as in Danny DeVito's *The War of the Roses*.

11. Internal narrators occasionally speak neither to the audience nor to another character—nor, as in the mindscreen narration to be described below, to themselves—but to a recording apparatus. In Wilder's *Double Indemnity* the tape-recording process is a dramatized narration, its last part overheard by the intended narratee. In *The Testament of Dr. Cordelier*, the tape is not seen being made but is listened to by others after the protagonist's death; a classic instance of the *acousmêtre* discussed in chapter 4, it may also be compared with letter narrations as a form of communication with other characters through a material medium. In a similar procedure, a character employs movie equipment in Nagisa Oshima's *The Story of a Man Who Left His Will on Film* (as described in Edward R. Branigan, *Point of View in the Cinema: A Theory of Narration and Subjectivity in Classical Film* [Berlin, 1984], pp. 147ff.). And a character videotapes her narration in Patricia Rozema's *I've Heard the Mermaids Singing*.

12. This term follows the prevailing usage for the comparable storytelling situation in literature, where relative scale and position distinguish a briefly described encounter (frame story), where an extended narrative is told, from a main action in which briefer tales are interpolated. I adopt it for films with misgivings, for like other well-worn terms it may be metaphorically overburdened and ultimately confusing. Some of the difficulties have been set out in Linda Dittmar, "Fashioning and Re-fashioning: Framing Narratives in the Novel and Film," *Mosaic* 16 (1983): 189–203; for example, "It is hard to call the enclosing plots of *Hiroshima [Mon Amour]* and [John Hawkes's novel] *The Cannibal* 'frame stories' if by that we mean an auxiliary component of narration—a vestibule where we hang a coat or leave an umbrella before entering the main hall. In these works the frame is the main story" (p. 197). Beyond suggesting that "frame" and "main" are like the Gestalt psychologists' figure and ground, where perceivers shift awareness of their mutual relation under differing conditions, this and other analyses have not settled the issue.

13. Since climactic narration occurs in the course of the ongoing action, in a series of storytelling scenes, it can fulfill only gradually the

narration-code function of inducing a sense that the film is a narrated one. As we shall see in discussing *Hiroshima Mon Amour*, the series may gradually fill in a past story (the heroine's autobiography) while cumulatively developing the status of a sustained (though interrupted) narrational action.

14. Even the canonical examples indicate that these categories do not exclude the presence of the alternative modes: as we shall see in chapter 6, the fourth narrator of *Rashomon* extends the triply told tale in a serial manner; and paired narrators in *Kane* iteratively review certain segments of the story, both Kane's entry into journalism and Susan's opera debut.

15. A rare instance of an anthology film with anthology narration is *Dead of Night*, in which several narrators tell supernatural tales in the four directors' five episodes.

16. Intertitles are discussed briefly in the following chapter, for the subject is best approached in a historical context. I omit full exemplification of impersonal and pseudo-documentary voice-over, as they have been well described in studies mentioned in chapter 4. On-screen narration, both external and internal, is omitted for the admittedly selfish reason that I plan to pursue it in a subsequent book or articles. And I omit anthology narration because its most interesting varieties occur in films (mentioned above) that are difficult to obtain for study and not widely known.

Chapter 2
From Silence to Sound: Texts and Voices

1. Among the numerous histories that discuss the Lumière exhibitions, though without reference to their oral announcements, are David Robinson, *The History of World Cinema* (New York, 1973), and David A. Cook, *A History of Narrative Film* (New York, 1981).

2. Georges Sadoul, *Histoire de l'art du cinéma* (Paris, 1949), mentions an actual person placed behind the screen who delivered his own lines during the screening of an interview filmed in 1895—"premier et naïf essai du cinéma parlant" (p. 22).

3. The only statistical data I have seen is to be found in a contemporary journalistic piece by E. W. Sargent in *The Moving Picture World* (10 Aug. 1912), rpt. in George C. Pratt, *Spellbound in Darkness: Readings in the History and Criticism of the Silent Film* (Rochester, N.Y., 1966), pp. 92–93. Of the twenty-six short films whose scenes, verbal "leaders," and other inserts were counted by a Reverend Dr. Stockton, only one was without intertitles. Sargent's watchword: "Write only enough leader to cover the unexplained points."

4. The use of the *benshi* persisted into the sound era, if we are to accept the evidence offered by Yoji Yamada's *Final Take* (1986). In this fiction film about the Japanese cinema industry of the 1930s, a scene at a movie house shows such a narrator enthusiastically at work.

5. *To the Distant Observer: Form and Meaning in the Japanese Cinema* (Berkeley, 1979), pp. 75ff.; the quotation below is from p. 77.

6. Recent studies of Griffith have improved our knowledge of his practices, but scant attention has been paid the intertitles; see William M. Drew, *D. W. Griffith's Intolerance: Its Genesis and Its Vision* (Jefferson, N.C., 1986), and Joyce E. Jesionowski, *Thinking in Pictures: Dramatic Structure in D. W. Griffith's Biograph Films* (Berkeley, 1987).

7. Credit for the intertitles has been accorded to Anita Loos in David Bordwell, Janet Staiger, and Kristin Thompson, *The Classical Hollywood Cinema: Film Style and Mode of Production to 1960* (New York, 1985), p. 186b, but it is not clear how far her responsibility extends (many directors used their writers as adjuncts). The discussion of intertitles on pp. 183–89 is among the few to address the subject astutely; shifting trends are described on p. 186a, where Loos is associated with the "cleverly written" variety (featuring arch remarks on characters and action).

8. In the absence of a published scenario, I quote the film directly; I have not yet seen the restoration shown at the New York Film Festival in 1989.

9. On the "author"-narrator, see Seymour Chatman, *Story and Discourse: Narrative Structure in Fiction and Film* (Ithaca, N.Y., 1978), pp. 147–48, and my discussion on p. 23 above.

10. A balanced account of these intertitles is Pascal Mérigeau, *Josef von Sternberg* (Paris, 1983), p. 42: "Sans faire réellement pléonasme, ils alourdissent le récit et accusent les prétentions 'littéraires' de Sternberg." His later films employed specialist writers for the intertitles; by the time he directed *The Docks of New York* (1928), the intertitles were sharply reduced in number and extent.

11. While these films are well known for their distinctive (near-)wordlessness, I know of no discussion of their common project; Kirsanoff has been especially neglected. Carl Mayer, scenarist of *The Last Laugh*, had previously written two nearly titleless films: *The Rail* (a.k.a. *Shattered*: 1921) and *Sylvester* (a.k.a. *New Year's Eve*: 1923).

12. The lone intertitle makes a facetious statement to the effect that while in real life the protagonist would not stand a chance, the filmmakers will take pity on him. There follows the universally derided happy ending; see Lotte H. Eisner, *Murnau*, no trans. (Berkeley, 1973 [1964]), p. 158.

13. Brief attention to Ramsaye's intertitles is given in Peter Morris's

additional notes to his translation of Georges Sadoul, *Dictionary of Films* (Berkeley, 1972 [1965]), p. 136.

14. See Charles Ford, *Jacques Feyder* (Paris, 1973), pp. 46f.

15. The film's narration is variously described in Jean Béranger, *La grande aventure du cinéma suédois* (Paris, 1960), pp. 52ff.; Peter Cowie, *Swedish Cinema* (New York, 1966), pp. 24ff.; and Sandra Beck, in *The International Dictionary of Films and Filmmakers*, ed. Christopher Lyon (New York, 1985 [1984]), "Films" volume, pp. 243f.

16. Another Sjöström film, *The Kiss of Death* (1916), may be deemed a progenitor of multiple dramatized narration; according to Sadoul's *Dictionary of Films*, "It is significant in film history—mainly for a thematic development in which an event is described, through flashbacks, by various witnesses who have different or opposing points of view" (entry under *Dodskyssen*, the Swedish title). I have not seen this (medium-length) film.

17. Georges Sadoul, *Dictionnaire des films*, ed. Emile Breton (Paris, 1981), p. 272. The film is also discussed in Siegfried Kracauer, *Theory of Film: The Redemption of Physical Reality* (London, 1965 [1960]), p. 236, where a characteristic confusion between narrating and "point of view" (focalizing) leads to a muddying of the waters on novelistic narration. See also Bettina Knapp, *Sacha Guitry* (Boston, 1981), pp. 117ff.

18. Another putative genre, the "woman's film," displayed an awareness of the new narrational techniques. While Michael Curtiz's *Mildred Pierce* (1945) is partially narrated on the model of a criminal investigation, using dramatized storytelling and voice-over, another example of the type, George Cukor's *A Woman's Face* (1941), employs the *film noir* format (though with fewer of its other trappings) in a courtroom drama of multiple dramatized narration. A more intimate form of storytelling for a woman's film is, however, the mindscreen narration of Sam Wood's *Kitty Foyle* (1940; the year of Wood's imaginative transfer of the narrated play *Our Town* to the screen). Similarly introspective storytelling occurs in George Stevens's *I Remember Mama* (1948), this time in the form of written narration, the heroine reading aloud her reminiscental fiction.

19. Sara Kozloff, *Invisible Storytellers: Voice-over Narration in American Fiction Film* (Berkeley, 1988), pp. 28, 29.

20. The cinematic transmutation of Welles's theatrical and broadcasting experience is recounted in Barbara Leaming, *Orson Welles: A Biography* (New York, 1985), esp. pp. 173ff.

21. Despite its centrality in this, as in other aspects of cinema history, *Kane* was not the first multiple dramatized narration. A strong claim to initiate the mode can be made by Max Ophuls's *Tender Enemy* (1936), in which the narrators are the ghosts of a woman's husband

and lover. Shown in superimposition among the chandeliers at her daughter's wedding party, they reminisce about their relationships with her, which are then enacted. Later, they are joined by another of her lovers, who changes the atmosphere by recounting her rejection of him and his subsequent suicide. Beyond acknowledging Ophuls's later techniques of narration—the impresario commentaries of *La Ronde* (1950) and *Lola Montes* (1955) and the complex reading-writing narration of *Letter from an Unknown Woman*—we should recall this prewar film as one of his most searching exercises in storytelling.

22. Bordwell, Staiger, and Thompson, *Classical Hollywood Cinema*, pp. 74–77, questions the status of *film noir* as a genre, much less a "nonconformist" one. The best discussion of these films' narration is J. P. Telotte, *Voices in the Dark: The Narrative Patterns of Film Noir* (Urbana, Ill., 1989).

23. A valuable effort to dispel critical resistance to unreliable narration in films is Kristin Thompson, *Breaking the Glass Armor: Neoformalist Film Analysis* (Princeton, 1988), chap. 5, "Duplicitous Narration and Stage Fright." Thompson discusses ambiguities in *Laura*'s narrational system in chap. 6.

24. There is even a *film noir* exercise in direct, on-screen narration: John Berry's *Tension* (1949), in which a detective addresses the audience to explain his favorite interrogating techniques, those that generate tension in his suspects.

25. Along with de Rochemont, Mark Hellinger may be considered an "onlie begetter" of pseudo-documentary narrational style; his story input into Raoul Walsh and Anatole Litvak's *The Roaring Twenties* (1939) may well have contributed to the film's early use of the documentary voice-over. Hellinger was influential in Jules Dassin's *The Naked City* (1948) as producer, voice-over narrator, and implicit role model—the hard-boiled former crime reporter who declares, "There are eight million stories in the naked city: this has been one of them."

26. An earlier autobiographical film that may have paved the way for the upsurge in the 1950s is John Ford's *How Green Was My Valley* (1941)—thoroughly described in Kozloff, *Invisible Storytellers*, pp. 53–62. See also her discussion of *All about Eve*, pp. 62–71.

27. A later Soviet development of this use of a writerly persona is Andrey Tarkovsky's *Mirror* (1974), in which a voice-over reading of poems by the filmmaker's father counterpoints the internal, autobiographical narration by the dying protagonist.

28. The practice was not invented in the 1950s; as early as 1939, William S. Hart re-released his 1925 film *Tumbleweeds* with an eight-minute introduction in which, dressed in characteristic cowboy garb, he sentimentalizes about the passing of the old West and the old, naive Western.

29. Tashlin was original, if nothing else, in his narrational strategies: *The First Time* (1952) is narrated by a character before birth, while *Susan Slept Here* (1954) is narrated by an object—an Academy Award Oscar!

30. An indication that narrational inventiveness, like many a postmodernist novelty, can quickly turn into cliché is the appearance in the same year (1986) of three internal on-screen narrations: Spike Lee's *She's Gotta Have It*, John Hughes's *Ferris Buehler's Day Off*, and Gene Saks's *Brighton Beach Memoirs*. My mention of *Omar Gatlato* is frankly intended to make better known an enormously appealing use of the mode.

Chapter 3
New Wave; Art Cinema; How It Is

1. On the interminglings of these two currents, see Bruce Morrissette, *Novel and Film: Essays in Two Genres* (Chicago, 1985). A useful collection of writings by some of the early participants is Peter Graham, ed., *The New Wave: Critical Landmarks* (Garden City, N.Y., 1968).

2. The distinction is summarized in Erik Barnouw, *Documentary: A History of the Non-fiction Film* (Oxford, 1983 [1974]), pp. 254ff. See also the reflections of the founder in Mick Eaton, ed., *Anthropology—Reality—Cinema: The Films of Jean Rouch* (London, 1979).

3. Another way of treating on-screen narrations by men-and-women-on-the-street was that of Chris Marker's *Le Joli Mai* ("The Lovely Month of May": 1962), which embedded them in voice-over commentaries expressing the political ideology of the filmmakers.

4. Perhaps the best brief discussion of Godard's theory and practice is found in two essays by Brian Henderson, in *A Critique of Film Theory* (New York, 1980). For an early sign of awareness that his films are distinctive in their narration, see Susan Sontag's review of *My Life to Live*, in *Jean-Luc Godard*, ed. Toby Mussman (New York, 1968), pp. 91–93.

5. *Alphaville: A Film by Jean-Luc Godard*, trans. Peter Whitehead (London, 1984 [1972]), p. 19; subsequent citations in text.

6. *Pierrot le Fou: A Film, English Translation and Description of Action*, ed. Peter Whitehead (New York, 1969), p. 52; subsequent citations in text.

7. The technique is more fully described and interpreted in Alfred Guzzetti, *Two or Three Things I Know about Her: Analysis of a Film by Godard* (Cambridge, Mass., 1981), pp. 25ff. See also the condensed but challenging discussion of the narrational status of Godard's performances as voice-over in his films (p. 357). The quotation of the scenario below is from pp. 24–30; subsequent citations in text.

8. The most illuminating statements on this phase are those of the filmmaker himself, in interviews collected in Colin McCabe, *Godard: Images, Sounds, Politics* (Bloomington, Ind., 1980). See also James Monaco, *The New Wave: Truffaut, Godard, Chabrol, Rohmer, Rivette* (New York, 1976), chap. 10, for descriptions of these hard-to-see films.

9. Robbe-Grillet's own films are a series of variations on the theme of unreliable narration; his cinema career is studied in André Gardies, *Alain Robbe-Grillet* (Paris, 1971), and in subsequent publications by Gardies.

10. Robbe-Grillet's position on the cinematic present tense is stated in the introduction to his scenario, *Last Year at Marienbad*, trans. Richard Howard (New York, 1962), pp. 12f.; it is developed in the essays collected in *For a New Novel: Essays on Fiction*, trans. Richard Howard (New York, 1965 [1963]). On this extraordinary film as an illustration of a general rule, the following remark seems decisive: "*Marienbad* takes as its starting-point Robbe-Grillet's assertion that film can only speak in one tense and then demonstrates what a film narrative limited to one tense would be like": Joan Dagle, "Narrative Discourse in Film and Fiction: The Question of the Present Tense," in *Narrative Strategies*, ed. S. M. Conger and J. R. Welsch (n.p., 1980), p. 58.

11. See Claude Bailblé, Michel Marie, and Marie-Claire Ropars-Wuilleumier, *Muriel: Histoire d'une recherche* (Paris, 1975); and David Bordwell, *Narration in the Fiction Film* (Madison, Wis., 1985), pp. 213–18, on *The War Is Over*.

12. This aspect of the film is well described in Freddy Sweet, *The Film Narratives of Alain Resnais* (Ann Arbor, Mich., 1981), pp. 87f. and 96f.

13. Resnais's later efforts include narration-as-lecture by an on-screen biologist in *Mon Oncle d'Amérique* (1978) and a collective effort to recount a seminal event in *La Vie Est un Roman* (1983).

14. Another New Wave specialist in a particular storytelling situation is Eric Rohmer, whose specialty is dramatized narration, usually climactic. His exercises in the dramatic interactions of characters engaged in storytelling and story receiving include *My Night at Maud's* (1969), *Claire's Knee* (1970), *Chloe in the Afternoon* (1972), *The Aviator's Wife* (1980), and *Summer* (1986).

15. The fullest account of the narration in this and other films mentioned below is Annette Insdorf, *François Truffaut* (Boston, 1978).

16. The elements of "art cinema" as a coded system, including its narrational code, are set out in Bordwell, *Narration in the Fiction Film*, chap. 10.

17. Another art cinema figure heavily engaged in narration was Pier Paolo Pasolini, whose anthology-like collections of tales (*The De-*

cameron, The Canterbury Tales, and *A Thousand and One Nights*) show less storytelling than do *Notes for an African Oresteia* (1969), *Pigsty* (1969), and *Salo—The 120 Days of Sodom* (1975). An equally wide range of narrational modes is exhibited in Jean-Marie Straub and Danièle Huillet's films, including the multiple dramatized narration of *Not Reconciled* (1965), the external voice-over delivering written texts in *Chronicle of Anna Magdalena Bach* (1968), and the on-camera readings by a novelist from his work in *Fortini/Cani* ("The Dogs of Sinai": 1976).

18. These and other early Bergmans with narrational elements are described in Jörn Donner, *The Films of Ingmar Bergman,* trans. Holger Lundbergh (New York, 1972 [1962]); also see Vernon Young, *Cinema Borealis: Ingmar Bergman and the Swedish Ethos* (New York, 1971).

19. For a closer analysis of this film, see Paisley Livingston, *Ingmar Bergman and the Rituals of Art* (Ithaca, N.Y., 1982), pp. 230ff.

20. Bergman's later narrated films do not come up to these achievements of the 1960s. Another experiment in direct, on-screen commentary in this period is *A Passion* (1969), in which the actors are interviewed about their interpretation of the characters. A number of narrational modes are deployed in *Autumn Sonata* (1978)—internal on-screen addresses and multiple-iterative versions of a mother's and daughter's traumatic past—but no unexpected insights emerge from their apposition. Nor do the *film noir*–like police interviews of *From the Life of the Marionettes* (1980) provide great penetration of a murderer's psychic depths.

21. The film is well studied in Robert P. Kolker, *Bernardo Bertolucci* (New York, 1985), pp. 17–18.

22. For the structure of storytelling here, see Bordwell, *Narration in the Fiction Film,* pp. 88–98.

23. Another stimulus toward personal narration was the filmmaker's on-screen account of his approach in the made-for-television documentary, *Fellini: A Director's Notebook* (1969).

24. The definitive study of the voice-overs of *India Song* as they relate to the texts of other Duras films, and to textuality itself, is Marie-Claire Ropars-Wuilleumier, *Le texte divisé: Essai sur l'écriture filmique* (Paris, 1981).

25. On this tendency, see Gilles Deleuze, *Cinema 2: Time Image,* trans. Hugh Tomlin and Robert Galeta (London, 1989 [1985]), chap. 8.

26. The authoritarian aspects of Kluge's narrational interventions have not escaped censure: see Thomas Elsaesser, *New German Cinema: A History* (New Brunswick, N.J., 1989), p. 136; this work supersedes previous studies of the school.

27. The technique has been termed "glideback" in Seymour Chatman, *Antonioni: or, The Surface of the World* (Berkeley, 1985), pp. 194f.

28. I shall develop the theoretical relationships of asides in relation to soliloquies and interior monologues in chapter 8.

29. The term is used for "omniscient" narration of psychological processes in Dorrit Cohn, *Transparent Minds: Narrative Modes for Presenting Consciousness in Fiction* (Princeton, 1978).

Chapter 4
Voice-over Narration: *Orpheus* and *Sunset Boulevard*

1. An alternative arrangement of the types of voice-over distinguishes "voice-off" ("the voice of a character who is not visible within the frame"), "voiceover during a flashback" ("a temporal dislocation of the voice with respect to the body"), "interior monologue" ("the voice and the body are represented simultaneously"), and "voiceover commentary" ("a *disembodied* voice"): Mary Ann Doane, "The Voice in the Cinema: The Articulation of Body and Space," *Yale French Studies*, no. 60 (1980), pp. 33–50. Doane's interest in the phenomenology of body and voice diverges from my own, but it bears on the issues of presence and absence discussed below. Another fruitful essay is Marc Vernet, "Figures de l'absence 2: La voix off," *Iris* 3 (1985): 47–56, which describes examples of the types mentioned below, but lacks a framework in which to call them anything but "voice-off."

2. See Michel Chion, *La voix au cinéma* (Paris, 1982), pp. 25ff. This useful neologism for the heard-but-not-seen character derives from the obsolete word *acousmatique* (whose English cognate bears another meaning); its further variation to *acousmère*, for the ventriloquistically presented Mrs. Bates in Hitchcock's *Psycho*, is perhaps excessive.

3. My contrasting of "external" and "internal" voice-overs is designed to avoid the terminological quandary discussed in Sarah Kozloff, *Invisible Storytellers: Voice-over Narration in American Fiction Film* (Berkeley, 1988), p. 6, where the objections to both "third-person/first-person" and Genette's terms "heterodiegetic/homodiegetic" are indicated. Much of the present chapter on voice-over was written before Kozloff's book appeared, and while I have taken account of her argument in the course of revision, the two remain independent treatments.

4. The received idea of external voice-over—one may consider it the official position in certain theoretical quarters—is succinctly expressed by Pascal Bonitzer (while employing, as do many of his compatriots, the term "voice-off"): "Voice off: the voice of his master. And there can be only one master. This is why, generally in this system, there is only one commentating voice on the sound track (and most of the time it is a man's voice)" (*Le regard et la voix* [Paris, 1976], excerpted in *Narrative, Apparatus, Ideology: A Film Theory Reader*, ed. Philip Rosen

[New York, 1986], p. 328). The partisan slant of such reflex aversions is revealed when Bonitzer adroitly excuses a leftist filmmaker's (very masculine) voice-overs: "What Chris Marker enunciates is the modern knowledge. . . . It is a layer protecting the filmic image, lubricating it and not forcing it" (p. 327). A similar impatience with the technique is registered in an otherwise helpful essay, Brian Henderson, "Tense, Mood, and Voice in Film (Notes after Genette)," *Film Quarterly* 36, no. 4 (1983), pp. 14f.

5. Elizabeth W. Bruss, "Eye for I: Making and Unmaking Autobiography in Film," in *Autobiography: Essays Theoretical and Critical*, ed. James Olney (Princeton, 1980), pp. 296–320, makes an intensive case against the possibility of autobiographical films, but the argument proves counterproductive by bringing under consideration the many resemblances between literary and cinematic autobiographies.

6. See Benveniste, *Problems in General Linguistics*, trans. Mary E. Meek (Coral Gables, Fla., 1971 [1966]), pp. 227ff., for a grammatical analysis of the pronouns, verbs, and deictic indicators that create this functional difference.

7. By the same token, there are subtle differences and resemblances between voice-over as a storytelling situation and the voice that accompanies acts of writing or reads out their texts. Voice-over as we have described it is nondramatized communicative speech, and the voice used for written narration is not a speaking voice that addresses others but a sonic equivalent of writing that the audience overhears. But in the case of letters, the text addresses other characters, and the voice is enlisted in dramatic action—in chapter 7 I shall claim that it can represent the reader's reception of the message. Diary narration has obvious affinities with noncommunicative interior monologue: the book as well as the writer is often visible to others, but the voice of writing is unheard by them. Indeed, most voices used for writing are independent of the degree of dramatization: whether or not the writer, text, or reader is shown, the voice of writing, perhaps because of its prose style, functions in much the same way. This distinct code should perhaps receive a name of its own ("writing voice-over"?).

8. Arthur Evans, *Jean Cocteau and His Films of Orphic Identity* (Philadelphia, 1977), refers to these films as an autobiographical trilogy, but the distinctions between their modes of self-embodiment are as significant as their common subject. For a comprehensive survey of the myriad literary versions, see Charles Segal, *Orpheus: The Myth of the Poet* (Baltimore, 1989); the emphasis is on antiquity, but a chapter on postclassical literature includes a brief discussion of Cocteau (pp. 163–64).

9. Jean Cocteau, *Two Screenplays: The Blood of a Poet [and] The Testament of Orpheus*, trans. Carol Martin-Sperry (New York, 1968 [1957]),

p. 8; subsequent citations in text. The personal style of Cocteau's scenario writing is also worthy of notice, as in *Testament*: "*After the credits I begin to draw Orpheus' profile in chalk on a blackboard.* / I SPEAK: It is the film-maker's privilege . . . " (p. 83).

10. For example, "*The author's voice*: 'The cloak, spread out like an ink stain, disappeared under the body of the supernatural being, who grew paler as he absorbed his prey' " (p. 50); this is to explain the boy's resurrection by his black guardian angel.

11. Genette, *Seuils* (Paris, 1987).

12. Cocteau, *Three Screenplays: L'Eternel Retour, Orphée, La Belle et la Bête*, trans. Carol Martin-Sperry (New York, 1972), p. 103; this edition does not contain the dedication and opening voice-over statement, which I quote below from the film itself.

13. Genette, *Narrative Discourse*, trans. Jane E. Lewin (Oxford, 1980), pp. 116f.

14. André Fraigneau, *Cocteau on the Film*, trans. Vera Traill (London, 1954); excerpted in *Film Makers on Film Making: Statements on Their Art by Thirty Directors*, ed. H. M. Geduld (Bloomington, Ind., 1967), pp. 147, 151.

15. *Cocteau on the Film*, in Geduld, p. 150.

16. Jacques Derrida has developed this critique of the "phonocentric" tradition in a series of works, most notably in *Of Grammatology*, trans. G. C. Spivak (Baltimore, 1976 [1967]).

17. For Wilder's earlier career as a scenarist, see Maurice Zolotow, *Billy Wilder in Hollywood* (New York, 1987 [1977]); also Steve Seidman, *The Film Career of Billy Wilder* (Pleasantville, N.Y., 1977).

18. Its closest contender in this respect is Wim Wenders's *Hammett* (1982), but this film shows the writer at work on his stories, not the scenarists who converted them into films.

19. A more recent instance occurs in Sidney J. Furie's *The Boys in Company C* (1978), in which the internal voice-over of a Vietnam soldier shown keeping a diary turns out to be that of a character who dies at the close; although the voice may be understood as the equivalent of a written text, its implied posthumous delivery marks it with the uncanny associations described here.

20. In the absence of a published scenario, I quote the film directly. The shooting script cited below can be consulted in typescript at a number of libraries; I quote the version dated 21 March 1949. For a brief account of the frame sequence, see Zolotow, *Wilder in Hollywood*, p. 165.

21. The sly appeal to a Hollywood cliché ("This is where you came in") not only indicates Joe's wry sense of his story and of himself but also expresses an attitude toward the milieu. He has gone from rags to riches to rags again; by the time *Sunset Boulevard* was made, this

variant of the Hollywood success-story pattern could be subtly jeered. But the finishing touch this line gives to the scene and to the film is to implicate the Hollywood language in which the tragicomedy is played out. In this subculture, individual lives are often conducted according to the symbolic patterns promulgated by the illusion industry in which they participate. The now self-aware hero registers this provenance of his life story by acknowledging our suspicion that we have seen it all before.

22. For further indications of the film's acute sense of language, see Bernard F. Dick, *Billy Wilder* (Boston, 1980), p. 156, which cites Joe's remark, "Audiences don't know somebody writes a picture. They think the actors make it up as they go along"—as well as Norma's hostility to the writer's craft, as manifested in the talkies: "They opened their mouths, and what came out? Words, words, more words!"

23. Opinions on the film's qualifications as tragedy are collected in Axel Madsen, *Billy Wilder* (Bloomington, Ind., 1969), pp. 85–86.

Chapter 5
Dramatized Narration: *The Cabinet of Dr. Caligari* and *Hiroshima Mon Amour*

1. Although narration in the theater has received little attention from narratologists—and, with such exceptions as Kristin Morrison's *Canters and Chronicles: The Use of Narrative in the Plays of Samuel Beckett and Harold Pinter* (Chicago, 1983), not much from drama scholars—a special issue of *Poetics Today* entitled "Semiotics and the Theater" (vol. 2, no. 3 [1981]) contains discussions of issues related to the question.

2. *The Haunted Screen: Expressionism in the German Cinema and the Influence of Max Reinhardt*, trans. Roger Greaves (Berkeley, 1973 [1952]), p. 18.

3. The tendency to join the scenarists in their complaint that the film was co-opted by authoritarianism is a perdurable one, given the persistence of similar libertarian ideologies. The director of a recent New York stage version of the film at the "La Mama Annex" is quoted in *The New York Times* (6 Dec. 1987): "I'm interested in extending the story along lines having to do with the corruption of power. . . . In the film, the communication breakdown centers around Francis, the narrator or protagonist, who is trying to piece the story together. . . . In the end, he is still not given credibility for seeing or knowing. He's considered insane and put into a straightjacket" (Arts section, pp. 5, 21).

4. Georges Sadoul, *Dictionary of Films*, trans. Peter Morris (Berkeley, 1972 [1965]), p. 48.

5. *The Haunted Screen*, p. 20; Eisner seems to be reporting an interview with her friend, Lang, but in the absence of corroboration this attribution of credit cannot be considered certain. An autobiographical statement by one of the co-scenarists has been published in Mike Budd, ed., *The Cabinet of Dr. Caligari: Texts, Contexts, Histories* (New Brunswick, N.J., 1990), pp. 221–39; this volume appeared too late for me to make full use of it.

6. The subtitle of Kracauer's book is *A Psychological History of the German Film* (Princeton, 1947); see the relevant chapter et passim. While the present approach represents a minority position, I am glad to find a supporting view in Bert Cardullo, *Indelible Images: New Perspectives on Classic Films* (New York, 1987), pp. 121–33.

7. I quote below the constructed scenario in the "Classic Film Scripts" series published by Lorrimer (London, 1972), which includes a translation of the intertitles and a "description of action" by R. V. Adkinson; subsequent citations in text. The instant sentence is omitted from this text, apparently because the intertitle does not appear in British versions of the film; a similar omission will be noted below.

8. The variable activities of early distributors are illustrated in Michael Budd, "*The Cabinet of Dr. Caligari*: Conditions of Reception," *Ciné-tracts* 3, no. 4 (1981), pp. 45ff., describing the U.S. exhibitors' addition of a live prologue and epilogue!

9. The problem with the mixture of styles in the film's set design, pointed out by Eisner (*Haunted Screen*, p. 25) and others, is thus not one of esthetic but of (occasional) narrational inconsistency.

10. Large doses of this material, mainly from German sources, are described in E. M. Butler, *The Myth of the Magus* (Cambridge, 1948).

11. For an analyst's reading of the film's portrayal of psychiatrists, see Catherine B. Clément, "Les charlatans et les hystériques," *Communications*, no. 23 (1975): 213–22.

12. I quote the scenario as translated by Richard Seaver (New York, 1962); subsequent citations in text.

13. *Narrative Discourse*, trans. Jane E. Lewin (Oxford, 1980), pp. 94f. and 35f. respectively; for Genette's system of coding story and narration units, comparable to the one I employ below, see pp. 37f.

14. René Prédal, *Alain Resnais*, in *Etudes cinématographiques*, nos. 64–68 (1968), pp. 138ff., develops a similar listing of the "ordre des séquences dans le film" and the "place réelle des séquences dans la chronologie du souvenir"; but he elides the two cellar seclusions into one event.

15. *Narrative Discourse*, pp. 83ff.

16. On interior monologue in the film, see Freddy Sweet, *The Film Narratives of Alain Resnais* (Ann Arbor, Mich., 1981), pp. 19ff. My use

of the term in chapter 4, distinguishing it from voice-over, is consistent with the circumstances of the scene, as well as with Duras's (and Sweet's) nomenclature; for a fuller discussion, see chapter 8.

17. Jacques Lacan, *Ecrits: A Selection*, trans. Alan Sheridan (New York, 1977), p. 47.

18. Resnais's (and Duras's) variations on these themes enter into almost every bibliographical item on their work; a concerted discussion is John Ward, *Alain Resnais: or, the Theme of Time* (New York, 1968)—addressed to the right phenomenological issues but theoretically wavering between Bergsonian and associationist psychologies of time in describing them.

19. Another film might have been made in which her narration is matched by that of the Japanese, telling of his combat experiences, loss of his family, return to Hiroshima, and so on. As it stands, we have a multiple dramatized narration manqué. Given his self-protective reticence, we may feel some ambivalence toward a protagonist who provokes so wrenching a narrative performance by the heroine and then egoistically exults in having been singled out to receive it.

Chapter 6
Multiple Narration: *Rashomon* and *Zelig*

1. This aspect of the film is played up in the 1959 stage version by Fay and Michael Kanin; as the former explained, "The film started to show the characters' fallibility and ridiculousness. And we said, let's push it to the final absurdity, . . . in which the husband trips and falls on his own sword." Perhaps this is what she meant by saying, "Rashomon—it's more than just a movie" (as reported in a *New York Times* review of the 1988 revival of the play).

2. *The Films of Akira Kurosawa* (Berkeley, 1970 [1965]), rpt. in *Focus on Rashomon*, ed. Donald Richie (Englewood Cliffs, N.J., 1972), p. 73; subsequent citations in text. The Akutagawa short stories are reprinted in this volume, as well as in the scenario text cited below.

3. Richie's interpretation of the characters' common motivation is expressed in terms reminiscent of existential psychology: "Each thinks of his character as being fully formed, of being a *thing*" (p. 83); he also uses the Sartrian term "bad faith" (p. 84).

4. Another way of describing these relations is to fall back on modifications of traditional film terms like "double flashback," as does Noël Burch in *To the Distant Observer: Form and Meaning in the Japanese Cinema* (Berkeley, 1979), p. 297.

5. The theft of the dagger is not narrated in the usual sense of the term, for the commoner exposes the deed by cynical aspersions in the

form of leading questions: "And so where is that dagger? That pearl-inlay handle that the bandit said was so valuable? Did the earth open up and swallow it? Or did someone steal it? Am I right? It would seem so. Now *there* is a really selfish action for you": *Rashomon: A Film by Akira Kurosawa*, trans. Donald Richie (New York, 1969), p. 161; subsequent citations in text. We might not ordinarily characterize a series of questions as storytelling, but in forensic situations they often function in that way.

6. This would be the chief criterion in distinguishing *Rashomon* from other films that follow the pattern, including a Western remake, *The Outrage*; a courtroom musical, *Les Girls*; and a structural predecessor, *Unfaithfully Yours*; see Robin Wood, article on *Rashomon* in *The International Dictionary of Films and Filmmakers*, ed. Christopher Lyon (New York, 1985 [1984]), "Films" volume, p. 385.

7. Welles's further excursions into multiple narration illustrate his continued experimental drive in this mode. After the letter narration of *Journey into Fear* (1942; credited to Norman Foster), *Mr. Arkadin* (a.k.a. *Confidential Report: 1955*) combines title cards, external and internal voice-overs, and dramatized narrations by a series of characters who inform and bamboozle the inquiring protagonist. In *The Immortal Story* (1966), the tale in question is reiterated in various degrees of detail by a number of characters; the insistence on live enactment by one of them—searching for immortality through fullness of narration—forms the film's dramatic plot and theme.

8. The film's thematic relation to *Citizen Kane* is neatly summarized in Nancy Pogel, *Woody Allen* (Boston, 1987), pp. 174ff. That its reference is not limited to the American success story is borne out by the statement that Zelig may be considered "the ultimate conformist": *Three Films of Woody Allen: Zelig, Broadway Danny Rose, The Purple Rose of Cairo* (New York, 1987), p. 67; subsequent citations in text.

9. The film's dedication, in an opening title card, to Dr. Eudora Fletcher, Paul Deghuee, and Mrs. Meryl Fletcher Varney suggests that real persons have lent their names to the fictional characters or play their present-day versions in the on-screen interviews. But the closing credits, reproduced in the scenario cited above, list the actors who play both the younger and elder versions of these characters.

10. The technique derives from Warren Beatty's *Reds* (1981), although color was not used there in contrast with black-and-white to distinguish present-day from historical sequences.

11. Frye uses both terms in *Anatomy of Criticism: Four Essays* (Princeton, 1957); Bakhtin's *Rabelais and His World* is his chief application of the latter term, but the texts cited in subsequent notes also develop the concept.

12. See *Problems of Dostoyevsky's Poetics*, trans. Caryl Emerson (Minneapolis, 1984 [1929]), passim. Since this chapter was written, there appeared Robert Stam's *Subversive Pleasures: Bakhtin, Cultural Criticism, and Film* (Baltimore, 1989). While valuable for its broad recommendation of Bakhtin's usefulness in film study—although somewhat tendentious in its choice of objects and goals for culture criticism—this work is particularly effective in its extended analysis of *Zelig* (chap. 6). While some of the points I make have been anticipated by Stam's discussion, I have opted not to interweave my own observations with his—preferring to allow them to second his where they repeat and, in turn, to draw support from his authority. I take this to be not only a familiar procedure in scholarship but a signal instance of dialogical relationships, highly appropriate in the present context.

13. See *Problems of Dostoyevsky's Poetics*, chap. 5, for Bakhtin's typology of prose discourse. Cf. Gérard Genette, *Palimpsestes* (Paris, 1981), for a systematic account of relationships among texts that is roughly equivalent to Bakhtin's intertextuality.

14. See Bakhtin, "Discourse in the Novel," in *The Dialogic Imagination*, trans. Caryl Emerson and Michael Holquist (Austin, Tex., 1981).

Chapter 7
Written Narration: *Letter from an Unknown Woman* and *Diary of a Country Priest*

1. The most strenuous effort to characterize the genre is Molly Haskell, *From Reverence to Rape: The Treatment of Women in the Movies* (Chicago, 1987 [1974]), pp. 153ff.; but its account of *Letter* is typical of *its* genre: Lisa "is radical in her refusal to follow the 'normal' path of a woman's destiny—to stop dreaming once she has married the proper man and settled down" (p. 186). Alan L. Williams, *Max Ophuls and the Cinema of Desire: Style and Spectacle in Four Films, 1948–1955* (New York, 1980), enlarges on the sympathy to be accorded a heroine for whom bourgeois marriage would be a fate worse than death: her "obsessive and self-deluding romantic 'vision' of Stefan is one of escape from a set of social roles even more threatening than the death which takes her" (p. 59). Stephen Heath, in *Questions of Cinema* (Bloomington, Ind., 1981), pp. 146ff., develops his argument on the specular exploitation of women using evidence drawn from this film; he also anticipates my terminology exactly, calling this "voice-over letter-narration" (p. 148).

2. *Letter from an Unknown Woman: Max Ophuls, Director*, ed. V. W. Wexman (New Brunswick, N.J., 1986), p. 185; subsequent citations in text.

3. Koch's comments on his scenario are informative regarding his

collaboration with Ophuls but not illuminating in the darker corners: see Richard Corliss, ed., *The Hollywood Screenwriters* (New York, 1972), pp. 125ff.; Corliss' introduction (p. 11) discusses the importance of letters as theme and narration in Koch's other scenarios.

4. Wood, *Personal Views* (London, 1976), pp. 116–22 (rpt. in the scenario volume cited above, esp. pp. 31–35); Wilson, *Narration in Light: Studies in Cinematic Point of View* (Baltimore, 1986), pp. 103–25 and 215, esp. pp. 105–6 and 120–21. After casting about for a source of objective presentation to complement Lisa's subjective one, Wilson's chapter comes round to the view that the added perspective is Stefan's: "Indeed, what is essential to the letter, within the framework of the film, is the way it expresses Lisa's cast of mind and the way it elicits Brand's vision of her while he reads it" (p. 123).

5. The theory and practice of flashback are discussed in Maureen Turim, *Flashbacks in Film: Memory and History* (New York, 1989), and in David Bordwell, Janet Staiger, and Kristin Thompson, *The Classical Hollywood Cinema: Film Style and Mode of Production to 1960* (New York, 1985), pp. 42–43. Their chief limitation is indifference to verbal modes of signaling time shifts, lumping together narrated and memory-coded transitions. I have used the terms "enactment" and "mindscreen" to distinguish, respectively, the past scenes these transitions signal; in the following chapter, a hybrid type will be labeled "mindscreen narration." The colloquialisms "flashback" and its cognate "flashforward" may, if the above distinctions are observed, give way to sharper rubrics.

6. Other letter-narration films that dramatize both writing and reading include François Truffaut's *Two English Girls* (1971), Alain Tanner's *In the White City* (1983), and David Jones's *84 Charing Cross Road* (1987).

7. John, the mute but observant butler, has been associated with the director's point of view by a number of critics, but the idea of an author-surrogate in the text is based rather on analogy (e.g., muteness implies the director's nonspeaking presence) than on narrational function. It may be best to count him as a symbolic wisdom figure—of which silence has traditionally been an attribute.

8. Some critics have been attentive to this doubled participation in the process, for example, Tania Modleski: "Throughout the long night [sic] it takes to read the letter the disembodied feminine voice is repeatedly shown to be speaking through the mute Stefan": "Time and Desire in the Woman's Film," *Cinema Journal* 23, no. 3 (1984); rpt. in the scenario volume cited above, p. 256.

9. See Caryl Emerson, "The Outer World and Inner Speech: Bakhtin, Vygotsky, and the Internalization of Language," in *Bakhtin: Essays and Dialogues on His Work*, ed. G. S. Morson (Chicago, 1986), pp. 21–40, on the theories of the Russian psychologists of inner speech.

10. *Narrative Discourse*, trans. Jane E. Lewin (Oxford, 1980), pp. 189–90. Mieke Bal's elaboration of Genette's focalization into a series of embedded perspectives might serve to describe the situation at hand, but its own assumptions and coding leave more loose ends than they tie up; see *Narratology: Introduction to the Theory of Narrative*, trans. Christine van Boheemen (Toronto, 1985 [1980]).

11. The term may suggest affinities with the "dual voice" at work in literary "free indirect style," as it has been studied by narratologists. But the voices doubled in this linguistic technique are those of the omniscient narrator and a favored character, rather than representing a relation of two characters. See Roy Pascal, *The Dual Voice: Free Indirect Speech and Its Functioning in the Nineteenth-century European Novel* (Manchester, 1977); also Ann Banfield, *Unspeakable Sentences: Narration and Representation in the Language of Fiction* (Boston, 1982).

12. A schematization may be useful to some readers, although it may alienate others; if N = narrator and F = focalizer (and with character-narrators, represented by NF):

"first-person novel" focalization: $NF\{F$;
dual-perspective focalization: $N\{F\{F$;
epistolary novels: $F\{NF$ [the letter reader{the letter writer];
letter-narration films: $F\{NF$ [same as above].

Note that many epistolary novels and all letter-narration films, according to the position taken earlier, lack a primary narrator who enunciates the text as a whole; unframed presentations of letters represent a non-narrated form of fiction that is assimilated to the diegetic mode only by convention (but not the less effectively).

13. Tony Pipolo, "The Aptness of Terminology: Point of View, Consciousness and *Letter from an Unknown Woman*," *Film Reader* 4 (1979): 166–79, is acutely sensitive to the several sources of subjectivity in the film, but opts for one or another explanation of the dominant source at various points in its argument: Lisa (p. 167), the camera (p. 173), Stefan (pp. 169–70), the "dual" elder and younger Lisa (p. 171), and the duality of Lisa and Stefan—an option considered only to be rejected (p. 170). All the elements are present, but an integrated view of their relationship is missing.

14. Here I follow and extend Wilson's remarks on Lisa's fatalism and its baleful influence on Stefan: *Narration in Light*, pp. 117ff.

15. There exists, as far as I can determine, no published scenario; I quote the English version of the film. The voice-over translation can be checked in many cases against the French text, given the shots of the diary in composition. There remains, of course, the possibility of motivated variance between the sound and image of writing (see the following note), but I have detected no gross differences.

16. Andre Bazin's "The Stylistics of Robert Bresson" (orig. pub. 1951), in *What Is Cinema?* trans. Hugh Gray (Berkeley, 1967), 1:138ff., is the starting point for discussing the relation between the voice-overs and the images of writing: "The most moving moments in the film are those in which text and image are saying the same thing, each however in its own way" (p. 140). A reconsideration of this sameness and difference within more recent theories—for example, Jacques Derrida's—of the relations between speech and writing remains to be done.

17. This is the second instance of a dramatized reading; the priest has previously been shown opening and reading the Countess's letter of submission and inner peace. We see her black-bordered stationery and the locket that falls from the envelope; we first hear the priest's voice-over intone the Countess's words, then see and hear him read the letter aloud.

18. Here too Bazin's brief remarks are the starting point for discussion (*What Is Cinema?* 1:140–41): "There is nothing more that the image has to communicate except by disappearing. . . . The black cross on the white screen, as awkwardly drawn as on the average memorial card, the only trace left by the 'assumption' of the image, is a witness to something the reality of which is itself but a sign."

19. To determine whether the priest has gained the power to transmit divine grace by virtue of his martyrdom lies, of course, beyond the purview of esthetic criticism and must be left to other enterprises in sign interpretation. There are hints, however, in the Vicar of Torcy's earlier request for Leydu's blessing, that his high spiritual gifts are already evident within the dramatic world of the film.

20. Another phase of the intertextual process is worth noting. One of the best accounts of the film's ways of conveying spirituality is to be found in Paul Schrader's *Transcendental Style in Film: Ozu, Bresson, Dreyer* (Berkeley, 1972). Schrader went on to employ aspects of the isolated, ascetic protagonist—and to foreground his writing of a diary—in his own scenario for *Taxi Driver* (1976), though its setting is, to say the least, rather different.

21. An additional possibility is presented by writing closeup 17: we see the hand write about hemorrhaging and waking to hear the cocks crow; we next see Leydu, in medium to long shot, go from window to bed and pick up the diary; we then see a continuation of the writing closeup. The sequence places us in the space of writing, though it does not show more than his hand in the act.

Chapter 8
Mindscreen Narration: *Brief Encounter*

1. Among the more lucid discussions of the subject is Nelson Goodman, *Of Minds and Other Matters* (Cambridge, Mass., 1984), esp. pp. 21ff., "On Thoughts without Words." The immediate issue here is the apparently still widespread behaviorist view that *all* thought is subvocal speech; Goodman holds out for at least some thoughts without words.

2. I borrow the qualifying term from Bruce F. Kawin, *Mindscreen: Bergman, Godard, and First-person Film* (Princeton, 1978), although without subscribing to its extension to authorial perspective. A summary on p. 190 gives a good relational definition of the term's application to character perspective: "1. Subjective camera (share my eyes). . . . 2. Point of view (share my perspective, my emphases). . . . 3. Mindscreen (share my mind's eye). . . . 4. Self-consciousness (share my reflexive perspective)." It should be noted that my use of the term is limited to this sense: film images coded as the mental images of a character.

3. By the same token, the seen/unheard requirements of interior monologue may be chipped away at the other end by special circumstances in a given film; Wim Wenders's *Wings of Desire* (1988) posits angelic characters capable of apprehending the mental processes of ordinary mortals. It would be absurd to consider the seen-and-heard heroine's meditations as voice-off; they are interior monologues even though "heard" by an angel in this special sense of the term.

4. This film may stand as the *locus classicus* of interior monologue, given its virtuoso usages; these include other soldiers' interior monologues (thus, multiple), the hero's second-person addresses to his wife and to a buddy, the imagined sounds of other voices in dialogue with or punctuating his own (mind-voice?), and a full repertoire of transitional and representational techniques for rendering it all.

5. Seymour Chatman, *Story and Discourse: Narrative Structure in Fiction and Film* (Ithaca, N.Y., 1978), pp. 179ff., gives a listing of soliloquy traits drawn from drama, from film, and from literature (for such two of the criteria of style and diction seem to be); there is also an enumeration of interior monologue characteristics on pp. 182ff., also oriented toward a fictional style, "direct free thought" (i.e., untagged quoted thought).

6. Edward R. Branigan, *Point of View in the Cinema: A Theory of Narration and Subjectivity in Classical Film* (Berlin, 1984), pp. 85ff., discusses "mental process narration," but because of his looser use of the

term "narration" this includes visual transitions to mental contents (dreams, fantasies, etc.) without verbalization. This would, in my book, be "mindscreen," but not mindscreen narration.

7. Some commentators minimize the capacity of films to render mental states like dream, memory, and imagination, given that bugbear, the "present tense" of all cinematic images; for example, George Bluestone, *Novels into Film* (Berkeley, 1957), pp. 46ff. Bluestone eventually gets off his essentialist high horse ("The film, having only arrangements of space to work with, cannot render thought, for the moment thought is externalized it is no longer thought": pp. 47–48) by acknowledging that this rendering, like all communication in cinema and elsewhere, is a product of coded symbol systems: "If, in an effort to bridge the gap between spatial representation and non-spatial experience, we accept such devices at all, we accept them as cinematic conventions, not as renditions of conceptual consciousness" (p. 48). Although not so good on space, Bluestone is very good on psychological time in the cinema, in the pages following.

8. Tense structure is an important, though not infallible, indicator for distinguishing interior monologue from voice-over, for reference to the present marks ongoing mental activity, while the past tense serves for retrospects. Mindscreen narrators do, of course, use the past tense within the encompassing present, just as voice-overs may drop a present reference into the predominating preterit. Leopoldo Torre-Nilsson's *The House of the Angel* (a.k.a. *End of Innocence: 1957*) begins with what appears to be voice-over, but the heroine describes her actions while performing them, with the implication that this is the interior monologue of the figure we see on-screen; when she turns to past-tense narration of the main story, this may be considered a continuation of her present mental activity, now reporting the past (as in *Brief Encounter*, as we shall see). The film returns to the scene of narration at the close, even repeating the last line of the opening sequence, as if to emphasize that the long enactment takes place in her mind, without the passage of time.

9. Two other Hollywood films of this kind are described by Bruce Morrissette, though in another context: "In the film *Slattery's Hurricane*, Herman Wouk's hero, a disgraced airplane pilot, recalls the past as he battles his way through a hurricane. . . . The film is a montage of flashbacks, each separated from the next by a shot of the pilot, accompanied by the pilot's voice on the sound track setting the scene through use of a narrative 'you' passage. The film *The Bribe* has roughly the same structure" (*Novel and Film: Essays in Two Genres* [Chicago, 1985], p. 139); I have seen neither work. A film that brings the mode into the romantic sphere is Sam Wood's *Kitty Foyle* (1940), in which the heroine recounts her past and present choices before a mirror.

10. Bazin's *"Le jour se lève* . . . Poetic Realism" was not included in the selection of his essays published as *What Is Cinema?* trans. Hugh Gray (Berkeley, 1967); a translation by John Mathews is to be found in the scenario volume cited below.

11. *Le Jour se Lève: A Film by Marcel Carné and Jacques Prévert*, trans. Dinah Brooke and Nicola Hayden (New York, 1970), p. 15; subsequent citations in text. The original of this last phrase is, "il évoque les circonstances, qui ont fait de lui un meurtrier."

12. *Brief Encounter* (New York, 1974), p. 80; subsequent citations in text.

13. Its predecessors in this respect include Germaine Dulac's *The Smiling Madame Beudet* (1922) and Ernst Lubitsch's *Lady Windermere's Fan* (1925); the latter's point-of-view sequences are discussed in David Bordwell, *Narration in the Fiction Film* (Madison, Wis., 1985), pp. 178–86.

14. Alain Silver and James Ursini, *David Lean and His Films* (London, 1974), pp. 42–48, discusses "subjectification" in *Brief Encounter*, including excellent accounts of the repeated opening scene, the fantasy sequence, and the "memories of memories" to be discussed in somewhat different terms below.

15. The inner life of the secondary characters is not, to be sure, explored, either by Laura or by Lean and Coward. The courtship of the trainman and barmaid is set up to contrast with the main story, not only in linguistic style but in the more overtly sexual and possessive content of lower-class mating rituals. (Laura's report may even reflect some envy of their robustness.) To explain the comic relief provided by the lower-class characters as serving to uphold the bourgeois values of the protagonists and their creators, as Roy Armes does (*A Critical History of British Cinema* [New York, 1978], pp. 214–15), is to supply the outlines of a new-left reading of the film.

16. The film's importance in celebrating the depth of the ordinary may be better appreciated when it is compared with the remake of 1974, where the services of Sophia Loren were thought to be required to make the housewife heroine sufficiently worthy of attention; this gain does not quite compensate for the loss of narration, of mindscreen, and perhaps of mind.

17. The scenario describes the film's initial transition from narration scene to story in a way that specifies the intended co-presence or dual state: "The [library] scene, with the exception of LAURA, slowly starts to dim out. LAURA remains a solid figure in the foreground. As the room fades away, the station refreshment room takes its place. LAURA, as well as being in the foreground of the picture, is also seated [at] one of the tables in the refreshment room, thus giving the impres-

sion that she is watching herself. Dissolve" (p. 24). It is regrettable that this elegant technique was not developed and varied as the film's code of mindscreen transitions.

Continuation:
Questions for Research

1. Hugo Munsterberg, *The Film: A Psychological Study* (New York, 1916), and Vachel Lindsay, *The Art of Moving Pictures* (New York, 1915), seem quaint by comparison with the Lacanian lingo of current discourse; one day the latter too will seem quaint.

2. Among the scanty generalizations about character in cinema are Béla Balázs, *Theory of the Film: Character and Growth of a New Art*, trans. Edith Bone (New York, 1952 [1945]), pp. 6off., on physiognomy; Raymond Durgnat, *Films and Feelings* (Cambridge, Mass., 1971 [1967]), pp. 173ff., on "human interest"; and Stanley Cavell, *The World Viewed: Reflections on the Ontology of Film* (Cambridge, Mass., 1979 [1974]), pp. 33ff., on types.

3. For a useful summary of current theorizing on, and suspicion of, subjectivity in film see Pam Cooke, ed., *The Cinema Book* (New York, 1985), pp. 244ff.

4. Magny, *L'âge du roman américain* (Paris, 1948), pp. 48–49; my translation (although the book has been translated). This study applies in a systematic way the phenomenological-existentialist response to American films and literary techniques current at the time.

5. Spiegel, *Fiction and the Camera Eye: Visual Consciousness in Film and the Modern Novel* (Charlottesville, Va., 1976). Other versions of the relationship are sketched in James Monaco, *The New Wave* (New York, 1976), pp. 99f., and in Robert P. Kolker, *The Altering Eye: Contemporary International Cinema* (Oxford, 1983), pp. 122f.

6. Cohen, *Film and Fiction: The Dynamics of Exchange* (New Haven, 1979), p. 192; the quotation following is from p. 170. Cohen disavows influence-mongering in favor of "fundamental isomorphic structures" (p. 108) that presumably govern both these arts, but even the explanation that follows indicates the direction of flow—writers responding to the new art of cinema.

7. *Narrative Discourse*, trans. Jane E. Lewin (Oxford, 1980), pp. 189ff. In the tour de force of "external focalization" the narrator may report only objective data, without indicating what the characters think or making other "authorial intrusions," but it would be a mistake to regard this period style and its masters (Hemingway, Robbe-Grillet, certain minimalists) as having achieved a non-narrated or "cinematic" fiction.

8. For an exposition of the argument that subjectivity is a conventionally induced and elaborately coded, rather than inherent or "natural," aspect of film images see Edward R. Branigan, *Point of View in the Cinema: A Theory of Narration and Subjectivity in Classical Film* (Berlin, 1984), esp. pp. 73f.

9. Among the largely anecdotal studies of screenwriting, Richard A. Fine's *Hollywood and the Profession of Authorship: 1928–1940* (Ann Arbor, Mich., 1985) stands out in studying the cultural orientation of the East Coast writers, as well as the institutional system in which they worked. More personal and circumstantial accounts include Tom Dardis, *Some Time in the Sun* (Harmondsworth, 1976); Tom Stempel, *Framework: A History of Screenwriting in the American Film* (New York, 1988); and Ian Hamilton, *Writers in Hollywood: 1915–1951* (New York, 1990). All the interest in the harried process of corporate writing has yielded little attention to the literary and cinematic qualities of the scenarios themselves.

10. The story of Faulkner's difficult assimilation, with indications of the narrational techniques he contemplated but rarely succeeded in employing, is told in Bruce F. Kawin, *Faulkner and Film* (New York, 1977).

11. See Donald Richie, *Ozu* (Berkeley, 1974), p. 231; there might be a fruitful paradox in Richie's comment that although *Citizen Kane* was Ozu's favorite foreign film, "it is impossible to imagine a picture more antithetical to his own." It may be stated as the problem of achieving character depth and fullness of milieu without Wellsian narration.

12. See Robert L. Carringer, *The Making of Citizen Kane* (Berkeley, 1985), pp. 3ff., for the details, including working sketches; but James Naremore, *The Magic World of Orson Welles* (New York, 1978), pp. 30ff., better explains their relationship to Conradian point of view.

13. A bibliography of film-and-fiction studies by F.-J. Albersmeier is included in the "Cinéma et littérature" issue of *Cahiers du 20e siècle*, no. 9 (1978). The journal *Literature/Film Quarterly* continues the discourse currently.

14. "Can Great Books Make Good Movies? 7 Writers Just Say No," *American Film* 12, no. 9 (1987), pp. 39–40.

15. And occasional maximalism, as in the collaboration of Terry Gilliam and playwright Tom Stoppard in *Brazil* (1985).

Index

Index

Designed by Ed King
Set in Palatino text and display by NK Graphics Baltimore, Inc.
Printed on 50-lb. Glatfelter Offset, eggshell finish,
and bound in Holliston Roxite by Thomson-Shore, Inc.

The term *narration* is often used to describe the process by which films communicate their stories. In *Narrated Films* Avrom Fleishman challenges the prevailing assumptions attached to this term in favor of a more concrete sense: spoken and written storytellings and the situations in which they are delivered.

Fleishman begins with theory and proceeds to history, surveying the changing narrational practices in cinema from its beginnings to the present. He covers the main storytelling situations: voice-over; dramatized narration (when one character tells another a story); multiple narration (when a number of characters do so); written narration, either through diaries or letters; and a problematic form known as "mindscreen narration," a cinematic version of the interior monologue of fiction.

Each of these situations is illustrated by close readings of pairs of classic films: *Sunset Boulevard* and *Orpheus; The Cabinet of Dr. Caligari* and *Hiroshima Mon Amour; Rashomon* and *Zelig; Letters from an Unknown Woman* and *Diary of a Country Priest; Daybreak* and *Brief Encounter*. A short conclusion points out further